Ukraine's Foreign and Security Policy 1991–2000

This book analyses Ukraine's relations with each of its neighbours in its first decade of independence. It examines the degree to which these relations fitted into Ukraine's broad objective of reorienting its key political ties from East to West, and assesses the extent to which Ukraine succeeded in achieving this reorientation. It shows how in the early days of independence Ukraine fought off threats from Russia and Romania to its territorial integrity, and how it made progress in establishing good relations with its western neighbours as a means of moving closer toward Central European sub-regional and European regional organisations. It also shows how the sheer breadth and depth of its economic and military ties to Russia dwarfed Ukraine's relations with all other neighbours, resulting in a foreign and security policy which attempted to counterbalance the competing forces of East and West.

Roman Wolczuk is a specialist on Ukrainian foreign and security policy. He has written extensively on Ukraine's international relations since independence and is a regular contributor to Jane's Sentinel on Ukrainian Affairs.

BASEES/RoutledgeCurzon Series on Russian and East European Studies

This series is published on behalf of BASEES (the British Association for Slavonic and East European Studies). The series comprises original, high-quality, research-level work by both new and established scholars on all aspects of Russian, Soviet, post-Soviet and East European Studies in humanities and social science subjects.

1. Ukraine's Foreign and Security Policy 1991–2000
Roman Wolczuk

Ukraine's Foreign and Security Policy 1991–2000

Roman Wolczuk

RoutledgeCurzon
Taylor & Francis Group
LONDON AND NEW YORK

First published 2003
by RoutledgeCurzon,
an imprint of Taylor & Francis
11 New Fetter Lane, London EC4P 4EE

Simultaneously published in the USA and Canada
by Routledge
29 West 35th Street, New York, NY 10001

RoutledgeCurzon is an imprint of the Taylor & Francis Group

Typeset in Times New Roman by
Keystroke, Jacaranda Lodge, Wolverhampton
Printed and bound in Great Britain by
Antony Rowe Ltd, Chippenham, Wiltshire

British Library Cataloguing in Publication Data
A catalogue record for this book is available from the British Library

Library of Congress Cataloging in Publication Data
Wolczuk, Roman, 1962–
Ukraine's foreign and security policy, 1991–2000 / Roman Wolczuk
p. cm. – (Basees/Curzon series on Russian and East European studies)
Includes bibliographical references and index.
1. Ukraine–Foreign relations–1991–. 2. National security–Ukraine.
I. Title. II. Series.

DK508.849 .W65 2002
327.477′009′049–dc21 2002031600

ISBN 0–7007–1740–4

Contents

Tables

Acronyms

AIOC	Azerbaijan International Oil Consortium
BSEC	Black Sea Economic Co-operation Forum
BSF	Black Sea Fleet
CEES	Central and East European states
CEFTA	Central European Free Trade Area
CFE	Conventional Forces in Europe
CIS	Commonwealth of Independent States
CoE	Council of Europe
EBRD	European Basis for Reconstruction and Development
GUAM	(Georgia, Ukraine, Azerbaijan, Moldova (and later, with Uzbekistan, GUUAM)
IPA	Interparliamentary Assembly
NACC	North Atlantic Co-operation Council
NATO	North Atlantic Treaty Organisation
NIS	Newly independent states
NISS	National Institute for Strategic Studies
NPT	Non-Proliferation Treaty
OSCE	Organisation for Security and Cooperation in Europe
PCA	Partnership and Co-operation Agreement
PfP	Partnership for Peace Programme
PTA	Preferential trading agreements
RSC	Regional security complexes
RSFSR	Russian Socialist Federal Soviet Republic
SSR	Soviet Socialist Republic
TMR	Transdniester-Moldova Republic
WTO	World Trade Organization

Introduction

When in August 1991 Ukraine unexpectedly stumbled into independence, nobody, perhaps least of all the Ukrainians, really knew what further to expect. Indeed, the event was as much of a shock to the Ukrainians as it was to the rest of the world. Up until it actually happened, they did not really demand it, expect it, or prepare for it. As a result of its suddenness, fundamental questions had not even been asked, let alone answered. How would Moscow respond? For that matter, how would the West respond? What was going to be the likely reaction of the huge Russian minority in Ukraine to being 'cut off' from ethnic brethren? What was going to happen to the nuclear weapons on the territory of Ukraine – surely the commitment to denuclearise, made in 1990, was a declaration rather than a statement of intent? How would the Soviet military forces in Ukraine be dealt with? In the days and weeks that followed independence, Ukrainian policy-makers had to hazard a guess as to likely answers. It was this guesswork that guided policy-making and policy-implementation in the days and weeks that followed, as the Ukrainian national–economic–political elite grabbed with both hands the opportunities presented by independence. The fact that Ukraine lacked a foreign policy elite compounded the problem of not knowing the answers.

However, the inability to find solutions was not merely a matter of time and personnel. Ukrainian independence reflected a much more profound change, namely, the collapse of bipolarity on the European continent. With the breakdown of bipolarity, regions gained a hitherto subordinated prominence, at least in Europe. As has been pointed out 'the world has now changed. The regional level stands more clearly on its own as the locus of conflict and co-operation for states and as the level of analysis for scholars seeking to explore contemporary security affairs'.[1] This book will argue that the solutions to Ukraine's problems lay at the regional level.

From Ukraine's point of view, the key date, which reflected the completion of the transition of regions from obscurity to prominence, was probably 1994. That was the year in which Ukraine signed a Partnership for Peace Programme (PfP) with the North Atlantic Treaty Organisation (NATO), and a Partnership and Co-operation Agreement (PCA) with the European Union (EU); it was the year in which Ukraine institutionalised the role of the United States (US) in its relations with Russia through the signing of the Trilateral Agreement which finally terminated Ukraine's nuclear status; it was also the year in which the Central and East European states (CEES) started to demand NATO membership. While all of these events suggested that Ukraine was 'regionally aware', deteriorating relations with Russia and NATO enlargement compelled Ukraine to adopt regional solutions to local problems, especially after efforts to persuade the Poles not to join NATO failed. All of the above-mentioned events reflected the increased salience of regions in international politics, along with the new threats and opportunities that emerged within them. As will be seen, Ukrainian foreign and security policy implementation in 1994 and the years that followed reflected this shift of emphasis to regions and the role Ukraine could play therein. With ever-increasing assertiveness, from that time on, Ukraine sought solutions to security threats in regional policies and approaches. This book will explore these policies and approaches. The book consists of four parts. The first part develops a theoretical context useful for examining Ukraine's policy of responding to security threats by attempting to participate in or explicitly avoid participating in regional security complexes along each of three azimuths (the North-eastern, Western and Southern) and the extent to which it achieved a degree of success in preserving its security and enlarging its freedom of manoeuvre by so doing. This examination will involve a review of the three theoretical perspectives that purport to explain regionalism, namely systemic-, regional-and domestic-level theories.

Part II of the book will examine Ukraine's regional policy along its North-eastern azimuth. Chapter 2 will focus on Ukraine's relations with Russia and Kyiv's efforts to come to terms with the ramifications of ties with Moscow, and the challenges these ties presented to the attainment of Ukraine's proclaimed objective of integrating with Western institutions. The chapter also examines Ukraine's relations with Belarus, a particular challenge for Kyiv in the light of Minsk's deference to Moscow's demands and needs. It will be seen that their respective relations with Moscow have largely shaped Kyiv's relations with Minsk. Chapter 3 will start by examining the fruitless efforts by Minsk (and to an extent Moscow) to draw Ukraine into a subregional Slavic Union with them. The chapter will focus in particular on Kyiv's response to economic and political pressures exerted by Moscow to integrate Ukraine more deeply with the Commonwealth of Independent States (CIS).

Part III examines Ukraine's regional ambitions along the Western azimuth. Chapter 4 analyses Ukraine's bilateral ties with its Central and East European neighbours. It will be seen that each of Ukraine's western Central and East European neighbours had an invaluable role to play in Ukraine's intended reorientation from East to West.[2] None were as important as was Poland, Ukraine's hitherto perennial enemy, and potentially crucial partner. As Brzezinski has argued, 'tight co-operative relations [between Ukraine and Poland] that strengthen each other's vitality and economic development would caution Germany and Russia from the temptation which has encouraged imperial ambitions in Eastern Europe in the past'.[3] It might be argued that, as a corollary, Ukraine's ties with the remaining CEES are of secondary importance. This is to an extent true of Ukraine's relations with Hungary and Slovakia, though this is not to devalue the role that these states played in facilitating Ukraine's reorientation. Ukraine's relations with the two CEES along its south-western border, Romania and Moldova, were more complicated. Ukraine's ties with Romania were poisoned from the very beginning by a long-running territorial dispute that Kyiv inherited with independence. Indeed, relations were unable to develop beyond the barest of contacts until this territorial spat was resolved in 1997, an achievement in which NATO enlargement played no small role.[4] Relations with the fifth of Ukraine's Central and East European neighbours, Moldova, were complicated primarily because of the presence of the relatively powerful former Soviet 14th Army there, something that once again threw into focus Ukraine's relations with Russia. While Moldova does not form a 'natural' Central and East European state owing to its status as a former Soviet republic and its somewhat southerly location, it has been included along the Western azimuth because of its proclaimed political objectives of membership of Western regional institutions and strong ties with Romania.

Bilateral relations with the CEES along the Western azimuth were also perceived as stepping-stones toward integration with the subregional and regional institutional structures of Europe.[5] This is strongly suggested by the willingness with which Ukraine used bilateral ties to pursue membership of subregional institutions such as the Central European Free Trade Area (CEFTA), the Visegrad group, and to recruit supporters for its own initiatives for new formations, as examined in Chapter 5. The ultimate goal for Ukraine was membership of the big regional institutions, the EU and, possibly, NATO, relations with which are the focus of the remainder of Chapter 5. Chapter 5 will also assess the extent to which this westward focus impacted on relations with Russia. The Western azimuth of Ukraine's policy reflected a will on the part of the new state to discredit the forces of the apparent geographical and historical determinism of integration with Russia, which had dominated in Ukraine for the last seven centuries. In turn, the extent to which Russia, using its economic might and Ukraine's dependence on it, tried to prevent this westward lunge will also be analysed. However, ties with the West were not to be simply at the expense of ties with the North-east; neither were ties with the North-east to be at the expense of ties with the West. As Sherr points out, 'Ukraine's mainstream, centrist political establishment (as opposed to *Rukh* and a number of other "national democrats") believe that Ukraine's integration into the West will not be achieved without success along the second vector: a "special partnership" with Russia . . . just as internal stability and Western support have been seen as the precondition for securing friendly relations with Russia, so friendly relations with Russia have been seen as the precondition for drawing closer to the West'.[6] Objectives along both azimuths were thus compatible, balanced and not mutually exclusive.[7]

If the Western azimuth to Ukraine's regional policy reflected a means of counter-balancing and even counteracting the overweening influence of Russia on Ukraine, the Southern azimuth, the basis for the fourth part of the book, represented a qualitatively different set of opportunities for Ukraine. As Ukraine struggled to balance the opportunities and threats presented by East and West, the Southern azimuth offered Ukraine the chance to pursue other avenues by forming closer ties with all non-Russian Black Sea littoral states, and this is the focus of Chapter 6.

Particular attention is paid to relations with Turkey, a potential competitor to Russia in the region and a budding ally for Ukraine in the evolving geopolitics of the region. Along this azimuth, Ukraine was also able to provide a semblance of support and a form of protection for former Soviet Republics around the sea, in particular Georgia and, by extension, its neighbour Azerbaijan. In doing so, Ukraine strove to undermine Russia's influence in the region and within the CIS. The most explicit evidence of this was Ukraine's contribution to the development of subregional institutions, which will be examined in Chapter 7. Ukraine supported the lead of Turkey in creating the Black Sea Economic Co-operation Forum (BSEC), and took a particularly proactive role in the creation of GUUAM (an acronym made up of the initials of its member states), which originally included Georgia, Ukraine and Azerbaijan, and which was soon joined by first Moldova, and then in 1999 by Uzbekistan. The emergence of GUUAM is particularly significant in terms of its negative reverberations for the CIS. The Southern azimuth needs to be seen in the context of the above 'North-east–West' dimension. Simply put, exploiting the Southern azimuth was a means for Kyiv to avoid over-reliance on Russia, and one which could contribute to Ukraine's integration into Western institutional structures. The final chapter of the book brings all of these themes together, arguing that Ukraine's regional policies along the three azimuths outlined above combined to form a coherent strategy to reduce Ukraine's traditional vulnerability located between North-east and West, that is to 'escape' from the North-east (or at least reduce its energy dependence on it), and 'join' the West. Throughout the book, the theories outlined in the first part of the book will be used to analyse the empirical data presented in order to explain Ukraine's regional behaviour.

Part I

Regionalism and Ukraine's foreign and security policy

1 A theoretical context

Independent Ukraine has variously been referred to as a pivot or keystone.[1] A pivot refers to a bearing on which something oscillates or turns. A keystone is the central, stress-bearing stone or crown at the very peak of an arch that locks the remaining parts of the arch into place. The common theme therefore is that of load-bearing centrality: the importance of the pivot lies in the central location of the support it provides to the whole and on which the balance of the whole depends; the centrality of the keystone is critical to the very existence of the structure of which it is an integral part. Without a pivot, no oscillation takes place, turning becomes impossible; with the removal of the keystone, the arch collapses. To refer to Ukraine, then, as a pivot or a keystone is to confer a rare honour: Ukraine is seemingly the pivot on which the European continent 'revolves'; it is the keystone that locks the remaining members of the European geographical arch into place. Ukraine is thus seen as a central and even critical feature in the European security structure: if at the end of the twentieth century 'geography and geopolitics still matter', Ukraine's geography and geopolitics seem to matter more than most, at least on the European continent.[2]

Up to a point, it is self-evident that the emergence of any new nation-state in Europe was going to be an event of no small significance. However, Ukraine was not just 'any' nation-state. First, Ukraine is one of the largest states in Europe at 603,700 square kilometres. Second, it is one of Europe's most populous states with over 50 million citizens. Third, on independence, Ukraine was, after Russia, Europe's most powerful state, in the sense that it possessed (if not actually controlled) the third largest nuclear arsenal in the world; even after denuclearisation, its military might remains formidable. Finally, it is probably Europe's most well-endowed state in terms of resources, possessing an estimated 5 per cent of *total* world mineral resources.[3] To paraphrase the second president of Ukraine, Leonid Kuchma, Ukraine is no Switzerland. These four features, in conjunction with the fact that Ukraine is located in what is historically a volatile part of a geopolitically critical region, between 'East and West', or between Europe and Eurasia, or even between Germany and Russia, help contextualise the importance of Ukraine's independence in 1991.[4] This is because geography remains important as 'geography defines the players (which are territorially organised states or would like to be), frequently defines the stakes for which players contend and always defines the terms in which they measure security relative to others'.[5] If so, the emergence of an independent Ukraine not only redefined the geography of the region it also introduced new stakes into the reckoning and fundamentally challenged the hitherto long-established regional security norms.[6] The upset of such norms is problematic at the best of times; it is especially problematic 'when states are surrounded, or are bordered by states with historical grudges or by states that have previously used their power against weaker states'.[7] Independent Ukraine was such a bordered state.

However, beyond mere geography, the measures adopted by Kyiv to integrate with Western institutions following independence in 1991 reflected the continuation of an evolving phenomenon, namely the emerging salience of regions in general and the Central and East European states in particular in international politics.[8] If it is true to suggest that the end of the Cold War contributed to the newfound prominence of Central and Eastern Europe, the diminished stature of Russia and the reduced inclination of the US to intervene in regional conflicts suggest that the end of Cold War hostilities opened up hitherto unexpected possibilities for regional co-operation. With the irrevocable breakdown of bipolarity, it has been suggested by Richard Rosecrance that 'autonomy has been restored to the separate regions of the world'.[9]

This book will argue that because of the restoration of this autonomy, Ukraine consistently pursued a policy of responding to the security threats that emanated from this context by attempting to integrate with or avoid integrating with regional security complexes (RSC). In particular, the book argues that Ukraine sought to integrate with RSCs along the Western azimuth and avoided integrating with RSCs along the North-eastern azimuth. Furthermore, Ukraine's objective of integration along the Western azimuth was pursued *in conjunction* with the pursuit of a special relationship with Russia and highly circumscribed relations with the CIS along the North-eastern azimuth. The book will further argue that participation in RSCs along the Southern azimuth was pursued insofar as they facilitated the achievement of the previous two objectives.[10] It is further hypothesised that Ukraine achieved a degree of success in preserving its security and enlarging its freedom of manoeuvre by integrating or avoiding integration with RSCs, bearing in mind the numerous internal and external obstacles it faced.

Buzan defines a security complex as a 'group of states whose primary security concerns link together sufficiently closely that their national securities cannot realistically be considered apart from one another'.[11] In addition to the security interdependence between member states that the conception of RSCs implies, geographical propinquity and an autonomous existence apart from the global system are also deemed characteristics of RSCs. In a considerable refinement of the conception of RSCs, Lake introduces the notion of externalities to address what are seen as flaws in the conception of RSCs, namely their inability to sufficiently distinguish between regional- and global-level interaction.[12] Externalities are benefits (positive externalities) and costs (negative externalities) that are conferred on actors other than those that are the sources of such externalities and thus help delineate more precisely the parameters of that which may be defined as an RSC.

This book identifies three geographically based RSCs in which Ukraine participates, although other conceptualisations exist.[13] These three azimuthial RSCs are the North-eastern, Western and Southern.

The role of Ukraine along each azimuth will be analysed on two levels. First, it will be examined in terms of Ukraine's regional bilateral relations with a particular neighbour along a given azimuth, or within a given RSC. Second, it will be assessed in terms of Ukraine's relations with subregional and regional institutions along a given azimuth, or within a given RSC. In pursuit of analytic clarity and academic utility an institutional definition of the terms 'regional' and 'subregional' will be utilised.[14]

As far as the term 'regional' is concerned, it has been pointed out that 'Europe is now defined by the membership of different clubs. Today you are what you belong to. We are no longer governed by history or geography, but by institutions'.[15] These different 'clubs' or institutions have different objectives and geographical scope. For example, the EU and NATO are clearly within the European/transatlantic geographical area, something that the CIS, in the widest geographical sense, is not. Yet clearly, in terms of geographical scope, they are all regional institutions, adequately satisfying the criteria of 'regionship' referred to above. Furthermore, their functions and objectives affect or impact upon the fundamentals of individual states – security, defence and sovereignty. Integration with institutions such as the EU, NATO and the CIS profoundly affects the most fundamental aspects of the character of the member states. This distinguishes these regional institutions from other ostensibly regional institutions such as the Organisation for Security and Cooperation in Europe (OSCE) and the Council of Europe. The functional scope of the latter two is notably less intrusive (statehood is not encroached upon to anything like the same extent as occurs in the case of membership of the EU or CIS) and the criteria for membership are notably less stringent and hence less discriminating.[16]

Subregional institutions, in the area covered by this book, turn out to be institutions whose members have either the explicit or implicit goal of membership or avoidance of membership of the regional institution of the geographical area within which the subregional institution finds itself. Thus, CEFTA and the Visegrad group (originally made up of Poland, Hungary, Slovakia and the Czech Republic) were patently subsets of the NATO/EU region, drawn as they were to the West from the earliest days of the collapse of the Soviet Union. In addition, CEFTA and Visegrad had as a functional goal membership of the EU for its member states. Similarly, the BSEC and the informal GUUAM are subregional formations in that they function in the shadow of the regional institutions (i.e. the CIS), and have as a functional objective the intention to impact either positively or negatively on the regional institution. Thus the BSEC, formed under the leadership of Ankara, was designed to facilitate Turkey's chances of integrating with the EU. It is for this same reason that Ukraine is an enthusiastic supporter and participant in the institution. GUUAM, on the other hand, has had as one of its explicit goals the transportation of Caspian oil by its member states beyond Russian control. Kyiv hoped to facilitate its chances of membership of the European Union by becoming part of the energy transportation system taking Caspian oil westward. It was also hoped that the emergence of

GUUAM would inhibit Kyiv's further integration into the CIS to the extent that GUUAM actively contributed to the unravelling of certain aspects of the CIS. Defining the proposed Slavic Union as subregional is somewhat more problematic in light of the sheer size and importance of Russia, one of its constituent states. However, if it were ever to emerge, a Slavic Union would be distinctly subregional in the sense that its main proponents see it very much as forming a core within the CIS. As such, the Slavic Union has always been envisaged as an albeit important subset of the CIS.

In sum, three azimuths will be examined, along which are found three RSCs, each of which will be analysed on two levels:

The North-eastern azimuth/RSC:

A. bilateral relations with Russia and Belarus
B. subregional level – Slavic Union
   regional level – relations/membership of the CIS

The Western azimuth/RSC:

A. bilateral relations with Poland, Hungary, Slovakia (and formerly Czechoslovakia), Romania and Moldova
B. subregional level – relations with CEFTA, the Visegrad group
   regional level – relations with the EU, NATO

The Southern azimuth/RSC:

A. bilateral relations with the Black Sea littoral states: Russia, Georgia, Turkey, Bulgaria, Romania
B. subregional level – relations with the BSEC, GUUAM
   regional level – relations with the EU, NATO, CIS

Ukraine was motivated by externalities on the bilateral and regional levels. On the bilateral level, Ukraine was reluctant to renew Soviet-era military, political and economic ties with Russia. Thus Kyiv sought a special, but circumscribed relationship with Moscow. Above all, however, Kyiv was focused on avoiding deep integration with the CIS, a negative non-security externality to the extent that it was seen in Kyiv as synonymous with continued industrial ossification. Such integration was likely to be accompanied by risks to Ukraine's independence and sovereignty, a clear negative security externality.

Conversely, along the Western azimuth, Ukraine was motivated by the positive security and non-security externalities that would accrue from harmonious bilateral ties with CEES and, eventually, from ties with Western subregional and regional institutional structures.

The Southern azimuth bridges the two above-mentioned azimuths. On the one hand, Ukraine was driven by the positive non-security externality that might accrue if Ukraine were to be involved in the transportation of Caspian energy, a prerequisite of which were strong ties with 'key' Black Sea states. The institutionalisation of these ties in Southern subregional institutional structures, such as the BSEC and

GUUAM, was one of the means with which Ukraine hoped to attain goals along this azimuth. The Southern azimuth was important for two other reasons. First, these subregional goals might facilitate the attainment of regional goals along the Western azimuth, namely membership of the EU. Second, Kyiv hoped that membership of subregional institutions along the Southern azimuth might inhibit Ukraine's deeper integration along the North-eastern azimuth.

In sum, each of the two levels of analysis identified above, namely Ukraine's bilateral ties with neighbours, and relations with subregional and regional institutions, will be examined in order to assess the extent to which Ukraine achieved regional goals along the North-eastern, Western and Southern azimuths.

Regional orders

In order to measure 'success' or 'failure' within a given RSC, an assessment will be made of the extent to which Ukraine influenced the dominant pattern of security management, or regional orders, along each of the azimuths. There are five forms of regional orders which can be placed in a hierarchy of ideal types requiring increasing levels of co-operation with regional neighbours: power-restraining power, concert, collective security, pluralistic security community and, finally, integration.[17]

Power-restraining power refers to the classic pursuit of security through the achievement of balance of power. In an RSC where security is primarily pursued via balance of power, stability is sought in either a unipolar/hegemonic (hegemonic stability theory), bipolar or multipolar regional order. With the collapse of bipolarity on the European continent, and the instability that has ensued, a new regional order has been sought by the CEES. CEES are unambiguous as to what sort of order they desire:

> in Eastern Europe there is a strong reluctance to trust other forms of security management in view of Russia's past behaviour and uncertainties about its political future. Poland, the Baltic states, and others have been eager to join NATO *as an alliance against Russia*, seeking security in a traditional power-balancing way [italics in original].[18]

All available evidence suggests that such an unambiguous choice was not available to Ukraine if Kyiv was to avoid the wrath of Russia: Moscow would never countenance Kyiv's membership of an alliance against it.

Hegemonic stability theory predicts that a hegemon will establish order or pursue security in a given region by dominating or exploiting smaller states. However, Ukraine's gravitation towards the Russian pole, as predicted by the hegemonic stability theory, was not an appealing option to Kyiv, as the benefits to Ukraine of order or security presented by hegemonic stability were outbalanced by the fact that domination or exploitation by the hegemon threatened its independence.

A concert refers to regional great powers adopting collective responsibility within a regional security complex. While concerts primarily benefit the most powerful states of the concert, the stability that ensues benefits the 'lesser' parties of the region. However, by virtue of the fact that great powers allow for each other's 'vital influence' in a region, concerts are perceived by the 'subjects' of the concert to have negative ramifications. In the European theatre, for example, Ukraine reacted with abhorrence to the Russian offer for such a concert in its 'near abroad' when in February 1993 Yeltsin argued that 'the moment has arrived for authoritative international organisations, including the United Nations, to grant Russia special powers as the guarantor of peace and stability in this [i.e. the former Soviet Union] region'.[19] In technical terms, as will be argued, the negative externality of the risk posed to Ukraine's sovereignty and independence by such an offer was too great for Kyiv to countenance.

The collective security approach is a more inclusive alternative to a great power concert. By reducing the prerogative of the great powers to manage regional security, regional powers seek to influence regional decisions. Such powers agree to abstain from the use of force in resolving differences, and instead revert to collective responses to rule out violations by an aggressor against a victim.[20] The common interests which motivate such co-operation include 'shared fears of unrestricted violence or unstable agreements, or insecurity about independence or sovereignty'.[21]

Certainly, the collective security approach is one on which Ukraine has put great store, pinning its hopes on the conversion of NATO into a regional collective security system along the Western azimuth. To an extent, these hopes have already been realised: the establishment of the Partnership for Peace Programme (PfP), and the creation of North Atlantic Co-operation Council (NACC) are significant moves in this direction. It is precisely through the creation of institutions such as these and the subsequent enlargement of NATO in 1997 that it has been argued that 'NATO's founding mission of collective defence organised against the Soviet threat has been fundamentally transformed . . . NATO's enlargement may have . . . set the alliance on a trend in the direction of a diluted collective security institution'.[22] In addition it will be shown that Kyiv's ambitions along the Western azimuth were bolstered by a lack of willingness on the part of Ukraine to participate in the Tashkent Treaty, a collective security system headed by Russia along the North-eastern azimuth. The underlying rationale of collective security, namely the recognition of common interests among states, implies that Ukraine perceived a greater degree of common interest with states along the Western azimuth than with states along the North-eastern azimuth.

Ukraine was interested above all in the last two of the five options, namely either joining a pluralistic security community or, ideally, integrating with institutions, though in both cases only along its Western azimuth.

A pluralistic security community is characterised by 'a sense of community and of institutions and practices strong enough and widespread enough to assure, for a long time, dependable expectations and peaceful change'.[23] This socially constructed and identity-driven approach involves a commitment to the non-use of threats or force, inviolability of borders, arms and force reduction, defensive military postures, and greater transborder flows. In simple terms, force becomes unthinkable between community members. A perusal of the history of post-Cold War Central and Eastern Europe and Ukraine, suggests that such a community is some way off, both along the Western and North-eastern azimuth. The friction between Ukraine and Russia between 1991 and 1997 is ample testimony to the elusiveness of the notion of community between two nation-states that had hitherto regarded themselves as 'fraternal'.

Integration implies the subordination of state prerogatives to those of a supra-national institution in pursuit of security. As Morgan points out, 'many governments in Eastern Europe regard membership in the EU (an integrated security community) as the ultimate guarantee of security'.[24] This included Ukraine, which as early as 1996 had set itself the goal of integration along the Western azimuth in the form of membership of the European Union. By contrast, neither membership of a pluralistic security community nor integration along the North-eastern azimuth was desirable to Kyiv.

To summarise, the extent to which Ukraine influenced the dominant pattern of security management, or regional orders along the North-eastern, Western and Southern azimuths, will be assessed on two levels, namely in terms of bilateral relations with regional neighbours, and relations with subregional and regional institutions. Along the North-eastern azimuth, it will be argued that Ukraine sought to establish harmonious bilateral relations with regional neighbours, but impede subregional and regional institutional developments to the extent that such developments negatively impacted on Ukrainian sovereignty. Along the Western azimuth, it will be contended that Ukraine utilised bilateral ties with regional neighbours in pursuit of membership of subregional and regional institutions. The Southern azimuth needs to be seen in the context of the previous two azimuths. The case will be made that Southern developments, i.e. bilateral ties, and relations with subregional and regional institutions, were pursued to the extent to which they facilitated the achievements of objectives along the aforementioned two azimuths.

While the two levels (bilateral and subregional/regional) are ostensibly discrete, the interaction between them was explicit as expressed in Ukrainian foreign policy objectives along each of the azimuths. An effort will be made to explore two-level interaction (bilateral–subregional, subregional–regional, bilateral–regional) and hence gain an albeit limited insight into factors involved in policy-objective formation in Kyiv and the impact these objectives had on influencing regional orders. Multi-level interaction analysis (i.e. the interaction between all three – bilateral–subregional–regional, etc.) has been avoided owing to its inherent complexity.[25]

Defining security

On independence in 1991, Ukraine immediately faced a number of major security dilemmas. As will become clear, the threats were not only those of a classic military type. Despite appearances and the invective flying around Kyiv and Moscow in the post-independence phase, Ukraine was not at any time faced with the prospect of a Russian assault, attack or invasion, despite the 'realist' thinking that characterised

Ukrainian strategic planning. Instead, the narrow military–defence conception of Ukraine's national security, i.e. that the military power of other states presented the main threat to the security of the state and that the state was only defensible with military power, was merely the pinnacle of a pyramid of concerns that could be labelled security issues. Barry Buzan elaborates a conceptualisation of security that lends to itself to Ukraine's predicament particularly well.

Buzan argues that the security of what he calls human collectives consists of five types of threat sectors: military, political, economic, environmental and societal. The placing first of the military threat reflects Buzan's acknowledgement of the primacy of the assumptions of realism, namely, the anarchy that characterises the international system of states. As such the military sector 'concerns the two-level interplay of the armed offensive and defensive capabilities of states, and states' perceptions of each other's intentions'.[26] Undoubtedly, as will be explored below, threats to Ukraine's security existed from the very earliest days of its independence. These took a number of forms ranging from a direct challenge to the territorial integrity of Ukraine by both Romania and Russia, to a refusal by Moscow to countenance the unilateral decision of Kyiv to nationalise all forces on Ukrainian territory, especially the Black Sea Fleet.

The second sector, political security, 'concerns the organisational stability of states, systems of government and the ideologies that give them legitimacy'.[27] On these criteria, on independence Ukraine was a *highly* vulnerable state burdened with the task of simultaneous and yet urgent nation- and state-building. The organisational stability of the state was missing. In the immediate aftermath of the coup in Moscow in 1991, the Communist party, the very backbone of stability throughout the Soviet Union, was banned and its property confiscated. While independent Ukraine inherited a system of government, it was soon deemed as incongruent with the needs of the new state. Mere tinkering to modify rather than replace it began soon after independence. This consisted of creating new institutions such as the presidency, and eliminating old ones like Communist party rule. Such tinkering also included the manipulation of existing institutions, such as first changing the existing Soviet era constitution, and then abandoning them altogether. All the while, the new-found prominence of the Ukrainian parliament, the *Rada*, threw into sharp focus the structural and ideological divides that permeated Ukrainian society: the ongoing battles between the dominant left-wing and the reformist national democrats were to blight Ukraine's political scene from day one. In turn, the parliament was in conflict with the presidency, an institution the Communists were vehemently opposed to.[28] The fact that all of this took place in the context of an economy which was experiencing a collapse of disastrous proportions and an increasingly unfavourable international environment merely exacerbated the situation. For all of these reasons, Ukraine lacked organisational stability.

The third sector, economic security, concerns 'access to the resources, finance and markets necessary to sustain acceptable levels of welfare and state power'.[29] With the collapse of the Soviet Union, Ukraine's access to resources, finance and markets collapsed. Indeed, Kyiv and Moscow had regular conflicts on the issue of access to the market – trade between them was characterised by the sudden imposition of tariffs, and counter-tariffs. In terms of economic security, Ukraine was sorely lacking.

Because of a past scarred by industrial and nuclear pollution, Ukraine was vulnerable in the fourth sector, namely that of environmental security, which according to Buzan, is 'the maintenance of the local and the planetary biosphere as the essential support system on which all other human enterprises depend'.[30] Furthermore it was a deteriorating situation, with an economy heavily dependent on unsafe nuclear reactors and vast swathes of South-eastern Ukraine littered with dirty and inefficient industries providing much needed employment to an underemployed population.

The fifth sector, that of societal security, 'concerns the sustainability, within acceptable conditions for evolution of traditional patterns of language, culture and regional and national identity and custom'.[31] Ukraine's internal structural divides have been postulated as the source of its greatest vulnerability, and hence threat to the integrity of the state. Ukraine is a nation-state geographically split, or perhaps more accurately, dividable along ethnic, linguistic, political, religious and political lines. In terms of societal security, Ukraine was susceptible on two counts. Internally, Ukraine was vulnerable to the centrifugal tendencies that tend to characterise states with minorities as large and as concentrated as the Russian minority in South-eastern Ukraine. As Buzan points out:

> if societal security is about the sustainability within acceptable conditions for evolution of traditional patterns of language, cultural and religious and ethnic identity and custom, then threats to these values come much more frequently from within the state than from outside it.[32]

This was certainly true as Ukraine pursued nation-building policies, which involved adopting the policies of what was termed a 'nationalising state'. Inevitably, such nationalising policies were seen as threatening to and by the minorities, something that could trigger centrifugal tendencies. Furthermore, these centrifugal tendencies were prone to further aggravation by powers intent on causing internal turmoil in Ukraine.

In themselves, no single one of these sectors presented an insurmountable security threat. Cumulatively, they were potentially overwhelming. Furthermore, the effects of the emergence of a challenge in any one of the five sectors could reverberate across to other sectors – the threat of a domino effect was ever present.

However, despite his misgivings as to the continued treatment of the state as the principal 'referent object of security' (that is an object the security of which is of primary concern), Buzan accepts the primacy of state security owing to the anarchical international environment. Despite his contention that threats to national security are more likely to be internally than externally generated, he acknowledges that the threats presented by external factors are the greatest source of danger. As he points out: 'Because the use of force can wreak major undesired changes very swiftly, military threats are traditionally accorded the higher priority in national security concerns. Military action can wreck the work of centuries *in all other sectors*.'[33] This concern with military threats, by implication, demands a focus on external determinants of threats to the national security of the Ukrainian state, something this book will primarily concern itself with, as well as the means Ukraine used to counteract them.

Theories of regionalism: frameworks for analysis

While the regionalisation of international behaviour is a phenomenon that has long received attention in international relations theory, theoretical interest in the phenomenon has been reinvigorated in recent years by the collapse of the bipolar system.[34] This book will employ a framework developed by Hurrell in which he sets out 'the major sets of theories that may be deployed to explain the dynamics of regionalism'.[35] Hurrell identifies three categories of theories – systemic-, regional interdependence- and domestic-level theories – each of which will now be examined.

Systemic-level theories of regionalism

Systemic-level theories provide the context within which the effects of wider political and economic processes on regionalism can be investigated. Thus 'systems theories . . . are theories that explain how the organisation of a realm acts as a constraining and disposing force on the interacting units within it. Such theories tell us about the forces the units are subjects to.'[36] However, by rejecting a reductionist approach to International Relations, systemic theories propagate the notion that regionalism and regional behaviour are products of systemic forces. Indeed, it has been argued that any attempt to define a region is little more than 'trying to put boundaries that do not exist around areas that do not matter'.[37]

Two broad approaches can be discerned that strive to contribute to an understanding of regional and subregional behaviour at the systemic level: the realist/neorealist approach on the one hand, and structural interdependence and globalisation on the other.

Realism and neorealism

For realists, regionalism is a strategy reverted to by weak states when their security is threatened by the presence of or stance adopted by stronger states or hegemons. Put succinctly, 'regionalist groupings are basically the natural response of weak states trapped in the world of the strong'.[38] Such a strategy is a corollary of a theoretical conceptualisation of international relations that makes stark assumptions about the international system of states.[39] First, the structure of international political systems is made up of interactions between states. Second, international systems are anarchic, lacking an overarching authority, forcing states to revert to self-help to ensure survival.[40] The formation and strengthening of alliances is thus a self-help strategy as states strive to balance against a perceived foe. Third, classic realists suggest that the prime objective of the state is power, although neorealists argue that power is only a means to an end, namely survival.[41] Fourth, states are deigned to pursue rational policies in pursuit of survival, security or power; such policies as a minimum include the use of military threat or actual force. However, survival, under conditions of anarchy, is not only a matter of the application of force – it is also a matter of continuous adaptation in a highly competitive environment. For the neorealist such adaptation involves the pursuit of economic and technological advantage in neomercantilist economic competition. From this perspective, the economic objectives that are believed to underlie 'regional integration do not derive from the pursuit of welfare, but from the close relationship that exists between economic wealth and political power'.[42]

For realists and neorealists, hegemons act as stimuli to the formation of regions. First, in pursuit of a balance of power, states may form regional groupings in response to the threat presented by a hegemon. As such, the formation of regional alignments corresponds to that of Walt's alliance formation.[43] Such formations, Walt argues, do not just strive to balance against states that are more powerful, especially when a state is perceived as either threatening or as having aggressive intentions. Second, the formation of regional alignments may reflect 'an attempt to restrict the free exercise of hegemonic power through the creation of regional institutions'.[44] Indeed, this very objective was behind Ukraine's insistence that Russia be granted membership of the Council of Europe (CoE). In particular, Kyiv hoped that Moscow's activities in Chechnya might be in part curtailed by the requirements of membership of the CoE. However, it is an isolated example. Russia, as the realist's realist, was unlikely to ever allow itself to be severely constrained in this way. Third, the sheer proximity and overwhelming power of hegemons may elicit the formation of alliances of neighbouring states with the hegemon. This process of 'bandwagoning', or aligning with the hegemon, is predicted to occur in the absence of any alternative to that of seeking accommodation with the hegemonic power. In fact, the entire underlying objective of Ukraine's foreign and security policy can be characterised as a search for an alternative to alignment with the hegemon. Fourth, in the case of declining hegemony, there may exist the tendency for the regional group and the hegemon to collaborate in the establishment of common institutions. Declining hegemons are said to institute co-operation in pursuit of burden-sharing and problem-solving, as a means of legitimising and garnering international support for policies in pursuit of interests. Such a process can be seen at work in Russia's desire for a post-Soviet institution and Ukraine's opposition to it. For all of these reasons, it is anticipated that realism will provide some powerful insights into Ukraine's regional strategy along all three azimuths.

Structural interdependence

The theory of structural interdependence strives to address what it sees as an oversimplification and mischaracterisation by realists of the international system. The analytical approach of the theory consists of three key themes, interdependence, complex interdependence and regime change, each of which impacts on the degree of integration.

Interdependence, the first theme, is defined as the mutual dependence that derives from international transactions across boundaries. In Ukraine's case, on independence, its economic, political and military interdependence with Russia was profound. This was more than mere interconnectedness as 'where there are reciprocal (although not necessarily symmetrical) costly effects of transactions, there is interdependence. Where interactions do not have significant costly effects, there is simply interconnectedness.'[45] The break-up of this extremely close relationship would prove to be costly for both parties, with Ukraine especially vulnerable. This vulnerability was caused by the asymmetry in the degree of mutual dependence between the two actors (i.e. the extent to which one actor depends on another and vice versa) that determines the amount of power any one actor possess in an interdependent relationship. As a provider of much of Ukraine's energy and raw materials, Russia was on this measure by far the more powerful of the two. There are two dimensions to dependence: sensitivity interdependence and vulnerability interdependence. Sensitivity interdependence is defined as the 'liability to costly effects imposed from outside before policies are altered to try and change the situation'; vulnerability interdependence is the 'liability to suffer costs imposed by external events even after policies have been altered'.[46] On these two measures, Ukraine was not only sensitive but it was especially vulnerable to its interdependence with Russia. Indeed, empirical findings not only support the theoretical affirmation that vulnerability interdependence is more important than sensitivity interdependence in establishing power relations between actors but also, more importantly, the contention that asymmetrical interdependencies are sources of power among actors.

The second theme of structural interdependence theory, namely complex interdependence, builds on simple interdependence by emphasising three key features: multiple channels of contact or access between states (interstate, transgovernmental and transnational), the absence of a hierarchy of issues to be addressed between states (that is, military security does not dominate the agenda), and a low salience of the use of military force. Clearly, where these three features are present, prospects for integration are enhanced. In the case of relations between Kyiv and Moscow, the fact that military security dominated the agenda in the development of relations in the first few years following Ukrainian independence was sufficient to discourage Ukraine's renewed integration with Russia, notwithstanding the multiple channels of contact that continued to link the two states (extensive familial ties, elite ties, educational/training co-operation). The fact that Kyiv was guided by the perception that military force on the part of Moscow had a high salience merely reinforced Kyiv's conviction.

The final theme, that of regime change (where a regime is defined as networks of rules, norms and procedures that regularise behaviour and control its effects), aims to explain how regimes undergo transition from one type (e.g. interconnectedness) to another (e.g. integration). It focuses on the distribution of power (predominantly military power) among states as a determinant of the nature of the prevailing international regime. As a result, it is argued that 'as the power of states changes . . . the rules that comprise international regimes will change accordingly'.[47] Thus a collapse in the power of the hegemon compels it not only to become more accommodating, but is accompanied by an increase in assertiveness on the part of secondary powers, the net result of which is a change in the economic regime, albeit in the absence of either significant shifts in the balance of power or war. Interdependence theorists attribute a prominent role to issue structure as an explanation of regime change, an area neglected by realists. Thus although Russia attempted to impose rules within a given issue area, the uneven distribution of its military and economic strength meant that attempts to link issue areas by Moscow were often unsuccessful, something which was exploited by Ukraine in order to pursue its regional ambitions and bolster its security. Despite its inherent complexity and lack of parsimony, the theory of structural interdependence highlights the important role of key variables affecting Ukraine's relations with Russia, which are perhaps underestimated by realism. By underlining the significance of these variables, the theory of structural interdependence will have provided a powerful insight into Ukraine's regional behaviour, at least along the North-eastern azimuth.

Globalisation

The final systemic approach to regionalism is that of globalisation, an 'informal integration which consists of those intense patterns of interaction which develop without the intervention of deliberate governmental decisions, following the dynamics of markets, technology, communications networks and social exchange, or the influence of religious, social or political movements'.[48]

Four interrelated features distinguish the process of globalisation. First, it refers to a growth in the primarily economic interconnectedness and interdependence between nation-states. Second, interconnectedness and interdependence leads to a diffusion of technology, in particular, transport, information and communication technology, which in turn reinforces the existing economic links between the nation-states and eventually leads to a growth in social exchange between their citizens. Third, and building on the previous two points, the resulting material infrastructure leads to a growth of societal interdependence. This interdependence, when bolstered by

> the integrating and homogenising influence of market forces, facilitates increased flows of values, knowledge, and ideas, and increases the ability of like-minded groups to organise across national boundaries, creating a transnational civil society that includes both transnational policy communities and transnational social movements.[49]

The result is a single global community.

Globalisation contributes to the emergence of regionalism in a number of ways. First, the need to tackle issues that exceed the ability of individual nation-states to cope imposes a requirement for collective management. The institutionalisation of such collective management is a more feasible prospect when undertaken at the regional level, where the actors share a world outlook, social system, historical and cultural experiences, strive for political and security convergence and are characterised by homogeneity of norms and values. Second, despite the apparent global nature of many problems, the solutions are often regional; additionally, any enforcement of standards agreed at the global level is likely to take place at the regional level. Third, the incongruity between the forces driving, on the one hand, integration and globalisation (e.g. market pressure, technological diffusion), and, on the other, the trend toward fragmentation is likely to be resolved at the regional level. Finally, globalisation drives regionalism by impacting on policy goals adopted by states. For example, in the competition for the finite foreign investment and technology available and the hoped-for economic development that follows in their wake, governments are driven to adopt ever more mercantilist market–liberal policies which are increasingly homogeneous with those of competitors in an ever more crowded market-place. Conversely, global forces are forcing states to congregate or join forces in larger units in pursuit not only of economic efficiency but also the political weight necessary to ensure that they are treated with sufficient seriousness in world economic institutions.

However, despite the growing appeal of globalisation as a theory in the context of an ever integrating or regionalising world, it is expected to offer little in terms of explanatory power regarding Ukraine's regional predicament in the first decade of its independence. This is because Ukraine's regional behaviour was geared toward consolidating its sovereignty and integrity, rather than tapping into global flows of capital or technology which it was incapable of absorbing, let alone attracting in the absence of a proper regulatory framework.

Regional-level theories of regionalism

An alternative to the systemic approach is provided by regional-level theories. By emphasising the role of institutions, regional cohesion and pluralism, these theories attempt to link regionalism with the interdependence that characterises regional-level interaction.

(Neo)functionalism

The essence of (neo)functionalism is that rising interdependence demands co-operation which in turn leads to integration in the shape of some form of supranational institution. While initially the role of the institution is limited to some predetermined issue-area, with time the influence of such an institution 'spills-over' into other areas, a process which again moves the independent states along the spiral of further integration. Functional spill-over, the first of three types of spill-over, occurs when integration causes problems the solution to which is further integration. Political spill-over is the tendency for the political elites that 'inhabit' supranational institutions (and whose loyalties have perhaps shifted to the institution) to encourage further integration, perhaps via institution-building. Cultivated spill-over refers to the role central institutions play as mediators in negotiations, a role which then may spill-over into an upgrading of the common interest, the result of which is greater integration.[50] Overall, integration is believed by (neo)functionalists to be a self-perpetuating process – as integration occurred in one area, it would expand into others. Haas, in his seminal work on European integration between 1950 and 1957, argues that his findings were sufficiently general to explain the formation of political communities subject to, first, the participants being industrial economies, tightly linked to international trade and financial flows, and, second, being pluralist societies governed by identifiable elites under conditions of democracy and constitutionalism.[51]

Yet as Hurrell points out, 'despite its [neofunctionalism's] influence on both the theory and practice of European regionalism, its relevance to contemporary regionalism elsewhere is rather less clear'.[52] Indeed, its relevance to Ukraine between 1991 and 2000 will be seen as distinctly marginal.

According to Hurrell, there are three criticisms supporters of the theory need to address. First, and especially relevant in the case of Ukraine's regional efforts, is the fact that while (neo)functionalism is relatively successful in explaining the evolution of regional institutions, it struggles to explain the emergence of regionalist schemes. Second, the prominence attributed to regional institutions by (neo)-functionalists contrasts sharply with the distinctly secondary and declining role states are deemed to play. Third, by neglecting the distinction between 'high' and 'low' politics, neofunctionalists fail to recognise that 'high' politics remain the realm of the state, and that only issues of 'low' politics lend themselves to integrationist schemes.[53]

Neoliberal institutionalism

In contrast to (neo)functionalism, which de-emphasises the role of the state, for neoliberal institutionalism the state remains important as the interface between domestic and international fora. However, because of the limitations of unilateral action and the growing interdependence of states, institutions are seen as the solution to the demands thrown up by problems of collective action such as the free-rider problem or the dangers of defection. For example, collective defence collaboration, when institutionalised, is not only deemed an effective means of deterring attack; it also provides cohesion to a group that might otherwise be liable to fragment. As such, institutions are more than a means to an end – they are fora for reciprocal feedback by providing information, facilitating communication, maintaining transparency, repeated interactions, sanctioning and allowing monitoring; they also provide a forum in which threats can be signalled, promises made, intentions transmitted and capabilities assessed. In sum, institutions enhance security by reducing uncertainty. And while strategic interdependence – that is, the interdependence between security strategies of states – is a zero-sum game in realist theory, for institutionalists it leads to more informed and hence more efficient security strategies.

Institutional theorists acknowledge the potentially divisive efforts that relative gains can bring about. However, while some issues tend to result in zero-sum relative gains (competing territorial claims, expansionism), the comparative rarity of issues that lend themselves to forceful resolution allied to the eroding utility of military force renders the relative gain problem mainly a worst-case scenario issue. Clearly a distinction needs to be made between Ukraine's objectives along the Western azimuth – namely, membership of key institutions – and its stated desire to avoid integration with institutions along the North-eastern azimuth. According to Wallander, institutionalists would explain this divergence through the relative density of the network of institutions along the respective azimuths. Along the Western azimuth, institutions such as the Council of Europe, the OSCE, the NACC, the EU and NATO reinforce

> the availability of defensive strategies in the face of shifting intentions or exploitative behaviour. States can afford to participate in security institutions designed for transparency and mediation if they can count on the monitoring and sanctioning capabilities of an institution designed for collaboration as well . . . In contrast, Russia lacks a similar network of strong security institutions. If multilateral strategies were to fail, Russia would be left with little but traditional military and diplomatic responses to exploitative strategies.[54]

With this point alone, neoliberal institutionalism contributes to an understanding of why Ukraine pursued membership of Western subregional and regional institutions so vigorously, yet so vehemently sought to avoid all but the most shallow terms of membership of the CIS.

Overall, co-operation, rather than simply being driven by a need for alliance formation or concerns about balance of power, is a process of intergovernmental bargaining the result of which is ever greater co-operation within an increasingly more complex whole. As has been pointed out, 'patterns of success in effective multilateral security co-operation cannot be explained solely by power and interests but must take international institutions into account'.[55]

Constructivism

In contrast to both (neo)functionalists and neoliberal institutionalists, both of which stress the institutional dimension of regionalism, cognitions are at the root of the constructivist approach to regionalism. Such a cognitive approach resonates strongly in Ukraine in two mutually exclusive ways. Simply, the stress Ukraine places on its Central European roots is at odds with the emphasis Russia places on its common East Slavic extraction with Ukraine. According to constructivists, the development of 'cognitive regionalism' is a result of the psychological dynamics that interdependence brings about. Both of the two different constructivist approaches focus on the sense of community that emerges from interdependence.

The first approach, based on the integration theory of Deutsch, argues that the emergence of an inter-state community is based on two platforms.[56] The first platform is a sense of community between the states, a degree of sympathy for and loyalty to one another, a commonality of norms and understanding and a sharing of principles. The second platform consists not only of a compatibility of political and economic values (which contribute to a sense of community) but also the (inter-societal) communication that results from transactions taking place between states or societies. In Ukraine's case, the latter, namely the lack of communication with its Western neighbours for the past fifty years, precluded the development of compatible political and economic values, all of which meant that on independence in 1991 Ukraine had a weak sense of community with its Western neighbours. This was a series of deficits the Ukrainian elite tried to rapidly rectify on independence. The fact that this community-building took place at the same time as the long-established community with its north-eastern neighbour was being disbanded has empirical resonance the theory must deal with in order to reaffirm its validity.

The second, Wendtian approach also gives prominence to processes that contribute to community formation. However, it also allows for the actors' interpretation of the world, and the influence of culture and history, something which explains Kyiv's concerted efforts to emphasise its European heritage as it mapped out its 'return to Europe'. Wendt's view that 'states are not structurally or exogenously given but constructed by historically contingent interactions' was quickly latched onto as Ukraine's political elite sought to create a *European* Ukraine.[57] If Ukraine wanted to join a CEES community, it had to share a CEES identity. Wendt identifies at least three mechanisms that lead to the formation of collective identities. The first, the structural context, consists 'of the shared understandings, expectations, and social knowledge embedded in international institutions and threat complexes, in terms of which states define (some of) their identities and interests'.[58] For Ukraine, the creation of such a context meant, above all, joining European institutions, even if only Central and East European subregional institutions, a key determinant in the formation of a European identity at the end of the twentieth century. The second mechanism, systemic processes, encourages collective identity formation through, first, rising interdependence, and second, transnational convergence. Interdependence rises as a result of both a growth in intensity of capital and trade flows, and the emergence of a common threatening 'other', all of which intensifies the propensity to form a collective identity. Indeed, the weight Ukraine placed on a growth in interdependence with its Western neighbours and the emphasis it repeatedly placed on Russia as the 'other' speaks volumes about Ukraine's regional ambitions in the area. The transnational convergence that results from the increasing homogeneity of outlook that comes with a confluence of cultural and political values, and cross-cultural or cross-border learning, was a long-term goal for Kyiv as it sought to 'Europeanise'. The functioning of the third mechanism, strategic practice, suggests that repeated instances of co-operation may lead to collective identity formation and the emergence of communities. Indeed, Ukraine's effort to ensure repeated instances of co-operation with its western neighbours is indicative of the extent to which Kyiv was intent on being part of any emergent Central and Eastern European community. As will be seen, constructivism was at the heart of Ukraine's efforts along the Western azimuth, and as such provides a powerful insight into the strategies Ukrainian policy-makers adopted in pursuit of membership of subregional and regional institutions.

'New Wave' regionalism

By examining the extent to which power relations guide the formation and development of regional institutions and their economic effects, 'New Wave' regionalism attempts to fill a gap left by Hurrell's framework.[59] New Wave regionalists examine regionalism as a '*political* process characterised by economic *policy* co-operation and coordination among countries' [italics in original].[60] They highlight the extent to which regionalism is a *politico-economic* phenomenon. Accordingly, the proliferation of preferential trading arrangements (PTAs) across regions of the world represents not only the economic arrangements between member states of that region but also is reflective of the inter-state politics within that region. This relationship between politics and economics will be made explicit in the following chapters as it will be seen that along the Western azimuth, Ukraine sought to participate in separate PTAs with both CEFTA and the EU precisely because of the political ramifications of such participation. In contrast, along the North-eastern azimuth, Ukraine sought to tightly circumscribe the political dimension of the CIS PTAs and to limit them to economic matters only. In other words, the extent to which Ukraine has tried to participate in PTAs reflects the political dimension it perceives as underlying that particular regional arrangement. As has been stated, 'states do not make the decision to enter a PTA in an international political vacuum'.[61] Rarely can New Wave regionalism have had more resonance than for Ukraine, a country which following independence found itself on the cusp of two regions, each of which were forming PTAs for clearly interrelated political *and* economic reasons.

Crucially, while welfare considerations underlying regionalism are a key feature of the study of the phenomenon for New Wave regionalists, considerations which were in fact very important to Ukraine, Kyiv was, perhaps for understandable reasons, inordinately preoccupied by the political dimension of the process.[62] In fact Ukraine's stance on the PTAs of the CIS needs to be seen in the political context of the vastly attenuated power of its key member, Russia, and with an eye on all of the attendant implications for that state's security relations and Moscow's efforts to minimise the pernicious effects of its decline in power. Conversely, the EU PTAs 'have been used with increasing regularity to help prompt and consolidate economic and political reforms', something which affected Ukraine's relations with that institution and Kyiv's prospects for membership.[63] The different objectives underlying the policies on which the PTAs of these two regional bodies are based have conditioned Ukraine's stance towards regional developments on its borders and will be explored in the following chapters.

'Subregional' regionalism

Within the study of regionalism, a growing body of research has sought to focus on subregional developments (again beyond the scope of Hurrell's theoretical framework) as a distinct yet complementary subset of larger integration processes. The very existence of subregional institutions in Central and Eastern Europe is a product of a dichotomy on the European continent. On the one hand, subregional institutions emerged in the area to help fill the political vacuum which followed the end of the Cold War. On the other hand, their existence (and membership of them) was based on the strict premise that subregional institutions should neither replace regional institutions nor replicate their functions, which, as shall be elaborated on below, were a potential impediment to their evolution.[64]

Although research on subregional integration adopts a normative approach, and does not aspire to the status of theory, it strives to highlight the factors or variables driving subregional integration. First, for the newly independent or recently 'de-satellitised' states of Central and Eastern Europe, membership of subregional institutions ostensibly offered the means of attaining proportionally greater influence – collectivism carries greater weight than individualism. Second, subregional institutions potentially provided those same states with convenient staging posts between the individualism and isolation of the immediate post-Cold War era, and the distant prospect of membership of the major regional institutions in Western Europe. (Indeed, for some CEES, in particular Ukraine, membership of subregional institutions was the only option on offer along the Western azimuth in terms of institutional membership functionally important in the pursuit of membership of key regional institutions.) Third, subregional institutions offered the prospect of providing all-too-rare fora for CEES to participate in *equal status* negotiations and exchange of information not only with member states but also other institutions.[65] Perhaps above all, 'subregional groups had the potential to sustain co-operation and help to avert the development of potentially dangerous divisions in the new Europe'.[66] If the 'benefits (of such co-operation) for the small and more remote states are particularly clear' they were equally evident to *weak* and remote states such as Ukraine.[67] It is worth reiterating that it was evident to policy-makers in Kyiv from the very first days of independence, that because NATO and EU membership was precluded, participation in subregional groupings was effectively the only avenue open to Ukraine along the Western azimuth if it wanted to 'return to Europe'. As has been pointed out, 'today you are what you belong to'.[68] Above all, subregional co-operation is believed to increase security by 'promoting confidence and trust between states and peoples of the region, reinforcing mutual dependence, strengthening democratic structures, reducing economic differences, promoting economic and social development, reducing region-specific risks and threats, and promoting further regional co-operation'.[69]

Despite the high hopes held out for the success of subregional institutions, particularly in Central and Eastern Europe, in attaining the goals outlined above, they would have to surmount a number of inherent flaws. First, certainly along the Western azimuth, subregional institutions would be placed in direct competition with the regional institutions to which CEES aspired. Yet, where a member state was intent on joining regional institutions, subregional institutions were unlikely to be an adequate substitute. This presented Ukraine with the prospect of joining institutions which were subsequently abandoned by founding and key member states. Second, in pursuit of membership of regional institutions, and lacking 'mediating' mechanisms put in place by regional institutions which might discourage individualistic approaches, subregional member states were likely to be in competition with each other for entry into regional institutions. It is evident that in the absence of an unambiguous message from regional institutions that 'a good record of co-operation at [the] subregional level will help not handicap states which otherwise meet the conditions of membership' it was unlikely that subregional institutions would prosper.[70] Ukraine needed them to prosper. A third point is that membership of subregional institutions potentially condemns the group to collectively move at the pace of the slowest member, amongst which Ukraine would inevitably find itself, certainly along the Western azimuth.

Although the ramifications of these inherent contradictions were potentially profoundly negative for Ukraine's prospects for membership of subregional institutions, the contradictions were not irreconcilable if 'the larger European organizations, including NATO, should articulate policies which more clearly support the sub-regions'.[71]

Domestic-level theories of regionalism

Domestic-level theories aim to explain the emergence of regionalism in terms of the experiences shared by polities of a given geographical space. Among such experiences are religion, culture, race, ethnicity and even extraction, a similarity of language, and an awareness of a shared history and heritage. While ostensibly similar to neofunctionalism (which also stresses certain domestic prerequisites to regionalism), domestic-level theories highlight the internal political make-up of states or the internal dynamics that take place within states as the independent variable. Two versions of domestic-level theories will be examined.

Regionalism and state coherence

The state coherence approach suggests that the very integrity, viability and coherence of states in a given region are a prelude to integration and regional co-operation between those states. Conversely, partaking in regionalism does not appear to be a viable option for states that are themselves disintegrating under the burdens imposed by a lack of internal legitimacy, ineffective or deleterious state structures and economic and political mismanagement. Ukraine was such a state. Owing to political and social fragmentation and the marginal internal legitimacy that ensued, let alone the economic and political mismanagement that has characterised the Ukrainian landscape in the first decade of independence, Ukraine's greatest security threat was and remains internal rather than external.[72] Specifically, because of different historical trajectories, the experiences of Western Ukraine have been very different to those of 'Greater Ukraine'. While 'Greater Ukraine', under Russia, was over the centuries exposed to Russification, mass immigration of ethnic Russians, collectivisation and rapid industrialisation, Western Ukraine was only subjected to Russian/Soviet practices from 1939 onwards.[73] As a result of these divergent historical paths, on independence Ukraine was (and continues to be) a highly fractured state. Ethnically, Ukraine is essentially a nation of two parts: 72.7

per cent or 37.4 million Ukrainians, and 22.1 per cent or 11.4 million Russians; 80 per cent of the Russians are urban dwellers based in the South and East. Ethno-geographically, it is a mixed nation with sizeable Russian minorities in Central, Eastern and Southern regions, an outright Russian majority and a fast growing Tartar minority in Crimea, and small but significant Russian minorities in Western regions. Linguistically it is also a nation of two parts – 43.4 per cent are Ukrainophones and 56.6 per cent Russophones.[74] It is noteworthy that a large proportion of ethnic Ukrainians are in fact Russophones. As a broad generalisation, Central, Eastern and Southern Ukrainians tend to be Russophone, while Western Ukrainians are predominantly Ukrainophones. Furthermore, there is a strong correlation between language used (the so-called language of convenience) and attitudes toward the 'Russian issue' and political affiliation.[75] For example, the Ukrainian Left, with its strong pro-CIS, pro-Russian, anti-capitalist and anti-West orientation, tends to be elected by the ethnically Russian and Russophone constituency in the cities and rural areas of Southern, Eastern and Central Ukraine. In contrast, leaning toward the right of centre, the National Democrats have their power base in Western Ukraine with some support in Kyiv. The extent to which this internal fragmentation influenced Ukraine's regional behaviour will be assessed where relevant.

The state coherence approach also suggests that prospects for regionalism are likely to be further damaged in the absence of mutually agreed and accepted territorial boundaries between states of a given region.[76] Therefore the impact on regionalism of the historically-legitimised threat Ukraine faced from some of its neighbours, in particular Romania and Russia, will also be explored.

Regime type and democratisation

The essence of the Democratic Peace Theory (or more accurately Hypothesis) as applied to regionalism is that the noted lack of wars between democratic regimes is conducive to regionalism. Two versions of the theory have been postulated.[77] The first suggests that the very nature of democracy, and the power it confers on the populace, constrains the elected government from pursuing actions the material consequences of which are then borne by the population. The second argues that the very institutional structures inherent to democratic regimes (that is the 'checks and balances' so beholden to political scientists) render war-making a last resort option for politicians. Furthermore, the norms and practices for conflict resolution within democratic regimes seem to be applied to external issues. Thus, when two such democratic states face up to each other, not only are they limited by the same structural and normative constraints on their own behaviour, but crucially, they *perceive* each other as such. As Russett points out '*the culture, perceptions and practices* that permit compromise and the peaceful resolution of conflicts without the threat of violence within countries come to apply across national boundaries toward other democratic countries'.[78] The net result of these two theories is that democracies do not conduct war with each other even though democracies may wage war with non-democratic regimes, which they do not perceive as limited by these same internal constraints.[79] From the Democratic Peace Hypothesis/Theory, it is but a short step to the argument that democratisation is a precondition of regionalism. The fact that the difference between a *democratising* state, and a fully *democratised* polity has yet to be fully elaborated, is highly pertinent in Ukraine's case as a less than fully democratic state.

Methodology

Foreign policy outcomes are not the prime focus of this book – strategies are, although outcomes are convenient dependent (i.e. measurable, or assessable) variables. As a result, where possible contemporaneous evidence has been employed. The main sources of such evidence are primarily newspaper articles (including interviews with key actors), interviews with involved actors and public government documents. The use of secondary sources has been kept to a minimum.

The book has sought to understand Ukraine as a regional actor as well as explain its behaviour. The onus will however be on 'understand'. Rather than simply seeking to identify specific causal factors as leading to particular outcomes, the book has sought in the words of Woods to

> search not so much for the cause of an event as for its meaning. Scholars seeking to understand will prefer to investigate a particular event or state of affairs, rather than a set of cases, delving into history not as a bank of information which might falsify a theory, but as a narrative which permits a greater appreciation of the origins, evolution, and consequences of an event.[80]

The case study approach adopted in this book has sought to comment as objectively as possible on events, while at the same time give some meaning to those events, a meaning gleaned from the wider context in which those events took place. Inevitably the interpretation of events is a more fraught exercise than is the interpretation of data, as the former tends to be experiential and even impressionistic while the latter employs operationalised variables, controlled conditions and predetermined independent and dependent variables. While there is clearly a danger that the interpretation adopted may be a fallacious one, it is hoped that the problem may be minimised by ensuring that the final product consists of 'strictly determined findings' but only 'loosely determined assertions'.[81]

Ultimately, by definition, the approach adopted is rationalist–constructivistic, i.e. the end product reflects the author's perception of events. Thus, rather than 'knowledge' having been discovered, it has been constructed. Nevertheless, the objective throughout has been that even this constructed version of reality bears some correspondence to a reality the reader may recognise. This has in part been ensured by the book having been guided, though not determined, by other work in the field.

Part II

The North-eastern azimuth

At the root of all Ukraine's objectives along its North-eastern azimuth lay the resolution of its troubled relationship with Russia. Thus, from the very earliest days of independence, Ukraine pursued the normalisation of political, economic and military ties with Russia. This was an essential objective along the North-eastern azimuth as the nature of Kyiv's ties with Moscow would invariably impact on Ukraine's relations with Russia *within* the CIS. In turn, the nature of relations with Russia would also help define Ukraine's status within the CIS. A bilateral relationship with Russia in which Ukraine was the self-evident junior partner would demean the latter's status within the CIS and impose on Kyiv undesired institutional constraints.

Within this context, Ukraine's relations with Belarus on a bilateral level were always going to be of secondary importance. They were, however, not unimportant. In particular, there is some evidence to suggest that both Ukraine and Belarus took advantage of each other when it came to resolving difficulties each was having with Russia. Although relations between Kyiv and Minsk were inevitably dwarfed by their respective relations with Moscow, they are particularly interesting in the light of Minsk's efforts to instil some life into the idea of a Slavic subregional institution, a Slavic 'brotherhood'. While this idea aroused some interest in Moscow, in Kyiv it fell on deaf ears. Kyiv was wary of any device that might drag it too deeply into institutional relationships with former Soviet republics that were not of its making, choosing or shaping.

2 Ukraine's relations with Slavic states

Relations with Russia

Following the coup in Moscow in August 1991, and the subsequent proclamation of Ukrainian independence, the political elite in Kyiv immediately started to implement the foreign and security policy which was enshrined in the Declaration of Sovereignty of 1990. The main impetus behind this policy was an unravelling of the hugely complicated network of economic, political and military ties that bound Ukraine to Russia.

As Garnett correctly noted in 1997, there were two sets of objectives underlying policy, namely 'a long and difficult agenda of issues relating to both the legacy of the break-up of the USSR and the contours of future state-to-state relations'.[1] Only by resolving the problems of the past could Kyiv influence the shape of future relations, and only once these two separate aspects to relations had been dealt with effectively did the possibility of genuine participation in European structures open up; without a normalisation of relations, the European option was precluded. Kyiv's relations with Moscow were critical in terms of their impact on Ukraine's ultimate participation in the wider scheme of things taking place in the West. Furthermore, only by establishing the contours of 'normal' bilateral relations could Ukraine hope to avoid being overwhelmed by the institutional constraints of membership of a CIS in which Russia was by far the dominant member.

Garnett identifies five key issues that were crucial in the resolution of 'the past' and preparation for 'the future': the recognition of borders, the military balance between Ukraine and Russia (including the Black Sea Fleet problem), economic and, in particular, energy relations and CIS integration. Each of these will now be examined in detail. Special attention will also be paid to each of these issues in terms of how they impacted on Ukraine's subregional and regional objectives along the three azimuths under examination.

Problems in the recognition of Ukraine's borders

If 'there is no more fundamental aspect of sovereignty than international respect for existing borders', then there was no clearer example of Russia's inability to come to terms with Ukraine's sovereignty than Moscow's procrastination over the unconditional recognition of Ukraine's borders.[2] An insight into the mindset of at least one member of Russia's political elite is provided by comments made by Yevgeny Ambartsumov, the chair of the Russian Supreme Soviet's Committee on International Affairs, who argued that it is possible to '"overrate the principle of the inviolability of borders" and that changing the borders of the newly independent states can be justified by both human rights considerations and "the general geopolitical interests of Russia"'.[3] It was precisely this type of stance, adopted by a member of the Democratic Russia Movement, that made the recognition of borders such a pressing issue for Kyiv.

While technically Ukraine was a sovereign state, on independence in August 1991 its sovereignty remained circumscribed by the November 1990 Treaty on the Basic Principles of Relations between the Russian Federation and the Ukrainian SSR which 'acknowledge(d) and respected the territorial integrity of the Ukrainian Soviet Socialist Republic (SSR) and the Russian Socialist Federal Soviet Republic (RSFSR) inside the borders presently existing *within the framework of the USSR*' [italics added].[4] In the absence of a new bilateral treaty specifying the mutual unconditional recognition of borders, the qualification of the latter part of the Article was far from satisfactory from Kyiv's point of view. Yet the willingness to sign a new more 'equal' treaty was far from forthcoming on the part of Moscow. While Yeltsin, in his fervour to bring about the demise of the Soviet Union and deprive Gorbachov of a power base, supported Kyiv's pursuit of independence, the collapse of the Soviet Union in December 1991 was not accompanied by an unconditional and mutual recognition of borders on the part of Russia. Instead, rather than formalise in a treaty the new ties that had arisen between Ukraine and Russia since their independence, Moscow continued to insist on the recognition of Ukraine's territorial integrity and the inviolability of its borders within the context of the newly formed CIS, the successor to the USSR. An effort on the part of the Ukrainian parliament to eliminate this conditionality by unilaterally amending the agreement establishing the CIS and, instead, bilateralising the recognition, respect and inviolability of mutual borders was summarily dismissed by Russia in a subsequent barrage of attacks on Ukraine's sovereignty and integrity.

Ostensibly, the essential problem preventing Russia's recognition of Ukraine's borders was the status of Crimea. More pointedly, Ukraine's relations with Russia were from 1991 complicated by Russian aspirations to Crimea *in toto* and Sevastopol in particular, along with the Black Sea Fleet based there. In theory these issues were not inextricably connected – they only came to be so through the efforts of Moscow.

Russian claims to Crimea and Sevastopol

Technically, Crimea was indisputably Ukrainian territory, at least since 1954 when it was 'donated' to Ukraine by Khrushchev.[5] This decision was effectively validated in the referendum on independence in 1991, when Crimea voted for the independence of Ukraine, albeit by a narrow majority – 54 per cent, the smallest majority in all of the *oblasts* of Ukraine.

However, despite Ukraine's technical ownership of Crimea, the Russian parliament (without the input of the presidency, which remained much more restrained on the issue), from the very earliest days of Ukrainian independence, launched a campaign using a combination of moral and ethical arguments to reclaim Crimea by questioning the legitimacy of Ukraine's possession of the peninsula. In May 1992, the Russian Supreme Soviet issued a resolution challenging the 1954 decision by Soviet authorities to change the status of Crimea from that of a Russian to that of a Ukrainian autonomous republic. This was followed on 5 December 1992 by an adoption of the Congress of the People's Deputies of the Russian Federation, of a decision to authorise an examination of the issue of the status of Sevastopol by the Russian Supreme Soviet.[6]

The latent rationale behind Moscow's desire for the rusting armada that made up the Black Sea Fleet (BSF) was the basing rights that came with the fleet: ownership of the fleet also conferred ownership of the infrastructure that went with it. The two apparently disparate threads of fleet and territory were deliberately linked by Moscow: a refusal by Kyiv to divide the fleet meant that a treaty could not be signed; the consequence of a lack of a treaty was Moscow's non-recognition of the territorial integrity of Ukraine. On the other hand, an agreement to divide the fleet automatically legitimised Russia's military presence on Ukrainian territory. Ukraine was in a no-win situation. As was pointed out by Vladimir Lukin, the head of the Russian Parliamentary Committee on Foreign Affairs and Foreign Economic Relations, 'the Ukrainian leadership will be confronted with a dilemma: either it agrees to the transfer of the fleet and [its] bases to Russia or [the status of] Crimea as part of Ukraine will be called into question'.[7] Yet by transferring the fleet, the status of Crimea would be automatically brought into question because of the legitimisation of the presence of Russian forces on Crimean territory. It was this dilemma that was to haunt Ukrainian policy-makers as they sought a resolution to the deadlock in the following years. As the Ukrainian deputy foreign minister put it 'we don't see a reason to tie the question of the division of the fleet with [sic] the signing of the treaty'.[8] Unfortunately for Kyiv, Moscow could see a reason for tying the two issues.

Summits on the basing rights of the BSF – the territorial dimension

The original agreement on the BSF in January 1992, in the immediate aftermath of the dissolution of the Soviet Union, for Ukraine to take 30 per cent of the BSF (excluding nuclear capable warships), was never implemented. No decision was made as regards basing or territorial rights.[9] Instead, there followed a 'war of decrees' between the two parties, which further muddied the already murky waters.[10]

The first serious attempt to bring about reconciliation between the two parties was in Dragomys on 23 June 1992, the result of which was an agreement on 'the creation of Ukrainian and Russian Navies based on the Black Sea Fleet, the details of which are to be worked out in continuing talks'.[11] The deferment of the BSF issue, along with the demurral of the associated matter of the 'ownership' of Crimea, meant that fundamental features of Kyiv's relations with Moscow, namely Ukraine's territorial integrity and the recognition of it as such, were not addressed. While the subsequent Yalta agreement in August 1992 introduced a semblance of calm into relations, in that a fifty-fifty division of the fleet was agreed, a fundamental stumbling block remained: a lack of agreement on the division of the infrastructure on land. Only too aware of the implications of allocating Russia 'ownership' of the infrastructure, the Ukrainians remained steadfast on the agreement for a fifty-fifty division of the fleet as applying only to the military craft/ships and vessels, and not infrastructure. Unsurprisingly, this was something Moscow was firmly against.

An uneasy peace reigned until the summit in Moscow on 17 June 1993, which ended in an agreement which reiterated the fifty-fifty division of the fleet. More importantly, it also provisionally accepted the concept of leasing Sevastopol to Russia, something which reflected Ukraine's deteriorating negotiating position. Indeed, so strong was Russia's position, that following the Massandra summit in September 1993 Yeltsin triumphantly announced that Russia was taking ownership of Ukraine's portion of the BSF in return for a reduction in its gas debt to Russia (though apparently, this deal was presented in the form of an ultimatum).[12] While it is accepted that the Russians 'were excessively optimistic' in their far-reaching conclusions, Kravchuk indeed 'favoured selling part of the BSF and leasing Sevastopol to Russia'.[13] Kravchuk conceded, as it would have increased the likelihood of the signing of a friendship and co-operation treaty. The signing of a treaty would have been very welcome as by that stage Ukraine had discovered that the desire to hang onto its nuclear weapons aroused the wrath of the West, rather than elicited its support. Indeed, not only was the West marginalising Ukraine because of its stance on nuclear weapons, but, according to Smith:

> the Massandra summit reveals that it has become difficult for Ukraine to break away from Moscow's orbit. Its economic and political weaknesses have forced Ukraine's leaders to the realisation that the ties binding them to Moscow are more constraining than previously thought.[14]

A significant milestone in the resolution of both the nuclear and borders issues was the 1994 Trilateral Agreement signed between Ukraine, Russia and the United States. Crucially, the agreement removed the clause that made Ukraine's territorial recognition by Russia conditional upon Ukraine's participation in the CIS.

The conditions contained in the Sochi accords, signed on 9 June 1995, included significant concessions on the part of Kyiv and again reflected the weak negotiating position of Ukraine. In particular, the agreement that Sevastopol be the main naval base of the Russian portion of the BSF (Article 2) was a direct contradiction of the Ukrainian constitution, and in fact legitimised the presence of Russian forces on Ukrainian territory. According to Ukrainian analysts, this decision was in effect an acknowledgement that the status of Sevastopol was open to negotiation and hence dispute.[15] Indeed, they argue that it was the Sochi accords that legitimised Russian claims that Sevastopol was a Russian city.[16] In turn, doubt over the city's national status came to legitimise Moscow's insistence that Sevastopol remain for the exclusive use of the Russian portion of the fleet. On 9 September 1995, Yeltsin again cancelled his visit to Kyiv to sign a treaty on the grounds that 'a resolution of the BSF issue has been postponed'.[17]

From the point of view of Ukraine, with the signing of the Sochi accords, the two issues, namely that of Ukraine's sovereignty over Sevastopol and Crimea on the one hand, and the division of the BSF on the other, became, if anything, even more tightly interconnected. Despite the signing of an agreement on the technicalities of the division of the fleet (and a number of other issues including military co-operation, the transfer of strategic bombers to Russia, transit rights for the 14th Army from Moldova to Russia, the establishment of a common policy on changes to Conventional Forces in Europe [CFE] flank restrictions), in November 1995, again in Sochi, disagreements soon arose.[18] While the first stage of the handover took place with some misgivings on the part of the Ukrainians, who accused the Russians of stripping material off ships to be handed over to the Ukrainians and of tampering with the inventory of the BSF, the second stage stalled for a number of reasons.[19] The key one remained, as ever, an inability to come to an agreement on basing rights.

President Yeltsin's planned visit to Ukraine on 4 April 1996 to sign the Friendship and Co-operation Treaty was postponed for the sixth time on the grounds that 'Russia wants to see Sevastopol as the exclusive base for the Russian portion of the fleet'.[20] (It is worth pointing out that Yeltsin also had a domestic constituency to play to, especially in light of the upcoming elections in June/July 1996; significantly, the above planned visit was cancelled soon after the Russian Duma's vote on 15 March to abrogate the Belovezha accords.) Soon after, an unexpected concession of a legislative nature was made on the part of the Ukrainians, triggered in part by their fear that a Communist might come to power in place of a visibly ailing Yeltsin. The long-awaited passing of the Ukrainian constitution on 28 June 1996 and the inclusion of a Transitional Provision (Point 14) providing for 'the use of existing military bases on the territory of Ukraine for the temporary stationing of foreign military formations . . . on the terms of lease' avoided an overt contradiction of Article 17 of the constitution which expressly forbids foreign military bases on the territory of Ukraine. This provision finally allowed for the possibility of a leasing arrangement.[21]

By the autumn, following a Yeltsin victory in Russia, relations between the two states had again started to deteriorate. On 16 October 1996, the Russian Duma virtually unanimously (334 voted in favour, one against, and three abstentions) barred the division of the BSF, and challenged the status of Sevastopol as a Ukrainian city. The vote was non-binding on the Russian president, and the latter distanced himself from the judgement. Then, on 24 October, the day preceding the planned summit between Kuchma and Yeltsin, the Russian Duma passed a resolution warning Ukraine '"against a unilateral approach" to the status of Sevastopol and announced that Sevastopol remained under the jurisdiction of Moscow'.[22] Soon after, on 26 November, Igor Rodionov, the Russian defence minister, suggested that Russia could not agree to the joint basing of both the

Russian and Ukrainian portions of the fleet at Sevastopol.[23] The Ukrainians, despite the pressure, refused to agree to a change of status of Sevastopol.

It has been argued that Ukraine's intransigence suited some segments of the Russian political spectrum. In fact, it has been suggested that 'the signing of a Ukrainian–Russian treaty was uncomfortable for Moscow. Because . . . its signing will allow Ukraine to enter the North Atlantic alliance, entry to which is barred for those states which have unresolved difficulties with neighbours.'[24] In fact, Russia was forcing Ukraine into an apparent corner, 'despite the Ukrainian effort to persuade Russia that its policies were driving Ukraine into the arms of NATO'.[25] Difficulties with Russia were behind the evolution of Ukraine's relations with NATO, which were progressing better than anyone had dared expect when negotiations first started between Kyiv and Brussels. Furthermore, NATO enlargement in general was looming as an ever more likely possibility, while Belarus' integration with Russia was at a virtual standstill, despite Minsk's enthusiasm. Russia's geopolitical position was deteriorating to the extent that the signing of a treaty with Ukraine was by 1997 emerging as a desirable objective. Indeed, Mykhailo Pohrebynsky, the director of the Kyiv Centre for Political Studies and Conflict Research, has suggested that Moscow started to seek a *quid pro quo*: in return for the signing of a treaty, the Russians sought a commitment on the part of Ukraine not to enter NATO.[26] The signing of the treaty and NATO enlargement had seemingly become interlinked.

The signing of the treaty – a resolution of the border problem?

According to Sherr, up until that point it was the very public nature of the discussions that contributed to their ultimate failure. This mistake was not repeated in the series of meetings leading up to the final signing of both the Friendship and Co-operation Treaty in May 1997, and the officially unrelated agreements on the division of the fleet and its infrastructure. Yet, even in the final days leading up to the signing of the treaties tricks were tried. At the last minute the Russians voiced reservations about the joint basing of the two fleets as this 'would disrupt command and control and, worse, provide Ukraine with a formula that might be used to allow NATO to lease facilities in Crimea at some future date'.[27] Russia was even then seeking to limit the sovereignty of Kyiv over parts of the territory of Ukraine.

Yet with the imminence of NATO enlargement, and the signing of a charter between Ukraine and NATO which was to take place at the July 1997 Madrid summit, Russia's room for manoeuvre was limited. On 31 May 1997, a Friendship, Co-operation and Partnership Treaty was finally signed as an inter-state document between Ukraine and Russia. According to Volodymyr Chumak of Ukraine's National Institute of Strategic Studies, Russia signed the agreement with Ukraine because of the latter's successes in signing bilateral agreements with neighbours, and because of the fact that Ukraine was becoming more prominent within the CIS.[28] (Three agreements on the fate of the BSF were signed as inter-governmental documents somewhat earlier on 28 May 1997. Of most import was the one specifying the status and conditions of the stationing of the BSF on the territory of Ukraine, which will be discussed later.)

As far as the recognition of borders was concerned, the treaty was seen as a major achievement for the Ukrainians, as Article 2 of the treaty was an unconditional commitment on the part of both parties that they 'respect the territorial integrity of each other and affirm the inviolability of the borders that exist between them'. However, despite the apparent success, Ukrainian analysts remained suspicious of Russia's commitment to respect Ukraine's territorial integrity for a number of reasons. Two types of border problems were distinguished: land and marine. As far as the 2,063 kilometre land border between Ukraine and Russia was concerned, a number of objections were raised.

The only borders that existed technically up until that point were those that were recorded on large-scale Soviet-era maps; these maps were designed to reflect administrative differences between republics (indeed the thickness of lines drawn on the maps was estimated to literally extend up to several kilometres when transposed from paper to territory).[29] Furthermore, according to a Ukrainian interpretation, the Russians insisted that Kyiv acknowledged any demarcation that took place as demarcating internal, porous CIS borders, thereby excluding them from the constraints imposed by the Helsinki treaty regarding the recognition of international boundaries.[30] Although some preliminary, even token, discussions had taken place, the actual delimitation of land borders had not yet been started; yet the treaty presupposed the existence of such formally delineated and demarcated borders.[31] The Ukrainians claimed that proposals to resolve the issue had been rebuffed on at least 'eight, maybe even ten occasions' by the Russians.[32] Inevitably, the issue of demarcation and delineation was tied to the status of the BSF and the signing of the treaty between the two states, i.e. the border issues could only be resolved once the BSF issue had been dealt with. Threats by Kyiv to unilaterally delimit and demarcate the border were acknowledged by the Ukrainians as effectively unviable owing to the fact that there was no guarantee that the Russian side would accept any decisions made.

As far as marine borders were concerned, the sticking point was the status of the Sea of Azov and the Kerch Straits. The problem lay in the fact that the Russians rejected any moves that would remove the sea's 'internal' status. It was believed by Moscow that such a move would remove barriers to its exploitation by 'foreign forces'.[33]

However, Kyiv's greatest concern was reserved for the fact that the signing of the various documents could negatively affect Ukraine's subregional and regional objectives. In particular, Ukrainian analysts argue that the signing of the treaty and the associated agreements could be interpreted as abandoning neutrality and effectively entering a military alliance with Russia. The corollary of such an interpretation is that Ukraine has precluded itself from NATO membership for the duration of the period for which Sevastopol is leased to Moscow, that is the twenty years until 2017. It has also been argued that the stationing of Russian military forces in Crimea make Ukraine a likely target in the event of a war between Russia and a third party.[34] This is indeed so, as under the resolution of the twenty-ninth session of the UN General Assembly, Ukraine could be regarded as a co-aggressor if Russian warships stationed on its territory take part in combat operations. Furthermore, no provision was made in the treaty for Ukraine to ban the use of the BSF against other states.[35] And while the treaty expressly forbade the deployment of nuclear weapons in Crimea by Russia, there is some evidence to suggest that by striving to locate tactical nuclear weapons in Crimea, Russia has sought to provide *de facto* evidence that Ukraine is prepared to accommodate its military and political interests, thereby turning Ukraine into a potential military ally in its confrontation with NATO.[36] Ukraine appeared to have paid a heavy price in the resolution of its territorial dispute with Russia and the preservation and protection of its territorial integrity. Nevertheless, Ukraine ratified the treaty on 14 January 1998, although not the BSF accords. On 25 December 1998 the Russian Duma ratified the treaty (though only after four postponements). However, the Federation Council (the upper house) postponed its vote on the treaty.[37] Yet even then, long after the signing of the treaty, the Russians continued to link the treaty and the Black Sea Fleet. Moscow refused to exchange ratification documents concerning the treaty until Ukraine had ratified the accords on the Black Sea Fleet legitimising Russia's military presence on Ukrainian territory. This Ukraine duly did on 24 March 1999 with a small majority.[38]

Overall, the signing of the treaty was in the main a symbolic political success from Ukraine's point of view, though with some well-scored points. The key Ukrainian success was the unconditional recognition of the territorial integrity of Ukraine on the part of Moscow, something that was not to be underestimated, especially in light of the tortuous process needed to reach that stage. However, in many other respects the treaty was a Pyrrhic victory for Kyiv.

The first and most immediate cost incurred by Ukraine was the 'temporary' accommodation of the BSF on Ukrainian territory. Having gained basing rights, Russia obtained a significant foothold on Ukrainian territory. This in turn led to another series of costs. The most tangible of these was a significant diminution of Ukraine's portion of the fleet. In addition, despite the fact that the stationing of Russian forces was a temporary phenomenon, it still was a direct contravention of Ukraine's constitution. In addition, the inclusion of the provision in the joint declaration on the part of both parties to 'co-operate in ensuring the security of the southern borders of our two countries' is interpreted by Sherr as showing that 'in resonance if not in substance . . . border co-operation can be a slippery slope from non-alignment to military alliance'.[39]

The military balance between Ukraine and Russia

Two days after the coup attempt in Moscow, the Ukrainian parliament, keen to avoid the mistakes of the previous independent administration, created its own armed forces in one fell swoop on 24 August 1991 by placing under its jurisdiction the Soviet forces on its territory.[40] This was a blow to Russia in four regards. First, it represented a failure in Moscow's attempts to maintain a unified military body. Second, it left gaping holes in Moscow's much cherished 'common defence space' due, in particular, to the loss of the Ukrainian component of the strategically critical early warning system. Third, it represented the loss of its first echelon defence forces, along with some of the best Soviet military equipment available, including nuclear weapons. Above all, it demonstrated Kyiv's intention to pursue independence in its fuller sense.

The resulting Ukrainian forces were significant by any standards. According to data based on Soviet inventories compiled prior to the August 1991 coup, Ukraine inherited some 30 per cent of the Soviet tank inventory, 20–30 per cent of infantry vehicles, and 25 per cent of the USSR aircraft inventory on the European side of the Urals. On sea, the Soviet legacy to Ukraine was in the form of the Black Sea Fleet. Based on the Crimean peninsula and with fifty-five major surface warships and twenty submarines, the BSF not only patrolled the Black Sea coast but was also the backbone of Soviet sea power in the Mediterranean. Incorporated within the fleet were substantial aviation (some 450 combat aircraft) and ground forces (with approximately 1,240 armoured vehicles of various types including tanks).[41] The fact that both states ratified the CFE treaty in July 1992 represented an acceptance on the part of Moscow of Ukraine's appropriation of the former Soviet forces on its soil. Despite the relatively straightforward transfer of Soviet forces to Ukrainian jurisdiction, a problem emerged in two key areas – the transfer of nuclear forces and the Black Sea Fleet.

The division of nuclear forces

The Ukrainisation of Soviet forces did not extend to nuclear forces, as separate provisions for these weapons were made early on by Kyiv. In December 1991 Kyiv volunteered for destruction all 176 Intercontinental Ballistic Missiles (ICBMs) based in Ukraine, and their 1,180 warheads. At the same time, Ukraine agreed to sign the nuclear Non-Proliferation Treaty as a non-nuclear power, to eliminate all tactical weapons on its territory, transfer its strategic bombers to Russia, and take off alert status all strategic weapons on Ukrainian territory. However, as relations with Russia deteriorated in 1992, primarily owing to the territorial dispute and the associated matter of the status of the BSF, so Kyiv came to renege on what was seen as its unambiguous commitment to full denuclearisation. However, this was only in part an anti-Russian stance. Although the deteriorating state of relations between them was clearly a cause of concern for both Kyiv and Moscow, it was evident that 'other factors in Ukraine and Russia could be counted upon to prevent the nuclear issue from escalating to a nuclear confrontation'.[42] Despite appearances, problems with the resolution of the nuclear issue were not at the foundation of Ukraine's relations with Russia. Instead, the matter lay in other spheres, in particular the lack of attention and material resources Ukraine was getting from the West, especially when compared to the amounts expected, and the fact that Moscow was selling off the nuclear material from weapons already returned to Russia by Ukraine. This explains why the Trilateral Agreement signed in 1994 resolved the matter so relatively promptly.[43] And with nuclear weapons removed from the reckoning, Kyiv and Moscow could continue seeking a solution to the problem that lay at the foundation of their deteriorating relationship: disagreement over territory, or at a deeper level, an inability on the part of Russia to come to terms with Ukraine's independence, a problem that came to be crystallised in the matter of the BSF, which will now be examined.

The Black Sea Fleet (BSF)

As has been mentioned, the issue of the BSF was intricately tied up with the resolution of the Crimea/Sevastopol issue. While earlier it was touched on in the context of the territorial dispute between Ukraine and Russia, it will be examined here *per se*. (Only a brief overview will be provided here, as the issue has been examined in detail elsewhere).[44]

The early provisional agreements on the exact division of the BSF made on Ukraine's independence collapsed on the grounds that as a former constituent part of the Soviet Union, Ukraine felt it was entitled to a portion of *all* Soviet Union fleets, something which worked out as considerably more than the 40 per cent of the BSF being offered by Russia.

By mid-1992 the inability to come to an agreement on a basic division of the fleet, aside from the infrastructure, was indicative of the deteriorating state of relations between the two neighbours. In an effort to prevent further damage to the already strained relations, at a meeting in Yalta in August 1992 an agreement was signed between Russia and Ukraine 'On the principles of the Creation of a Ukrainian Navy and Russian Black Sea Navy on the basis of the former Soviet Union Black Sea Fleet'. This agreement removed the BSF from under CIS jurisdiction, thereby bilateralising a technically multilateral issue – in theory, up until that point, all CIS states could launch a claim to a portion of the fleet. Additionally, a fifty-fifty division was agreed, and until a final agreement on the basing of the fleet was made (planned for 1995), the fleet was to remain under the command of a jointly appointed admiral. At a subsequent meeting in Moscow on 17 June 1993, the two presidents signed yet another agreement 'On Urgent Measures on the Formation of the Russian and Ukrainian Navies on the basis of the Black Sea Fleet', in which both parties reiterated their support for a fifty-fifty division of the fleet.

Ukraine's deteriorating negotiating position was exposed at the Massandra summit in September 1993 when the Russian side announced that it was claiming the whole fleet, including Ukraine's portion. This meant that Ukraine would 'remain without a navy for many years to come' while Russia would place itself in the position of being able to 'control Abkhazia, Transdniester and Crimea, Moldova, and obviously Ukraine, and also the Balkans'.[45] The agreement on the part of Kyiv to give up its portion of the fleet *in lieu* of part of its growing debt to Russia was retracted as the full force of domestic opposition to the offer became clear.[46]

As Ukraine's economic crisis intensified throughout 1994, its negotiating position reached a nadir. As a result, its claim to 50 per cent of the fleet was dramatically watered down in the Sochi accords, signed on 9 June 1995 between the Russian and Ukrainian presidents.[47] The subsequent second Sochi accords of 25 November 1995 detailed the technicalities of the division of the fleet, the first part of which went, more or less, according to plan. The Ukrainians, however, had serious misgivings as to Russian conduct: they not only suspected the Russians of stripping arms off the ships, but also of reducing the inventory of the BSF prior to the division taking place.

Yet the prospects for progress were improving, as indicated by the acceptance of the new Ukrainian constitution in June 1996 and its provisions for the temporary stationing of foreign forces on Ukrainian territory, Yeltsin's presidential victory soon after, and above all progress in the NATO enlargement talks. In August 1996, a joint commission announced it was close to, but not yet at the stage of 'finalising agreements on the status and conditions for deploying the BSF on Ukrainian territory; parameters governing the division of the fleet and its infrastructure, and the allocation of Sevastopol's bays; and the term of the lease and the system of lease payments'.[48] In a flurry of events, key issues came to be resolved. As early as 28 May 1997, a day after the signing of the Founding Act between Russia and NATO on 27 May, Ukraine and Russia signed three inter-governmental agreements resolving the division, basing and costing of the BSF. This was followed three days later, on 31 May, by the signing of the long-awaited inter-state treaty between Ukraine and Russia (dealt with earlier).

According to Sherr, 'the political provisions of the agreements are highly favourable to Ukraine. The same cannot be said of the military provisions'.[49] Two separate issues stand out. First, the agreements allow for the leasing of port facilities in Crimea to the BSF for a period of twenty years, with scope for extension for a further five years subject to the agreement of both parties. Without doubt, Russia's concession on joint basing rights was a significant achievement for Kyiv, especially in the light of Moscow's fears that Ukraine's Crimean bases could in practice eventually be leased out to NATO forces, however unlikely that prospect appeared at the time. However, as far as the Russian side was concerned, the benefits could be argued to outweigh the disadvantages. Primarily, the legitimisation of the presence of Russian forces on Ukrainian territory for the next twenty to twenty-five years was a noteworthy achievement. Similarly, the actual subdivision of the fleet and, above all, its infrastructure was highly unfavourable to Ukraine, as were the limitations placed on the quantity and quality of berths available for the Ukrainian portion on the fleet.[50] Further rubbing salt into the wounds were the lamentably poor terms Ukraine obtained for leasing facilities, an additional premium paid by Kyiv for the political concessions obtained with the signing of the treaty.[51]

Sherr identifies three key 'uncertainties' resulting from the agreements. First, he argues that while the institutionalisation of the recognition of the territorial integrity of Ukraine by Russia was not unimportant, the fact that the accords 'did nothing to diminish Russia's principal levers of influence over Ukraine' was no less noteworthy. Second, the vagueness of accords means that they lend themselves to a variety of interpretations. Third, the unhindered implementation of the agreements has not followed in the wake of their signing. For example, ratification of the agreements was not a straightforward process, hindered as it was by Moscow on frequent occasions. In fact the Russians made the ratification of the treaty conditional upon the Ukrainians ratifying the BSF accords, duly accomplished by Kyiv on 24 March 1999.[52]

Nevertheless, in retrospect, the overall transfer of forces from Soviet to Ukrainian jurisdiction proved to be less troublesome than might have originally been expected. Problems were limited to two narrow, albeit important, areas: nuclear forces and the BSF. As far as Ukraine was concerned, behind the battles for the ownership of the nuclear weapons lay a contest for economic resources and the influence that such weapons were expected to bring. More problematic were the troubles regarding the BSF. Ultimately, the dispute over the BSF touched on more profound issues, in particular the exchange of unconditional recognition of the sovereignty and territorial integrity of Ukraine for the accommodation of Russian forces on Ukrainian territory and the writing off of a significant proportion of a fleet of doubtful value. Yet despite this, the alacrity with which Kyiv signed the treaty once Moscow had agreed to it suggests that Ukraine found that this was an exchange worth making.

Economic relations

The above record of intransigence and confrontation between Ukraine and Russia up until 1997 camouflaged a mutual economic interdependence from which neither side could easily escape, despite the posturing. There are four dimensions to these economic relations: asymmetries of interdependence, Ukraine's energy dependence on Russia, energy transportation issues and military–industrial co-operation.

Asymmetries of interdependence

As Table 2.1 suggests, Ukraine remains heavily dependent on Russia both as a source of imports (primarily energy) and as the destination of its exports. However, owing to the much larger size of the Russian economy, compared to that of Ukraine, Kyiv is much more dependent on Moscow for trade than vice versa. This remains true despite Ukraine's success in diversifying its trade away from Russia, as shown

Table 2.1 Ukraine's dependence on Russia for trade

	Main destination of Ukraine's exports[a] (in percentages)		*Main origin of Ukraine's imports* (in percentages)	
1995	Russia	43.1	Russia	52.3
1996	Russia	38.7	Russia	48.0
	CIS	54.1	CIS	67.8
1997	Russia	26.2	Russia	45.8
	CIS	42.9	CIS	58.4

Note: [a] Figures taken from *Ukraine – Country Report*, Economist Intelligence Unit (quarterly issues between 1996 and 1999).

by the relative fall in both exports to and imports from Russia since 1995, indicated in Table 2.1 (it should be noted that the figures fail to reflect a massive deterioration in Ukraine's export base and the fact that the reduction of exports to Russia was not a voluntary phenomenon). However, Ukraine's traditional dependence on Russian imports has remained substantial, primarily due to its heavy reliance on Russian energy supplies.

Economic theory suggests that Ukraine's traditional dependence on Russia is artificial, unhealthy and disfiguring of Ukraine's economy. The so-called gravity equation predicts that the amount of trade between two states is correlated with the geographical distance between them and their GDP – crudely, the closer the two states are geographically, and the richer they are, the higher is the amount of trade that tends to occur between them. Using this model, the Ukrainian–European Policy and Legal Advice Centre (a project funded by the European Union's TACIS Programme), suggests that Ukraine's exports should more 'naturally' gravitate toward Europe and only to a much lesser extent towards Russia. Indeed, extrapolating into the future, according to the model, the pattern of Ukraine's trade could look something like that in Table 2.2. In other words, Ukraine's economic integration with Central Europe and neighbours other than Russia is a 'natural' phenomenon if unimpeded. However, this westward integration remains impeded by existing ties with Russia, as it has been for much if not all of Ukraine's time as a modern industrialised state.

A number of strategies have been used by Moscow to prevent Ukraine's reorientation toward its 'natural' trading partners in the West. For example, Russia has tried to take advantage of Ukraine's indebtedness to prevent a westward drift. In particular, as Ukraine's debt to Russia has grown, Moscow has tried to convert this debt into assets by attempting to gain stakes in 'strategic' segments of Ukraine's infrastructure such as ownership of gas pipelines and oil refineries.[53] Not only would this maintain and even, with time, reinforce the structural ties linking Ukraine and Russia, it would also prevent independent moves on the part of Ukraine to take advantage of one of its few worthwhile assets – the vast transportation system linking the energy sources of the East with markets in the West. Furthermore, losing control of its infrastructure would impede Ukraine's reorientation from East to West as Kyiv would be deprived of control of a significant component of foreign policy formation.

Furthermore, Moscow has striven to undermine Ukraine's attempts at economic independence. This is something Ukraine is particularly vulnerable to, owing

Table 2.2 Structure of Ukrainian exports in time perspective (% of total exports)

	Russia	*Belarus*	*Moldova*	*ex-Comecon*	*Other*
1987	56.2	5.9	2.9	17.8	0.9
1995	44.1	4.3	1.2	8.8	36.8
Predicted long-term	8.0	1.4	0.5	6.9	81.8

to the nature of the production cycle that exists between Ukraine and Russia. Specifically, very few goods were produced in a closed production cycle in Ukraine with most goods produced in co-operation with Russia: Ukraine's exports are notable for the high proportion of either raw materials or goods needing low processing, with Russia completing production of most of them.[54] An example of Moscow's efforts to take advantage of this interdependent production cycle was the steps that it took to undermine Ukraine's ability to fulfil its contract to deliver 350 tanks to Pakistan (a contract worth $650 million) by refusing to issue export licenses for Russian firms involved in providing parts to the Ukrainian tank manufacturer.[55] This mutual production interdependence is argued to benefit the Russians:

> to a large extent, such an approach creates the danger of an artificial prolongation of the orientation of Ukrainian manufacturers toward the Russian market, manufacturing policy and economic infrastructure . . . which threatens the continuation of [Ukraine's] technological backwardness and lack of competitiveness on international markets.[56]

And, of course, its continued dependence on the Russian market.

However, the single biggest problem preventing a diversification away from Russia is Ukraine's dependence on Russia for energy.

Ukraine's weak spot – energy dependence on Russia

Ukraine's 'energy predicament' is serious, as the actual degree of dependence on Russian energy supplies is very high: Ukraine is the largest importer of natural gas in the world, most of it coming from Russia.[57] Specifically, of the roughly 80 billion cubic metres needed by Ukraine annually, in the six years between 1994 and 1999, Ukraine imported from Russia 69, 66, 70, 53, 56, and 55 billion cubic metres respectively; the balance was made up of domestic supplies and deliveries from Turkmenistan.[58] Ukraine is also heavily, though not as overwhelmingly, dependent on Russian oil, importing between 12 and 16 million tons between 1994 and 1999.[59]

The matter has been exacerbated by problems presented by 'the often inflexible infrastructural ties inherited from the Soviet period . . . "which effectively hinder switching to other suppliers"'.[60] This in turn has made Ukraine more vulnerable to other pressures. In particular, Moscow has striven to deprive Ukraine of badly needed investment currency by unilaterally imposing almost arbitrary prices on Ukraine, and as a result overcharging Ukraine for gas provided. The amounts involved are significant:

> Ukraine is overpaying Russia $2 billion annually, giving Russia a bigger net profit from gas sales to Ukraine than from its . . . exports to nineteen west European economies – hence its huge debt. The chairman of the Russian gas monopoly, Gazprom, Rem Vyakhirev, admitted to the Ukrainian prime minister, Valeriy Pustovoitenko, that the pricing policy was unfair and 'does not correspond to reality'.[61]

Indeed, it seems that during 1998, Ukraine paid $80 per 1,000 cubic metres, $3 more than Germany paid, despite the fact that the latter should have theoretically incurred substantially greater transportation costs, estimated at $25–35 for the additional 1,500 kilometres the gas had to travel.[62]

However, it is likely that Ukraine's energy dependence on Russia might be coming to an enforced end. Russia is facing an energy shortage of its own, something which is likely to have negative reverberations for Ukraine should Kyiv not diversify its energy supplies. Quite simply, both oil and gas extraction rates in Russia have been declining for some time, and are expected to continue to do so in the future as can be seen in Table 2.3.

Table 2.3 Oil and gas extraction rates in Russia

Oil extraction rates (millions of tons)[a]		*Gas extraction rates* (billions of cubic metres)	
1983	619[b]	1987	544
1990	516	1990	640
1991	461	1991	643[b]
1992	395	1992	641
1993	354	1993	619
1994	318	1994	607
1995	307	1995	595
1996	293	1996	575
1997	297	1997	544
1998	303	1998	559
1999	*280*[c]	1999	*554*[c]
2000	*220*[c]	2000	*534*[c]

Notes: [a] Figures taken from M. Honchar, O. Moskalets and S. Nalivka, 'Vidhomin Serpnevoho Strusu', *Polityka I Chas*, No. 2 February 1999, p. 40.
[b] peak extraction figures
[c] estimates

Thus as extraction rates decline, Russia will find itself in a dilemma. The desire to satisfy domestic consumers and Western customers paying in hard currency will undoubtedly be at the expense of non-hard currency paying consumers such as Ukraine and other former Soviet republics, though in turn this is likely to trigger centrifugal trends within the CIS.

Ukraine has tried both to reduce its energy dependence and to anticipate this energy shortfall in a number of ways. First, in order to deal with its immediate needs, Ukraine sourced energy from other members of the CIS, namely Turkmenistan, and to a lesser extent Kazakhstan. Similarly, Ukraine established partnerships with separate regions of the Russian Federation, in particular the Tuymen' *oblast* and western Siberia.[63] Second, Ukraine pursued ambitious long-term solutions. In particular, as will be explored in more detail in Chapter 6, it has also attempted to take advantage of the discovery of Caspian energy resources and Ukraine's key strength as a transit route for that energy.

Ukraine's ace: the transportation of Russian energy

If the downside of the structural ties that link Ukraine and Russia is the former's energy dependence on the latter, there is also an analogous downside for Russia. One of the strongest links binding Ukraine to Russia is the intricate network of pipelines for the transportation of both oil and gas westward. And, as has been pointed out, 'just as Russia's richest asset is its massive reserves of gas and oil, Ukraine's richest asset is its bottleneck on the export of Russian oil and gas to the West'.[64] This point is evidenced by the fact that '90 per cent of Russian oil and most of its gas is exported to Western and Central Europe through pipelines crossing Ukrainian territory'.[65] It has been estimated that Ukraine carries 17 per cent of all the EU's gas.[66] This Russian dependence on Ukraine has been exploited by Kyiv either to relieve some of the pressure exerted by Moscow or, in turn, exert pressure on Moscow. Either way, the strategy has been the same. For example, in January 1996 Ukraine temporarily closed the pipelines for a few hours in pursuit of higher transit fees.[67] Similarly, Ukraine has apparently not been averse to siphoning off westward-bound gas in 'times of need'.[68] Gazprom accused Ukraine of siphoning off 15 billion cubic metres of gas worth roughly $900 million in 2000 alone, a figure which Kyiv disputes.[69]

This strategy is, however, something of a double-edged sword. Russia is making substantial efforts to literally get around this problem, but the solution is expensive: plans to build a pipeline around Ukraine, via Belarus, on to Poland, have been estimated to cost $3.6 billion, and have as a result not been implemented. However, although there are doubts over the prospects for the completion of the whole project, 'completion of the European part of the pipeline, off the Torzhok pipeline north of Moscow, is indeed feasible, and it is this part of the pipeline which would affect Ukraine most directly'.[70] Russia has also tried another means of reducing this dependency, and one which would bind Ukraine even more closely to it. By buying segments of Ukraine's 34,400-kilometre gas transportation and 4,000-kilometre oil transportation infrastructure and storage/refinement capacity, Russia would gain a foothold in a 'strategic industry'. Needless to say, such controversial moves have been strongly resisted both by the Ukrainian parliament and the president.[71] Significantly, in this regard, Russia has a strong competitor in the West: in 1998 Shell offered to purchase a 50 per cent stake in UkrGazProm, the state-owned gas transportation company, for $2 billion.[72] However, on 16 October 2000, President Kuchma, at a meeting with President Putin, offered Gazprom a stake in Ukraine's gas pipeline system *in lieu* of Ukraine's gas debt to Russia.[73] The offer was also made in anticipation of an upcoming agreement between the EU and Russia. Specifically, later that month the EU and Russia signed an agreement on the building of a new pipeline designed to bring an extra 60 billion cubic metres from Russia to Western Europe. The pipeline would cross Belarus, Poland and Slovakia, bypassing Ukraine altogether.[74] When Poland promptly announced that it would do nothing to harm its 'strategic partner', Moscow nonchalantly hinted at a pipeline crossing the Baltic Sea, bypassing Poland as well. Moscow had called Kyiv's (and Warsaw's) bluff and Ukraine fell for it – Ukraine was not prepared to risk being totally sidelined in the energy transportation system between the EU and Russia.

Overall, in terms of the energy interdependence between the two, it is hard to dispute Smolensky's point that

> the proclamation of independence, the adoption of state symbols, and a national anthem, the establishment of armed forces . . . and even the presence on Ukrainian territory of nuclear missiles . . . amount to little if another power, Russia, controls access to fuel without which Ukraine cannot survive economically.[75]

This is certainly a profound predicament for Ukraine. However, it could be added that the wealth effect of Russia's energy resources is considerably reduced if they cannot be brought to market. In sum, there is a mutual interdependence between the two parties that continue to bind them, for better or for worse.

Military–industrial co-operation: aerospace and aeronautics

The fourth noteworthy aspect of the economic relations between Ukraine and Russia, in addition to the three identified, are the strong ties that continue to exist in military–industrial production.

Historically, the Ukrainian SSR in close co-operation with the RSFSR was virtually the sole source of space, aeronautical and missile technology within the USSR. Indeed, on independence, Ukraine possessed some 30 per cent of all of the former Soviet defence industry.[76] Nevertheless, as in most other areas of production, Ukraine and Russia were bound by integrated production cycles. For example, the Russian 'Proton' and 'Soyuz' rockets' control systems are made in Kharkiv, while the launch platform for the Ukrainian-built 'Cyclone' is built in Russia.[77] This co-operation has continued in the post-Soviet era, as in the case of the joint effort to build the Zenit-3 rocket used in the Sea Launch project – a commercial effort to launch and place satellites in space from a platform in international waters (successfully tested in 1999). The Zenit rocket used consisted of two lower boosters made by the Ukrainians (Yuzhmash) with the top one made by the Russians.[78] Similarly, the Ukrainians and Russians have great hopes for a common space project in which both parties have a fifty-fifty stake.[79]

A similar strain of interdependence continues to exist between Ukraine and Russia in aeronautics. On independence in 1991, Ukraine inherited the Antonov Aircraft Design Bureau based in Dnipropetrovs'k, the Motor Sich engine manufacturing plant based in Zaporizhya, and two aircraft assembly plants, the Kyiv Aviation Industrial Unit, and the Kharkiv Aviation Industrial Unit. There is a single helicopter manufacturing factory in Ukraine, the Dubove helicopter factory, which co-operates with the Russian Komov Design Bureau in the production of the helicopters. Because of the very high degree of integration in the manufacturing of parts and aircraft in the Soviet Union, on independence the Ukrainian sector was starved of supplies and even raw materials used in domestic manufacturing from other sectors of the former Soviet Union.[80] Ukraine's key prospect for the future, the extremely advanced AN-70 cargo aircraft, is heavily dependent on co-operation with Russia, both in terms of design and construction.[81]

In arms production the profound interdependence continues. As has been pointed out:

> without the partnership of Russia, it is very difficult for Ukraine to deliver complete systems – from designing projects to completing and delivering systems and after sales technical support. The time of individual successes has passed. It is impossible to break into markets and compete with the West without co-operation between CIS states.[82]

For this reason, in March 1997 an agreement was reached between Ukrspetsexport, the Ukrainian exporter of military production, and the Rosvoorouzhenie, the Russian equivalent, on payment policy and production in areas of co-operation on military production.[83] However, this agreement did not work out, leading Kuchma and Yeltsin to resolve the matter at a meeting in Moscow in March 1998, as a result of which it was announced that 'at last the question of military–technical co-operation between the two countries is resolved and they will enter world military markets together'.[84] The fact that such co-operation extended to a joint presentation at the Abu-Dhabi Military Show (Aidex 97) led Ukrainian Minister of Defence Kuzmuk to comment, 'I cannot say that I am happy with such companionship with the Russian delegation'.[85] Clearly, in relations between Ukraine and Russia, politics remain intricately intertwined with economics.

Inevitably, such close ties are perceived by the Ukrainian political elite as having negative ramifications for Ukraine's prospects for subregional and regional integration with the West. In particular, the Ukrainian National Institute for Strategic Studies (NISS) has taken the view that Ukraine's geopolitical stance, searching for a balance between East and West, at least in the early years following independence, is at odds with tight military–technical co-operation with any one side, or more specifically, Russia. The reality of such ties is at odds with strategic industrial objectives. This has been particularly true since 1995, when Ukraine started to pursue a less balanced and more pro-Western foreign policy stance. The model for such ties was provided by Central European states that found that the quickest way to participate in the European integration process was by first becoming integrated with pan-European security structures. In order to follow this same path, the NISS deemed it necessary that Ukrainian weapons become fully adapted to pan-European standards and procedures. According to the NISS it is envisaged that

> today's excessive ties with the Russian military–industrial complex will, with time be replaced with strong integration with European manufacturers, and a wider diversification of exports. A gradual "emergence from the orbit" of the Russian defence complex, is, for understandable reasons, the most complex,

> lengthy but also most principled [sic] duty . . . Russia's strategy is unacceptable to Ukraine.[86]

Particular emphasis is laid on the minimisation of Ukraine's dependence on Russia in the fields of rocket and space technology, and aircraft manufacturing, two areas in which the Institute views Ukraine's prospects as being particularly bright.

Overall, Ukraine's bilateral relations with Russia represented a problem from the very earliest days of Ukraine's independence. This was inevitable as Ukraine started to unravel the deep political, economic and military ties that existed between the two states. Russia's references to an *independent* Ukraine through gritted teeth, while acknowledging its formal status, demonstrates the difficulties Moscow had with bilateralising ties, at least on a political level. Nevertheless, the fact remains that there exists a strong vein of economic interdependence linking the two countries, on which Ukraine is more reliant than Russia. In recognition of the importance of these ties, Ukraine signed a ten-year economic treaty with Russia in 1998, which was designed to reinvigorate ties between the two states.[87] In theory such a treaty would reintroduce Ukraine to its perpetual dilemma: a restimulation of its economy, though at the expense of an intensification of Ukraine's dependence on Russia (though in practice such a restimulation was unlikely).[88] However, by signing up to such a treaty, Ukraine was in danger of returning to its former status of dependency on Russia. It appeared clear to Ukrainian commentators that

> If Ukraine accepts Russian integrationist initiatives, it will remain isolated from Europe and world processes. This will preclude the technological modernisation to the extent that the country will end up in an unfavourable economic environment. The closed CIS region will preserve the technological ossification of its participants. Under those conditions, Ukraine, as other countries of the CIS, will end up as a country condemned to chase the world outsider – Russia.[89]

In sum, it was believed in Kyiv that the maintenance of stronger ties between Ukraine and Russia would preserve existing production structures and their common technological backwardness, especially when compared to Europe, Japan and the US.[90] Such a predicament merely underlined Ukraine's geopolitical dilemma. On the one hand, 'a reanimation (of ties) would mean a return to the status of an internal colony', something policy-makers were intent on avoiding, despite the obvious economic mutual interdependence that linked the two neighbours.[91] On the other hand, it was argued that 'it is worth bidding farewell to the illusion that Ukraine is the breadbasket of Europe, which in fact is an agricultural over producer . . . Ukraine's most needy market remains Russia'.[92] Such realism was well-founded as Ukraine's relations with the EU failed to remotely meet its expectations, as will be explored in later chapters; and while something of an oversimplification, the quote neatly encapsulates the essence of Ukraine's dilemma along its Western azimuth, in the shadow of its Eastern azimuth. It is for reasons such as these that Garnett points out, 'under almost any future scenario imaginable coping with Russia and Russian power will remain the core element of Ukrainian foreign policy.'[93]

Relations with Belarus

From the outset, relations between Ukraine and Belarus were secondary to each of those states' relations with their common eastern neighbour, Russia. However, this is not to understate the importance of Minsk in Ukrainian perspectives. As has been pointed out, 'Ukraine's two biggest mistakes would be to either declare "cold war" on the Belarussians (that is, Oleksandr Lukashenko), or to toy with the regime in Minsk'.[94] In other words, Belarus was not an insignificant factor either on a bilateral level, or in terms of the role it could play in Ukraine's tussles with Russia. While the two were relatively closely allied in the early days of their respective independence, and hence could formulate policies relatively conducive to each other's needs, with the election of Oleksandr Lukashenko they followed widely different geopolitical trajectories. And yet, a curious empathy remained between them throughout, as will now be seen.

Russia – an ever-present shadow

It is noteworthy that in the early days Belarus' foreign policy followed a path that closely resembled that of Ukraine. For example, Minsk felt compelled to announce independence soon after Ukraine in 1991. Similarly, Minsk's commitment to neutrality, nuclear free status, along with its proposals for a nuclear free zone (put forward by the Belarussian Foreign Minister Pyotr Kravchenko), bore a strong resemblance to Ukraine's own adopted policies.

After independence, Ukraine's relations with Belarus were proper and cordial rather than 'brotherly'. There were a few minor agreements, but relations between Ukraine and Belarus were not formalised in grand treaties, although there were no outstanding disputes preventing relations from developing in the early days of their independence. This was primarily because both parties were focused on internal developments (in particular the economic crises which were endemic to both states) as well as on relations with their giant common neighbour. As a result, a treaty on friendship, good neighbourliness and co-operation between Kyiv and Minsk was only signed in July 1996 after prolonged but essentially trouble-free negotiations. Similarly, the signing of an agreement on the delineation and delimitation of state borders (the first such agreement within the CIS), signed in May 1997, was equally unproblematic. However, the relative paucity of bilateral relations between the two is in stark contrast to Belarus' (and Ukraine's) relations with Russia, which form an interesting contrast.

Even in the early years of independence, Minsk was always more focused on developing relations with Moscow than relations with Kyiv. In July 1992 an agreement was signed concerning economic and military co-operation between Belarus and Russia. Although Belarus along with Ukraine was not a signatory to the Tashkent Collective Security Agreement in May 1992, Russian pressure and the needs of the defence industry were such that Minsk eventually succumbed in December 1993.[95] However, this was not without the Belarussians negotiating an amendment whereby Belarussian personnel were excluded from service outside

Belarus without the explicit consent of the Belarussian parliament.[96] On the 12 April 1994, an agreement was signed on monetary union, granting Russia's central bank a monopoly over the right of currency issue and monetary policy; the agreement was never implemented. This focus on Russia left little space for an intensification of ties with Ukraine.

It this was true prior to 1994, then Belarussian relations with Russia took on a new dynamic with the election of Oleksandr Lukashenko as president in the middle of 1994, arguably at the expense of ties with Ukraine. At the same time, Belarus' role in the CIS integration process took on a renewed impetus as did Minsk's efforts at creating some kind of subregional Slavic grouping, in both cases starting with much closer ties with Russia. Kyiv could only stand by as a bemused onlooker as a whole series of measures instigated by Lukashenko were taken to bring about a reintegration of the two states. For example, as far as political relations with Russia were concerned, in February 1995 a treaty on friendship, good neighbourliness and co-operation was signed between the two states, followed soon after by an agreement on the creation of a customs union. Following a referendum in May 1995 in Belarus, the Belarussian–Russian border was effectively dismantled.[97] On the 2 April 1996, a treaty on the formation of a community of Belarus and Russia was signed. In April 1997 an agreement was signed to upgrade this to a 'union', a goal that was finally achieved in December 1999. Overall, relations between Belarus and Russia were characterised as consisting of a chain of 'economic unions, monetary unions, defence pacts, integration, restoration, "common social spaces" and so *ad infinitum*'.[98]

On military issues Belarus was guided by Russian priorities. For example, following Lukashenko's accession to power in 1994, the planned withdrawal of Russian secondary troops prior to a general withdrawal as required by the Belarussian commitment to neutrality, renounced in 1993, was halted.[99] More antagonistically, in July 1995 the withdrawal of the Russian Strategic Rocket forces was suspended, though this was finally completed in November 1996.[100] Furthermore, in a move clearly designed to speed up the glacial pace of the movement towards the political union for which Lukashenko so yearned, in February 1998 the Belarussian president offered to host Russian nuclear weapons as a countermeasure to NATO expansion.[101] This message was quickly taken up by Roman Popkovich, the chair of the defence committee within the Russian Duma, who suggested that the 'treaty setting up a closer union between Moscow and Minsk might give Russia the right to base nuclear missiles in Belarus'.[102] In April 1998 Minsk ratified a treaty of defence co-operation with Russia signed in 1997, which envisaged the harmonisation of defence policies and legislation in military affairs.[103]

Up to a point, Belarussian policy played into Ukraine's hands. Indeed, it facilitated the attainment of Ukraine's foreign policy objectives of closer ties with European and North Atlantic defence structures. As Minsk and Russia moved ever closer, especially in military terms, Ukraine became an ever more important factor in Western military planning. While the return of nuclear weapons to Belarus would have been a retrograde step by any standards of assessment of European military security, it would have been made immeasurably worse by a *de jure* or *de facto* reintegration of Ukraine into the Russian sphere. Such a move would be quite a coup and explains the insistence on the part of the Russian and Belarussian presidents that, as their two states got closer, Ukraine should join them in a *troika*.

Belarus' offer of military co-operation with Russia was not quite as altruistic as it was made out to be by Lukashenko. Belarus was suffering economically, and stronger economic ties with Russia were one of the few available escape routes for Minsk. The particular problem lay in the fact that in economic terms 'Belarus was exceptional in the degree to which it was integrated with the other Soviet republics, especially Russia and Ukraine'.[104] Almost inevitably, Belarus was virtually completely dependent on Russia for its energy, importing 90 per cent of its requirements from there. Thus, following his election and the intensification of the economic collapse, Lukashenko tried to instil some life into the moribund integration process. (Balmaceda argues that a deepened relationship was appealing to Lukashenko insofar as it strengthened his own position within Belarus, or conversely as long as it did not challenge his personal power.)[105] Yet by 1998, the proposed union was still very much at the discussion stage. At a meeting between Russian Prime Minister Primakov and Lukashenko, matters such as economic ties, joint economic institutions, a common currency, and Belarussian debt for energy supplies were still being discussed, despite earlier commitments to, for example, the common currency.[106] This was much to the consternation of Lukashenko, who lamented that Belarus and Russia might merge 'if Russians muster the will'.[107] Russia was not prepared to exchange the closeness in security ties with Belarus for taking on the burden of an effectively unreformed and bankrupt Belarussian economy. Although plans for integration were greatly set back with the Russian economic crisis of the summer of 1998, prospects for economic integration were dim even prior to that. The differences in the degree of reform in the two economies (such as degrees of price liberalisation, privatisation, the implementation of hard budget constraints, volatility of currencies and levels of inflation) made genuine economic unification a burden for Russia such that it would be hard pressed to bear. This stance has been reinforced by the new Russian president, Vladimir Putin, who has reaffirmed that Russia is only interested in the type of integration that might actually confer some advantage on Russia. Further disruption to the Russian–Belarussian relationship is likely following the opening of key segments of the Yamal gas pipeline in September 1999. While ostensibly a unifying feature of the Minsk–Moscow relationship, the inherent contradiction thrown up by the transportation of Russian energy across Belarus may prove insurmountable. For example, while the ownership of the Belarussian segment of the pipeline belongs *de facto* and *de jure* to Gazprom, the details regarding the ownership and leasing of the territory over which the pipeline passes remain murky and beyond scrutiny. In addition, while Belarus had been happy to lower transportation costs in exchange for cheaper Russian energy prior to the opening of the Yamal pipeline, such is the capacity (a potential quadrupling) and strategic importance of the new pipeline, now that Ukraine has been substantially marginalised in energy transportation, that Belarus might be impelled to return to a standard quantity-based charging system.[108]

For Ukraine, ties with Belarus were one of the means with which Kyiv could alleviate some of the pressure exerted on it by Moscow. This was particularly true in the field of economic relations. Tighter economic ties with Minsk were taken advantage of by Kyiv to alleviate the pressures of the *de facto* economic blockade placed on Ukraine following the imposition of VAT on Ukrainian goods in 1996 by Russia.[109] This restimulation of ties was something that the Belarussians were themselves not averse to, owing to their own economic crisis: any stimulation of the economy was welcome. Furthermore, in pursuit of its own wider objectives, Ukraine has offered to act as the West's representative in Belarus in order to prevent the total international isolation of Minsk.[110]

Relations between the *triumvirate* of Kuchma, Lukashenko and Yeltsin also worked in Russia's favour. In particular, Minsk was taken advantage of by Moscow as a counterweight to moves by Kyiv. Indeed, the more insubordinate Ukraine became, the more important Belarus became to Russia from an economic and military– security point of view.[111] According to the Russian Institute of Strategic Studies, 'closeness with Belarus, taking into account all possible negative and positive sides, on the whole, is in the best national interest of Russia, and gives a succession of geopolitical, and with time, economic advantages'.[112] It was simply that Russia was not yet willing to pay the economic price for these advantages.

Conclusion

Ukraine was the outsider in relations involving the three Slavic CIS states. While after 1994 Minsk appeared desperate for closer ties with Moscow, Kyiv seemed to have an almost pathological fear of any initiatives or moves emanating from Moscow. Anything and everything was interpreted in terms of its implications for Ukrainian independence and sovereignty. While the price to be paid for such a stance was in some ways relatively negligible (military and political independence were relatively cost-free and achieved quite quickly) it was profound in economic terms. Yet any moves to reanimate economic ties between the two states that could be taken advantage of by Russia in order to bring about a reintegration of Ukraine were avoided by Kyiv. These constraints on the development of economic ties meant that both economies suffered unduly from the collapse of the Soviet Union; there is little evidence that Ukraine was prepared to budge on its principles. Yet this stance toward Russia merely exposed the very vulnerability of Ukraine – in the absence of stronger ties with its neighbours other than Russia, it remained overwhelmingly dependent on ties with its Muscovite one. This is why relations along the Western azimuth were so important to Ukraine, as will be seen in Part III. And even as Ukraine's economic predicament worsened, Kyiv did not budge until it had at least received from Russia the unconditional recognition of its territorial integrity.

The sheer number of political, economic and military ties developing between Minsk and Moscow, and the relative paucity of such ties between Kyiv and Moscow highlight the gulf in geopolitical outlook that existed between Ukraine and Belarus especially in the years following Lukashenko's election. It could not be disguised by the Belarussian weak efforts to put a gloss on relations. The gap was at its most glaring on the international scene. A good example was the stance adopted by both states toward NATO enlargement. Belarus adopted an overtly oppositionist and confrontational stance toward NATO enlargement; indeed, this stance grew firmer to the extent that it showed to a willingness to accommodate nuclear weapons on its territory and form military alliances with Russia. This outlook contrasted with Ukraine's lack of objection to NATO enlargement. Similarly, Ukraine demonstrated a clearly pro-Western stance when it responded to US pressure by cancelling an agreement it had signed with Iran to help build a nuclear power station there in conjunction with Russia. The vacancy was quickly filled by Belarus.[113] More recently, while Belarus responded in bellicose tones to the NATO attack on Serbia, Ukraine adopted more measured tones, vowing to continue its participation in the Partnership for Peace Programme. This divergent geopolitical outlook was reflected in opposing geopolitical trajectories adopted by the two states on a subregional and regional level (see next chapter).

What light do the events recounted in this chapter shed on the relevance of the theoretical approaches described in Chapter 1? In theoretical terms, in the days and early years following independence, Ukraine implemented a strategy regarding Russia which was in line with that predicted by realist theory. Although Ukraine was never under a military threat from Russia, the pursuit of self-help through the creation of fully independent forces, irrespective of the disruption it caused in terms of relations with its Russian brethren (especially economic costs), spoke volumes about the mindset prevailing in Kyiv. However, it was also indicative of the determination of policy-makers to pursue independence in its fullest sense. Ukraine's decision to adhere to the commitment made in 1990 in the Declaration of Sovereignty to denuclearise can also be seen in this light – the maintenance of 'Ukrainian' nuclear forces imposed a dependence on Russia which was incompatible with independence. However, while for realists Ukraine's decision to denuclearise was counter-intuitive, Kyiv's subsequent decision to renege on that commitment in 1992–3 was more in keeping with realism, and apparently reflected the sense of threat Kyiv perceived to be emanating from Russia. In reality, the decision was not as strongly guided by 'realist' rationale as realists might believe. It was in fact more indicative of the real challenge Ukraine faced – nuclear weapons could be 'sold' and thereby help alleviate the bankruptcy brought about by the severe economic depression that had taken hold there.

The theory of structural interdependence helps fill the gaps left by realism. As Ukraine de-integrated from former Soviet political, economic and military structures, its interdependence (the first theme of the theory) with Russia was laid bare. However, this interdependence was asymmetrical – Ukraine was far more reliant on Russia than vice versa. In line with the tenets of the theory of structural interdependence, Ukraine was extremely sensitive and vulnerable to any changes in energy prices imposed by Russia (as Moscow introduced world energy pricing), especially in the context of the overall economic collapse. Yet the economic cost was a price Kyiv was willing to pay in order to distance itself from Moscow. This is because, first, Ukraine was concerned as to the frequency with which military solutions were reverted to by Moscow to 'resolve' issues in its 'near abroad' (i.e. there was a high salience of use of force – a tenet of the second theme of the theory – something which was damaging to the continued interdependence between the two states as was the fact that force tended to be high on the Russian political agenda). Second, it was indicative of Ukraine's resolve to take advantage of the changed power structure (a tenet of the third theme of the theory) of the post-Soviet space in pursuit of its own goals.

3 The North-eastern azimuth

Subregional and regional integration

Following the unexpected demise of the Soviet Union, there was a real danger that the collapse of institutional ties linking the former Soviet republics would result in an economic and political vacuum. The all-pervasive nature of the Soviet Union as an organising framework would have ensured such an implosion. From the very outset of discussions on the successor to the Soviet Union, it was apparent that the views of Ukraine and Russia were incongruent. Ukraine was adamant that participation in any successor institution was, at best, a temporary exercise to bring about 'a civilised divorce'. In this regard, Ukraine differed sharply from its two Slavic 'Eastern' neighbours. At the outset, both Russia and Belarus were intent on drawing Ukraine into a subregional *ménage à trois*. This early Ukrainian resistance was to become a permanent feature in its dealings with Belarus and Russia. These early subregional efforts on the part of Moscow and Minsk were only abandoned under pressure from other former Soviet republics, unwilling to be left outside such a post-Soviet grouping. This pressure resulted in the formation of the Commonwealth of Independent States. Yet as the CIS foundered, something which is at least in some measure attributable to Ukraine's obstructionism, the Slavic theme was returned to.

Subregional integration within the CIS

From the very earliest hours following the collapse of the Soviet Union, pressures were exerted on Kyiv to enter some sort of confederation with the original founding members of the Soviet Union, namely Russia and Belarus, to the exclusion of other former Soviet republics. Kravchuk, Ukraine's newly elected president, refused to join any sort of confederation, opting instead for a much looser commonwealth.[1] In fact, Minsk's objectives were subtly different to those of Moscow. Belarus was focused on tripartite co-operation with Russia and Ukraine; Russia was keen to involve all of the former republics.[2] For Minsk this was a matter of self-preservation, as there is some evidence to suggest Russian analysts rejected the notion of a community, recommending instead a formal annexation of Belarus by Russia.[3]

There were adequate grounds for an ethnically based Slavic subregional grouping. The three Slavic republics collectively constituted by the far the greatest contributors to the Soviet Union in terms of geography, population, and economic potential. They were further linked by interdependence, and a common Slavic extraction. This common extraction related to the fact that they were all eastern Slavs as opposed to the Poles and others in Central and Eastern European who were western Slavs. The fact that eastern Slavs shared a Cyrillic-based Slavic language, and Orthodoxy as a religion also differentiated them from other Slavs such as the Poles. Strong cultural and ethnic bonds, particularly the high number of Russians resident in both Belarus and Ukraine and Ukrainians in Russia, further reinforced this sense of commonness. Furthermore, as Pritzel points out:

> the fact that the decision to dissolve the Soviet Union and replace it with a Commonwealth of Independent States was made by the three Slavic Republics . . . was clearly a reflection of the marginal position that the Caucasus and Central Asia occupied in the minds of Russia's policy makers.[4]

The non-Slav republics simply did not figure prominently in policy-making, at least in the immediate days following the collapse of the Soviet Union, and there was a strong basis for a subregional, Slav-based grouping.

Following the initial rejection by Kyiv of the very notion of a subregional grouping made up of former Soviet Slavic states, the idea evaporated until the election of Oleksandr Lukashenko in 1994, who immediately started to push for closer ties between Minsk and Moscow. In pursuit of stronger sub-CIS ties, on 2 April 1996 a treaty was signed between Russia and Belarus on 'The Creation of a Community (or Commonwealth) of Sovereign Republics', something which Belarussian President Lukashenko characterised as the 'first stage' of the CIS. Ultimately a three-speed CIS was envisaged in which the 'big four (namely Russia, Belarus, Kazakhstan and Kyrgyzstan) made up the second stage, with the remaining member states belonging to the third stage.[5] While Belarus and Moscow were clearly keen that Ukraine should belong to this first group, it was evident from early on that at best Kyiv was going to be a reluctant participant in the third.

The new Belarussian–Russian Community was soon endowed with formal institutions such as a supreme council and executive committee, with a parliamentary assembly in the pipeline. Yet the rhetoric and institutionalisation of the new body failed to camouflage the vast discrepancy between the economic and political stances adopted by the two member states: authoritarianism and a centralised economy continued to be the main themes within Belarus as opposed to the flawed but nevertheless real Russian democratic system and market economy.

Minsk was lured by the prospect of Russian economic support for the collapsing Belarussian economy. Belarus was hopelessly reliant on Russia for energy, producing only two million of the 150 million tons of oil it had the refining capacity for, and the raw materials for its electronics industry and orders for its machine building factories. There is little doubt that Lukashenko believed 'that he was utterly indispensable to the Russian authorities, which would at any cost, even their own economic interests, please Minsk'.[6] For the immediate future the benefits were obvious. For Russia, the new union represented a countermove in advance of NATO enlargement. It was, however, also a move designed for the domestic electorate.

In March 1996, the Russian Duma denounced the 1991 Belovezha Agreements on the demise of the Soviet Union. By agreeing to the new union, Yeltsin was trying to appease the electorate in preparation for the upcoming presidential elections. Yet it was soon clear that the benefits, such as they were, were somewhat one-sided. While Belarus failed to gain either the much hoped for substantial credits or loans, Moscow, in addition to appeasing a tetchy electorate, also managed to gain free leases on substantial military facilities based in Belarus, low charges on the transportation of 80 per cent of all of its goods transported westward, and the opportunity to take an interest (meaning 'ownership') in strategic Belarussian enterprises.[7]

As ties between Belarus and Russia intensified, so did the pressure on Ukraine to join them in a formal union. Kyiv remained aloof. For example, when in the spring of 1999 Lukashenko proposed the creation of a pan-Slavic bloc to counter NATO influence in Europe, Ukraine responded by reiterating its commitment to the alliance and continued co-operation in the PfP.[8] Lukashenko was left clutching at straws when, following an outright rejection of Ukraine joining the union by Kyiv, he stated that he felt 'grateful that Kuchma supported . . . [the idea] . . . that we Slavic brothers, Russians, Ukrainians and Belarussians will hold consultations and work out a memorandum on our strategic partnership in all areas, not just economic' (RFE/RL, 22 July 1999). Minsk's hopes were exposed as hollow when in the run up to the 1999 presidential elections, the incumbent Leonid Kuchma was asked why it was that he did not want to join the Russian–Belarus alliance; he replied that 'When a pauper is joined by two others, they do not end up richer. Russia is simply not in a position to help Ukraine today. It has to deal with its own problems.'[9]

Overall, Ukraine refused to participate in any moves aimed at the creation of a subregional multilateral body within the CIS involving Russia. Kyiv was suspicious of any moves that might drag it into some form of integration process, especially as the subregional and regional processes were clearly linked in Belarussian and Russian minds. Lukashenko demonstrated this when he pressured the Ukrainians to join the Russia–Belarus union and the CIS customs union, arguing that 'Ukraine will get nowhere without tighter integration with the CIS'.[10] In the early days, Belarussian efforts at subregional structures were partially aimed at avoiding its own total subordination to Russia. However, following the election of Lukashenko, these efforts were really geared toward some form of a new Slavic Soviet union. Russia's goals were more far-reaching. Above all, Moscow was focused on Ukraine's full reintegration into the post-Soviet space by ensuring its membership of the CIS.

CIS integration: rationale, issues and milestones

The ongoing friction between Ukraine and Russia found resonance in their totally different stance and approach toward the characterisation of the post-Soviet space. Kyiv and Moscow approached the former Soviet space from incongruent and incompatible points of view. For Ukraine, the new geopolitical space was to be inhabited by sovereign and independent states. In contrast, Russia envisaged a new form of union based around the Ukrainian–Russian tandem. Indeed, evidence suggests that if necessary, this new relationship could have been shaped according to the demands of Kyiv – the prime goal from Moscow's point of view was that a formal relationship or 'partnership' continued.[11]

Ukraine's conceptualisation of CIS integration parallels that of Garnett, who suggests that CIS integration is a process of 'responding to the problems of a currently weak zone of states and instability on Russia's borders with a political and security structure shaped by Russian interests'.[12] For Kyiv, the CIS was inevitably going to be Russocentric, dominated by Russian perspectives on events. Furthermore, Kyiv was only too well aware that membership of the CIS meant an intense relationship with an economic, military and political heavyweight, something that was always going to have negative reverberations for Ukraine's own sovereignty and independence. The fact that the two key members of the CIS held diametrically opposed views of the CIS was thus highly problematic, both for Russia and the institution itself. This disparity of views was merely compounded by the structural, constitutional and financial inadequacies that plagued the CIS from its inception.[13]

Yet for Russia the very existence of the CIS was crucial. There were many reasons for this, but two stand out. First, at the very least the CIS slowed down the economic and social disintegration that was taking place in the structures linking the states of the former Soviet Union. Indeed, it has been postulated by some Ukrainian officials that the existence of the CIS was designed to prevent the break-up of the Russian Federation itself.[14] Second, the CIS legitimised the presence of Russian forces throughout the CIS.

The central importance of Ukraine to the CIS was made clear by Yeltsin, who openly admitted that creation of the CIS

> was the only way of pulling Ukraine into the orbit of some sort of new union-like relationship on a totally new basis, and therefore to cool the fervour of our military and national patriots, who threatened us with a new *putsch*, related to the exit of Ukraine.[15]

Ukraine was crucial to the success of the CIS for a number of reasons. Above all, Ukraine's size, resources, military–technical infrastructure, military might, socio-economic structure, historical and ethnic ties made the Ukraine–Russia tandem the obvious foundation on which to build the CIS as a multilateral forum. Alternatively, Ukraine's non or limited involvement in the CIS would strongly suggest a centrifugal tendency between the two key partners forging paths in different directions. As Garnett points out, 'Ukraine's participation is crucial to defining whether the CIS can meaningfully unite the key states of the former USSR'.[16] Such divergence would have clear negative ramifications for future integration, especially if Ukraine was to gain adherents to its cause. In addition, according to Garnett, Ukraine's participation would add 'a strong Slavic and European flavour to the CIS', as well as 'restore a European element to what could develop into a lopsidedly "Eurasian" organisation'.[17] The 'lack' of Ukraine would leave Russia locked out of the European space. Another benefit of Ukraine's participation in the CIS was that it would legitimise the institution. Conversely,

Ukraine's absence might embolden other CIS states to search for extraneous partners beyond the Commonwealth. Russia saw the CIS as a means of rebuilding ties between former Soviet republics, and in particular with Ukraine, on a new more voluntary basis now that the 'glue' of fear and ideology binding them had failed. Arguably, the success of this policy could be measured by the extent of Ukraine's involvement in the institution.

Ukraine's recalcitrance at being drawn in was a response to perceived Russian expectations as to what kind of vehicle the CIS was to be. In contrast to the *consultative* role (to bring about a 'civilised divorce') anticipated by Ukraine, Russia envisaged and developed the CIS as an *integrative* body along the lines of the European Union, on the origins of which it was modelled.[18] This divergence of views was to shape both the various institutions of the CIS, and the role each of the two key members were to play within them.

In Ukraine's favour, with regard to its objectives within the CIS, was the fact that there were a number of key factors working against the viability of the institution. First, member states were at vastly different levels of economic development. The Muslim states, with their low level of economic development, relatively underdeveloped infrastructure and limited industrialisation, contrasted with the economies of the Slavic republics. Second, the CIS region was neither ethnically, culturally, or in terms of religion, homogeneous. Third, the CIS was riven with internal disputes, of which the Russo-Ukrainian one was perhaps the most significant. Fourth, many member states were motivated by their own economic potential and therefore loath to retransfer power back to an imperial centre. Fifth, many states neighboured more prosperous, or potentially more prosperous regional groupings, and hence competitors to the CIS. This was particularly true in Ukraine's case. Sixth, many member states suffered internal ruptures, in most of which Russia's influence could be detected. If nothing else, this alienated those states from Russia. Seventh, member states had individual and indeed sometimes contradictory geopolitical objectives triggered by membership of different geographical regions. For example, Ukraine was westward looking, while Kazakhstan saw markets in the east. Russia wanted to keep them both close. So while Russia attempted to intensify the centripetal tendencies of the CIS by continuing to provide energy, encouraging the formation of CIS institutions, stationing troops on the outer borders of the CIS, Ukraine energised the centrifugal effects acting on the institution by not participating in CIS structures and emphasising the formation of bilateral ties with CIS member states and the formation of subregional institutions within and beyond it, frequently made up of CIS member states. Finally, the member states, including Russia, were just too poor to make it viable.

Three areas of CIS co-operation or integration were envisaged by Russia: political, economic and military.

Political co-operation

From the very beginning, Ukraine put obstacles in the way of the development of the CIS as a forum for political co-operation let alone as an integrationist structure. Despite agreeing to being a founding member of the CIS on 8 December 1991, at subsequent meetings the Ukrainian delegation overtly opposed the CIS developing either into a state entity or a supranational institution, preferring that it remain as a loose forum for independent states. Soon after the signing of the agreement it was ratified by the Ukrainian parliament on 12 December 1991 (and subsequently announced in a declaration on 20 December). However, ratification was only completed with a whole host of conditions and exemptions attached by Kyiv in order to preserve Ukraine's sovereignty and independence, and prevent full integration into the CIS in the face of what it saw as Moscow's attempts to renew former ties.[19] Of the twelve qualifying points made by the Rada, the most important included the recognition and respect of territorial integrity and immutability of *existing* national borders (as opposed to administrative–territorial borders within the CIS); a rejection of the co-ordination of foreign policy activities, and an offer of co-operation instead; and a rejection of unified CIS armed forces. In general, the Rada was against the formation of the CIS as a supranational institution, with its own executive organs and co-ordinating structures, deemed so essential by Moscow.

However, so unsatisfactory were the conditions of continued membership of the CIS, that in January 1992 Kravchuk threatened to leave because of what he saw as the continued violation of CIS agreements by member states, and Russian interference in Ukrainian affairs and those of other republics.[20] This was a response to the open threats made by the Russians as to the possibility of linking non-participation in CIS agreements and Russian interference in the internal affairs of former Soviet Union states. For example, Ruslan Khasbulatov, the chairman of the Russian Duma, suggested that the resolution of border issues within the CIS (with Moldova ostentatiously singled out as an example) was dependent on the republics' continued membership of the CIS.[21]

The proposal for the writing of a charter for the CIS in May 1992 was a natural progression for the institution as a supranational structure. In itself the document was important, as the CIS lacked a clear, useable statute, and was instead structured according to the documents and agreements signed up until that point. Indeed, until a charter was signed, CIS members, rather than linked according to a statute, were in fact linked according to common extraction (as former members of the Soviet Union), economic interdependence, and the rapidly deteriorating bonds that still nevertheless linked the former Soviet *nomenklatura* in power in many of the states.

Inevitably, any such charter was anathema to Kyiv. In general terms, Ukraine was against anything which locked it into anything other than a West European institution. In more specific terms, some of the provisions of the charter were undesirable *per se* for Ukraine. For example, Kyiv was against Article 4 on a common economic space, and common external borders (which implied that CIS 'internal' borders were administrative rather than state borders). Article 11, on collective military forces, directly contradicted the foreign and security policy of Ukraine; each article was an abhorrence to Kyiv.[22] Even the supposedly pro-Russian and pro-CIS Ukrainian Prime Minister Leonid Kuchma was against the charter, stating categorically at a CIS heads of government meeting in November 1992 that Ukraine would neither adhere to nor sign a charter in the form presented.[23] As a result, at the CIS summit in Minsk in January 1993, the CIS charter, providing for a new legal framework and closer relations, was left unsigned by Ukraine along with Turkmenistan, Moldova and Azerbaijan, while Georgia did not even attend the meeting.[24] This was despite the efforts of the Russians who, somewhat exasperatedly, felt that they had 'laid so much stress on independence and non-intervention (in the charter) that it would be useless'.[25]

Kyiv's tactics did not lead to Ukraine's isolation within the CIS. On the contrary, Ukraine's oppositionist stance consolidated its position within the body as an alternative pole to Russia. An early example of this was Moldova's siding with Ukraine in its opposition to the 'new centralism' and Kishinev's insistence that it would not sign the charter if Kyiv did not.[26] Thus, simultaneously, as the CIS failed to take on the cohesion to make it a meaningful body, a strengthening of ties was taking place between some of its members within the institution. Indeed, the start of a subregional sub-CIS formation was in the offing.

At the same time as the charter was being prepared, the formation of the Interparliamentary Assembly (IPA) was under way, agreed to by seven of the eleven member states of the CIS in March 1992. Fearful of the creation of a supranational institution, with all of its associated threats to Ukrainian sovereignty and independence, Kyiv proposed interparliamentary consultations rather than an assembly.[27] Nevertheless, despite Ukraine's objections, the IPA held its first session in Bishkek on 15 September 1992.[28] As a consultative institution, it was ostensibly designed to co-ordinate the process of co-operation between member states, the development of proposals for the activities of national parliaments, and the promotion of proximity and harmonisation between different national legislatures. However, Ukraine suspected alternative motives behind the institution.[29] It has in fact been argued that the IPA was the political superstructure being built on the economic foundation that the CIS was trying to recreate between member states; thus it was to act as a new union parliament, creating a new union legislature.[30] Indeed, the acceptance of the Convention of the IPA of the CIS in May 1995 allowed for the IPA to establish and sign treaties on behalf of member states. It had gained inter-state powers. Unsurprisingly, the Ukrainians rejected the proposal in September 1993 of the chairman of the Russian Duma for the setting up of a CIS parliamentary assembly – effectively a common CIS government – out of hand.[31] Ukraine's suspicions as to the intentions of the Russians were further confirmed in 1994 by the head of Russian Foreign Intelligence, Yevgeniy Primakov, who suggested that the organisation of the CIS

> lends to itself to the formation of a union under the leadership of Russia, to the supranational structures of which member states will delegate some of their

> defence and economic functions. Such a structure is very similar to the political make up of the former Soviet Union.[32]

Kyiv's suspicions and scepticism appear to have been well founded. Ukraine's reluctance to get too deeply entangled with the CIS economic and political structures was further reinforced by the belief that such structures would be effectively under the control of the Russians.[33]

As political integration progressed, President Kuchma, a supposedly pro-Russian president, unambiguously laid out Ukraine's antipathy toward political, economic, military or other forms of integration with the CIS. During his speech to the Western European Union in June 1996 he not only underlined his pro-European orientation, but also shut the door quite categorically on any hopes for a new supranational role for the CIS, let alone the revival of the USSR:

> I wish to underline the role of the CIS as a mechanism leading to a peaceful and democratic resolution of all the problems associated with the collapse of the USSR . . . and that it was on the initiative of Ukraine that the CIS was confirmed as neither a supranational nor state-like creation . . . Our country opposes any form of supranational activities on the part of the CIS. Furthermore, Ukraine is categorically against any efforts at reanimating in any shape or form the former Soviet Union.[34]

This sent a clear shot across the bows of the Russian Duma that had passed a resolution in March 1996, 'On the deepening of the integration of nations, that were united in the USSR, and a reversal of the resolution of the Supreme Soviet of the RSFSR from 12 December 1991', that is a reversal of the decision to abolish the Soviet Union in Belovezha. It is noteworthy that a change in the constellation of forces within Ukraine in 1999 brought about a change in Ukraine's status in relation to the IPA.[35] The election of the left-winger Tkachenko as speaker of the Ukrainian parliament led to Ukraine joining the IPA in March 1999 (up until then it had been an observer), with 230 votes in favour, just passing the 226 threshold necessary.[36] It is worth noting that in joining the IPA, Ukraine became a member of a body which is regulated by Article 36 of the Charter of the CIS to which Ukraine is not a signatory.[37]

Membership of this body had potential consequences for Ukraine's 'strategic' goal of integration with subregional and regional bodies along the Western azimuth. In particular, the national democrats in the Ukrainian Rada were concerned that the harmonisation of the legislature of the IPA member states might contradict the steps taken by Kyiv to harmonise Ukraine's legislature with Western institutions. For example, the Council of Europe has specific requirements for civil, criminal and procedural legislation, which might be at odds with those of the IPA. This potential problem was exacerbated by the fact that many IPA members (Kazakhstan, Uzbekistan, Turkmenistan and Kyrgyzstan) are never likely to be Council of Europe members, and thus need not agree to or abide by legislation moulded by the needs of the Council of Europe or some other such institution. Furthermore, Ukraine was already moving away from the demands of the IPA as Kyiv sought to harmonise its legislation with that of the EU and the OSCE.

Overall, Ukraine's joining the CIS IPA was one of the few meaningful positive political developments within the CIS involving Kyiv as, in the main, Ukraine was simply unwilling to delegate autonomy to the institution.

Military issues

If the military split between Russia and Ukraine was the source of acrimony between Kyiv and Moscow on a bilateral basis, the *frisson* continued between them within the CIS as a multilateral forum. Soon after the Belovezha Agreement, Kravchuk started ploughing a lone furrow gradually de-integrating Ukraine from its economic, political and, above all, military ties with the former Soviet Union republics. Ukraine was guided by a set of principles which precluded the reintegration of Ukraine's forces with those of Russia and the CIS, namely, Article IX in Ukraine's Declaration of Sovereignty which specified neutrality, non-bloc and non-nuclear status.[38] While the suitability of such policies for Ukraine is open to question, they did represent an unambiguous set of guidelines for Ukraine's leaders to pursue in their dealings with Moscow regarding the eventual shape of the military formations in the post-Soviet world.

As we have seen, as part of implementing these guidelines, on 12 December 1991 President Kravchuk decreed the transfer of all military material and forces in Ukraine to Ukrainian command, excluding those associated with strategic nuclear deterrence. By early 1992, irrespective of Russian efforts to create a CIS military budget, Ukraine was providing the bulk of finance for forces stationed in Ukraine.[39] At a meeting of CIS defence ministers, Ukraine, along with Azerbaijan, conspicuously refused to initial any of the eleven drafts presented that were to do with the creation of CIS common defence structures.[40] The depths to which relations between Ukraine and Russia had sunk was made more than evident when Kravchuk refused to attend the CIS summit in Tashkent in May 1992, citing a scheduled meeting as an excuse. Russia, Kazakhstan, Uzbekistan, Tajikistan, Turkmenistan and Armenia all signed the Tashkent Collective Security Treaty. This agreement was designed to work along the lines of NATO interrelations, whereby an attack on one member state was deemed an attack on all other states, thereby obliging them to render military and other assistance. Ukraine, Azerbaijan, Moldova and Belarus all refused to sign; Georgia was not a member of the CIS at that time.[41] With the exception of Belarus, the members of the latter group, along with Georgia, went on to form a subregional institution that came to be known by the acronym GUAM, later to be joined in 1999 by Uzbekistan (to form GUUAM). In October 1992 Ukraine and Moldova refused to initial a draft treaty 'On Defence and Collective Security'.[42]

As relations between Kyiv and Moscow deteriorated over the course of 1992, the frequency of clashes between them within the CIS increased. With the removal of the Black Sea Fleet from the jurisdiction of the CIS at the bilateral Yalta summit between Ukraine and Russia in August 1992, the nuclear forces stationed in Ukraine and the matter of joint air defences remained the most significant bones of contention within the CIS. While the nuclear issue was finally addressed in 1994 with the Trilateral Agreement signed between Ukraine, Russia and the USA, the matter of air defences became a more prolonged affair.

Joint air defences were a crucial factor driving Russia's interest in the formation of a military union with Ukraine. Following the collapse of the Soviet Union, Russia remained effectively undefended from missile attack. Of the eight early warning stations located around the Soviet Union, only three were located on the territory of the RSFSR. While the CIS Collective Security Treaty proposed in Tashkent in May 1992 was supposed to resolve the problem, it did not do so as Ukraine failed to sign it. Subsequent pressure in the form of arm-twisting over oil and gas supplies eventually resulted in Ukrainian Minister of Defence Shmarov initialling an agreement on participation in a common air defence system in February 1995.[43] It has been argued that not only did Ukraine effectively lose its non-bloc status with this move, but it also opened itself to uncontrolled incursions by flights from member states.[44] An agreement on the use by Russia of the two early warning stations based in Mukachevo and Sevastopol (which covered Europe and the Mediterranean) at a cost of $4 million per annum was finally signed in February 1997.[45]

Overall, so great were the tensions in the Ukrainian–Russian relationship from the very first days of the Commonwealth that according to the President of Kazakhstan, Nursultan Nazarbaev, the continued friction between Kyiv and Moscow as regards military issues was affecting the stability of the CIS.[46] The fact that the CIS failed to function effectively as a military alliance from there on ultimately undermined the credibility of the institution. This lack of credibility was amply demonstrated in April 1999 when owing to a refusal on the part of Azerbaijan, Georgia and Uzbekistan to sign a protocol to the treaty in order to prolong it, the Tashkent treaty effectively started to unravel. The fact that this was followed by an announcement at the NATO summit in 1999 of a commitment by the non-signatories to subregional integration in the form of a growth and hence consolidation of GUAM to GUUAM, only served to magnify the impact and significance of the event, a point which will be explored in some detail in Chapter 7. It reflected a further diminution in the stature of Russia and the CIS in favour of Ukraine's status within GUUAM, as well as of the Western Alliance. There can be little doubt that Ukraine contributed to the unravelling of the Tashkent treaty in two key ways. First, by adopting an oppositionist stance with no ostensible repercussions, Kyiv modelled a position that was clearly appealing to other CIS members. Second, by remaining in steadfast opposition to the CIS, Ukraine established itself as a leader of renegades within the CIS, of which GUUAM was the most powerful example. Without Ukraine, a GUUAM was effectively inconceivable. Without Ukraine (and its 'followers'), a military union of CIS states was rendered meaningless. Along with political integration, military integration was a key area in which Ukraine could reject Russian moves for greater ties with impunity. The same cannot be said for economic ties, the strongest glue binding Ukraine to Russia.

Economic integration

In October 1991, two months after the Ukrainian declaration of independence, and two months before the formal unravelling of the Soviet Union, a treaty on economic community was signed by eight of the twelve former Union republics. The treaty was designed to create a common economic space in which signatory states would co-operate on issues of trade and economic policy; the treaty also allowed for the setting up of inter-republican bodies that would regulate the economies. Highly significant, and indicative of things to come on the subregional dimension, was the fact that Georgia, Ukraine, Azerbaijan and Moldova (the GUAM states) all refused to sign the treaty. Ukraine's main objectives were to maintain bilateral ties with other republics, and avoid participating in a renewed Moscow-centred economic system. This was despite the fact that the Soviet Union was a major source of Ukraine's imports and a significant market for its exports. However, ties with Russia dominated this market. Russia took some 75 per cent of all of Ukraine's Soviet exports, and was the source of perhaps 80 per cent of its Soviet imports. As far as Kyiv was concerned, the problem lay in the fact that Moscow saw economic ties as a means to a political end. For example, the tight link between economics and politics was evident, as according to Smith it is the

> close knit economic integration, which reflects the Russian desire to tie economically the near abroad to the Russian Federation. This would increase the dependence of these states on Russia, and so make it more difficult for them to pursue foreign policies that Moscow might consider anti-Russian.[47]

In contrast, for Ukraine, economic relations, both on a bilateral basis with CIS states and on a multilateral basis within the CIS, were not meant to be as exclusive as they had been hitherto. While relations with former Soviet republics were clearly fundamental to an economy as heavily integrated with theirs as was Ukraine's, Kyiv's objectives along the Western and Southern azimuths demanded a reorientation of ties westward. As a result, the Russians were hesitant to make any proposals that might be perceived by Ukraine as directly impeding their drive westward. So although a central CIS bank was mooted as early as January 1992, Moscow was mindful of 'the general scepticism over Russia's role in the CIS, and the hatred of "central" anything [sic] among member states'.[48] Similarly, it was argued that

> the planned establishment of a consultative co-ordination economic council and economic court was extremely important to arrest the economic decline in the CIS states. The creation of the council seems unlikely, however, given President Yeltsin's reluctance to force the issue, presumably out of a desire not to antagonise Ukraine.[49]

Nevertheless, despite Ukrainian sensibilities, institutional CIS economic integration, with all of its political connotations and inherent institutional flaws, proceeded without Kyiv. Tighter relations with Ukraine, while important, were not indispensable to Russia. Repeatedly, Ukraine refused to participate in any steps toward economic integration despite the mutually binding ties that existed with Russia and other CIS states. At the Bishkek Summit in October 1993, Ukraine refused to take part in the Consultative Economic Committee, signing only five out of the fifteen documents presented at the summit. In May 1993, at the CIS summit in Moscow, while Kravchuk signed a joint declaration, which proposed greater economic integration and the creation of a common market for services and goods, he objected to the creation of an economic union. Thus, Ukraine did not sign the Agreement on an Economic Union, on 24 September 1993, which anticipated the creation of a free trade association, a customs union (the main benefit of which was duty-free import of Russian energy for non-Russian states), and a common market (for goods, work and capital, and a rouble zone) as a full member. Instead, Ukraine, along with Turkmenistan, joined only as an associate member, a status of an unspecified nature, in April 1994. Kyiv demonstrated similar recalcitrance when Ukraine joined the Interstate Economic Committee in October 1994, after posting a whole host of reservations. In particular, Kyiv insisted that a provision be made for each country independently to decide on exactly which functions would be delegated to the committee. The second precondition was that Ukraine remained outside the payments union, while the third was that national legislation should not be overridden by the rulings of the committee.

In January 1995, Russia proposed the setting up of the long-awaited customs union, with two prime conditions of membership. The first condition required the harmonisation of customs and economic (*hospodarche*) legislation with that of Russia; the harmonisation of external economic activity with that of the Russian Federation was the second condition.[50] While Russia was joined by Belarus and Kazakhstan in the union, Ukraine remained resolutely beyond it because it reduced the prospects for Ukraine's membership of Western subregional and regional institutions, from which it believed it would effectively be debarred.[51]

Subsequently, in March 1996, Russia, Belarus, Kazakhstan and Kyrgyzstan signed an agreement 'On Deepening Integration' that was regarded as a forerunner to a Eurasian Union, a CIS version of the European Union. As ever, Ukraine remained conspicuously to one side.[52] While the proposal to create a CIS free economic zone was endorsed by CIS prime ministers in November 1998, the suggestion for merging the CIS Interstate Economic Committee and the Executive Secretariat was rejected by Ukraine amongst others, despite Prime Minister Primakov's assurance that it would not become a supranational body.[53]

Past evidence suggested otherwise to Kyiv. Russia occupied leadership positions in key institutions, such as the Interstate Economic Committee, and maintained majority voting rights in others.[54] That Moscow took advantage of those institutions (e.g. the rouble-based accounts settlements of the Interstate Bank ultimately result in the provision of free credit for the Russian economy) was not Kyiv's only worry.[55] Above all, Kyiv was animated by concerns that Moscow's control over key CIS structures would help it convert the CIS into a vehicle which it would then use to return to its former hegemonic status, thereby undermining the sovereignty of individual republics. Furthermore, despite the ostensible focus of the CIS on economic integration, Ukraine suspected that political integration remained the covert objective. For example, there was an explicit link made by the Russians between the creation of a customs union, on the one hand, and 'reliable protection of the outer border of the CIS', on the other.[56] A common border defence system was mooted, something which was anathema to Ukraine and which it subsequently rejected.[57] Similarly, Russian Deputy Prime Minister Aleksandr Shokhin 'told journalists that Moscow was making it clear that joining the economic union "would result in a partial loss of not just economic sovereignty, but political sovereignty as well"', something that was unacceptable to Kyiv.[58] Threats against non-participants were not just implicit: Russia suggested that Ukraine join the CIS Customs Union as a means of avoiding the inevitable negative consequences of being beyond it.[59]

Evidence suggests that had the CIS maintained an economic rather than political focus, Ukraine might have been a more compliant partner. Kuchma, a much hoped for ally of Moscow, was critical of the absence of any real economic CIS integration, something which suffered at the expense of Russia's more political ambitions.[60] As an alternative, Kyiv came up with its own more economy-oriented proposals for a new style CIS. It proposed a reduction in CIS co-operation on political and military matters, on border protection, military–technical issues, and on issues concerned with collective security, and matters to do with humanitarian aid, legal issues, exchange of information and ecology. Instead, 'the Ukrainian representation wants to transform the CIS into a mechanism for economic co-operation, *provided that its structures do not duplicate those of other European and international bodies and hinder the integration of CIS member countries into those bodies*' [my italics].[61] Needless, to say, these proposals came to nothing.

Conclusion to Part II

Overall, the successful resolution of difficulties with Russia was to be the foundation on which all Ukraine's other foreign policy successes were to be built. Russia represented the single greatest threat to Ukraine's security and independence. In addition to using the Crimean issue to challenge the territorial integrity of Ukraine – no mean threat to a state as fragmented and fragile as Ukraine – Moscow also tried to bring about Ukraine's isolation. Kyiv was unlikely to garner many allies while it found itself in a drawn out and sometimes tense confrontation with a spurned and angered Russia.

The failure of Moscow's policy was not only indicative of the dire economic and political straits Russia itself was in. Failure was also a corollary of the successful implementation of Ukraine's foreign and security policy and Kyiv's refusal to buckle under the psychological and economic pressure exerted by Russia. Relations with Belarus were helpful in this regard. Furthermore, as Belarus drew ever closer to Moscow, Kyiv grew ever more important from the point of view of the West.

These bilateral level achievements were very much at the expense of the formation of the Slavic subregional institutions that were mooted by, in particular, Belarus. If anything, this was even more true of the CIS. The more issues that were resolved between Russia and Ukraine beyond the CIS, the lower became the credibility of the CIS as a forum designed to resolve issues.

According to one assessment of the development of the CIS in 1992, 'future relations among its component states will develop along three lines: as allies (Belarus–Russia); rivals (Ukraine–Russia); or adversaries (Armenia– Azerbaijan)'.[62] These predictions have certainly been borne out. Ukraine's rivalry with Russia is evident on the bilateral, subregional and regional levels. At each of these levels Ukraine has felt confident enough to either resist or challenge Russian objectives.

Admittedly, there is a real contradiction in Ukraine's attitude toward the CIS. Without a doubt Ukraine has been one of the most vociferous critics of the CIS, in particular of its failure to function effectively as an economic entity, incapable of integrating the separate and disparate functions of the member states of the CIS into a cohesive whole. Yet it is true to say that Kyiv is guilty of contributing to this failure. By blocking developments at every turn, Kyiv helped paralyse the institution. This blocking strategy was driven by Ukraine's suspicion, justified or not, that economic integration was a cloak for political reintegration. There is little doubt that Moscow was not very successful in allaying these fears. On the contrary, evidence suggests that such fears were well founded: unguarded public remarks by prominent Russian public figures are testimony to that. Furthermore, the Georgian president, Eduard Shevardnadze, suggested that the existence of the CIS had a deleterious impact on relations between CIS member states. Specifically, he argued that 'Russia and Ukraine would have found a rapport with each other but for the CIS'.[63] In a similar vein, in February 1997 Volodymyr Horbulin, the influential head of the Ukrainian National Security and Defence Committee, expressed the view that the CIS effectively had no prospects for the future, and that instead Ukraine should concentrate on developing its bilateral relations with other states.[64]

The divergence between Ukraine and Russia in terms of their attitudes toward the CIS threatens the institution: 'Russia must either deepen its hold on the more willing states, such as Belarus, and thus permanently divide and weaken the CIS as a structure covering the whole of the former USSR, or it must follow a path toward co-operation.'[65] Not only was this divide already in evidence as Ukraine sought ever-closer ties with Western institutions, it was exacerbated by other events taking place within the CIS. For example, at the beginning of 1997, Kyrgyzstan, Kazakhstan, Uzbekistan and Turkmenistan signed an agreement on 'eternal friendship'. The intensification of ties between the Central Asian republics (Turkmenistan, Uzbekistan, Kyrgyzstan, Kazakhstan and Tajikistan) was interpreted as a continuation of intra-CIS subregional activities initiated by GUUAM (and by early 1998 was referred to as the '5+4=9' process) conspicuously excluding Russia.[66] Furthermore, owing to Ukraine's reluctance to participate in the CIS as a full member, Russia was itself forced to go along this ultimately divisive route, as shown by the signing of the agreement 'On Deepening Integration' between Russia, Belarus, Kazakhstan and Kyrgyzstan on 29 March 1996 in preparation for a Eurasian Union, thereby creating an 'in' and an 'out' group. Furthermore, CIS summits were frequently characterised by the proliferation of both bilateral and subregional ties, at the expense of progress in the evolution of the CIS.[67]

Crude statistics reveal the sheer extent of the failure of the CIS. Between its inception in 1992 and 1997 the CIS approved 786 documents of various types. Of these, Ukraine signed 558 (or 70.9 per cent), though 81 of these were only signed with reservations attached (i.e. only 60.6 per cent of documents were signed unconditionally). In total, 228 documents went unsigned by Kyiv, while 65 of the 558 signed documents required either ratification or some form of processing. Of the 65, 15 had been ratified by the Ukrainian parliament, 14 confirmed by the president and the cabinet of ministers, while 27 needed further processing; the remaining 9 were regarded as 'inexpedient'. Of the 228 documents left unsigned by Ukraine, 71 pertained to organisation–administrative matters, 30 to economic and social affairs, while the remaining 127 were of a military–political nature. Of the 90 statutory structures established within the CIS, Ukraine participates in 58 (64.4 per cent); of these, 3 are based in Ukraine, and 50 in Russia.[68] Yet the quantitative dimension of the above-mentioned statistics, while starkly revealing Ukraine's recalcitrance at being drawn into the CIS, fails to reveal the qualitative nature of some of the documents which went unsigned. As of 2002, Ukraine remains beyond the Tashkent treaty, the economic union, and the customs union. The most important documents signed between Ukraine and Russia remain the bilateral Friendship Treaty with Russia and the BSF agreements, all resolutely beyond the framework of the CIS.

For a number of reasons remaining beyond the integrative grasp of the CIS was fundamental to Ukraine's future as a European state. First, porous borders with Russia, and the opportunity for illegal and economic migrants to wind their way westward through Ukraine, meant that a Ukraine firmly tied to Russia would be looked on unfavourably by the European Union, especially following Poland's accession. (It has been estimated that most immigrants from Asia and Africa heading for the EU enter through Ukraine, probably via Russia. In 2000, there were half a million illegal immigrants in Ukraine and two million in Russia.)[69]

Second, by joining any CIS free trade zones, or customs or payment unions Ukraine would not only prejudice its chances of joining the EU (which are negligible in any case) but would also in fact break the law on 'The Basic Direction of Foreign Policy of Ukraine', which forbids Ukraine's participation in 'the institutionalisation of forms of international co-operation with the CIS which are capable of transforming the Commonwealth into a supranational structure of a federal or confederative character'.[70] There remained a looming threat to such a strategy, which was pointed out by A. Migranyan, a member of the Presidential Council of the Russian Federation (and therefore decidedly *not* a representative of the Foreign Ministry), who argued that 'Russia would sooner destabilise the whole post-Soviet space, rather than allow the emergence of a number of anti-Russian centres . . . This is the basis of the existence of the Russian state'.[71]

It is misleading to suggest that Kyiv was responsible for all the moves that blocked deeper co-operation within the CIS. There were faults within the institution itself, primarily the poorly or vaguely defined mechanisms for the implementation of decisions, as has been extensively discussed elsewhere.[72] Exacerbating the problem was the lack of trust between partners, and the absence of any means of conflict resolution between partners who were often in confrontation with each other. It is hardly surprising that the CIS has been lampooned as the Community of Dependent States, and the CIS integration process itself has been condemned as 'a policy of condemning oneself to vegetate in the backyard of the world economy for the sake of the ideological stereotypes of the past' by the Uzbek president, Islam Karimov, in April 1996.[73]

Membership of the CIS has placed Ukraine in a profound dilemma, which has not been fully resolved. By eschewing ties with Russia and the CIS, Ukraine was in danger of cutting off its nose to spite its face – it lacks sufficiently extensive or strong economic ties with other states to take up the slack. Ties along Ukraine's Eastern azimuth were so fundamental to its needs that it could not afford to simply break them. Yet by rebuilding economic ties with Russia and with CIS member states, Ukraine was in danger of undermining its sovereignty and independence, and becoming debarred from the Western azimuth where it sought economic salvation in albeit limited access to credit and the technology of the future. According to Sherr, Ukraine's problems along the North-eastern azimuth lie in the fact that 'Ukraine's dependencies on Russia, and the failures of its own elite and of the West's reformers to shift the balance make Russia's power to damage seem greater than the West's power to deliver'.[74]

In theoretical terms realists would predict that Russia, as a declining hegemon, would be driven to create an institution such as the CIS to manage the regime change taking place in the post-Soviet space. Yet Kyiv was neither willing to bandwagon with Russia within the CIS, nor share the burden of managing the process of regime formation by helping bolster the CIS with its much needed support. Somewhat awkwardly for the realist theory, while Ukraine was not willing to participate in political or military co-operation, it continuously sought to expand the economic dimension of the CIS.

The fact that Kyiv would have preferred that the focus of the CIS be reserved for economic issues reflected Ukraine's economic interdependence not only with Russia, with which it was heavily interdependent (and thus sensitive and vulnerable to any changes introduced by Moscow), but all former Soviet states. Yet despite this interdependence with CIS member states, Ukraine refused to be drawn into the institution more deeply than deemed strictly necessary by Kyiv. This was because Russia, as the dominant partner within the CIS, imposed an agenda on the institution which accorded to Moscow's priorities, and which jarred in Kyiv. Thus for the CIS, as for Russia, military matters figured prominently on the CIS agenda and military power had a high salience (both tenets of the second theme of structural interdependence, namely complex interdependence). Furthermore, for policy-makers in Kyiv, integration with the CIS seemingly ensured the continued obsolescence of Ukraine's technological base and a prolongation of declining economic standards at the popular level at a time when the overall power structure of the world had decisively and unambiguously shifted in favour of the West (a tenet of the third theme of structural interdependence, namely regime change). Indeed, it was because the overall power structure had changed to the disadvantage of Russia that Ukraine was able to be so much more assertive within issue-areas (again a tenet of regime change), avoid the pressures for deeper integration into the CIS and pursue its own agenda along other azimuths.

As New Wave theorists might argue, it was precisely the *politico*-economic dimension of the CIS that conditioned Ukraine's stance towards that institution. The PTAs (such as the customs union or economic union), which Russia tried to get Ukraine to participate in, were seen by Ukraine as instruments designed to engender its renewed political subordination. Yet Kyiv was not prepared to countenance the political consequences of renewed economic integration with Russia within the CIS. That is not to say that welfare considerations were unimportant to Kyiv. In 1998 it attempted to transform the CIS, via tightly circumscribed PTAs, into a mechanism reserved for economic co-operation; the effort sank without a trace. In contrast, Russia, as one of the strongest states within the CIS, according to New Wave theorists, was likely to 'use PTAs as a means to consolidate [its] political influence over weaker counterparts'.[75] It is this 'misuse' which explains Ukraine's mainly unsuccessful attempts to impede the institutionalisation of the CIS, fearing that the interests of Russia, as the dominant state, would be more powerfully reflected within those institutions, to the detriment of the security of weaker states.[76] In the absence of a CIS shaped according to its needs, limited participation remained the only viable alternative for Ukraine.

Prospects for subregional level developments along the North-eastern azimuth were recognised as doomed to failure by 'subregional' regionalist writers, in view of the fact that 'Russian attempts to assert a hegemonic role have led other NIS (Newly Independent States) to conclude that EU-style integration among equals is unattainable, while Russian-dominated integration is not in their interests and the best option', which put paid to a Slavic union let alone Ukraine's participation in a CIS customs or economic union.[77]

Part III

The Western azimuth

Bilateral relations with the CEES, specifically, Poland, Hungary and Czechoslovakia (until 1994), and Slovakia and the Czech Republic thereafter, Romania and Moldova, formed the foundation of Ukraine's Western regional policy, the objectives of which extended to membership of Central and East European subregional institutions, and the EU on a regional level, along with stronger ties with NATO.

Establishing harmonious relations with the CEES was a key first goal if Ukraine was to achieve its strategic objective of integration with European structures. For reasons of size, geopolitics and history, Poland was by far the most important of these, and will receive the lion's share of attention. To suggest that relations with Budapest and Prague (up until 1994 and including Bratislava thereafter), were secondary would be to underestimate the collective role these CEES played in Ukraine's journey 'back toward Europe'. Nevertheless, relations with Warsaw remained a priority for Kyiv from a period that preceded independence. If anything, the importance of this relationship increased as the international environment changed and, in particular, as subregional and regional processes evolved. Ties with Poland were one of the few means available to Kyiv to avoid being locked out of the Western integration process. They were also a means of alleviating pressures from its north-eastern borders.

If relations along Ukraine's immediate western flank were a source of hope, the South-western azimuth was a source of potential threat. Relations with Romania and Moldova stood out because of the potential dangers. On independence, a territorial issue with Romania that had lain effectively dormant under the Soviet Union raised the spectre of confrontation and was only subdued because of the demands of NATO enlargement. Similarly, with the collapse of the Soviet Union the remnants of the heavily-armed 14th Army stationed in Moldova elicited disquiet in this once quiescent corner of the former empire, as Moldova sought to carve out a space for itself as a non-Romanian, non-Russian nation-state. Its proximity meant that it was not a region that could be ignored by Kyiv. Indeed, Kishinev actively sought Kyiv's help in tackling its problems to the extent that it allied itself with Ukraine in subregional formations.

In terms of subregional goals, Ukraine was particularly keen to participate in any groupings involving the CEES. This was because such groupings were invariably oriented toward joining key regional institutions along the Western azimuth. Kyiv was only too keen to join this bandwagon; alas, the CEES were only to keen to jettison any laggards. In this regard, the helping hand provided by NATO, which was willing not only to form a partnership with Kyiv but also sign a charter, was a welcome development. In contrast, the development of Ukraine's relations with the EU would prove to be disappointment, in spite of Ukraine's high hopes of eventual integration with that body.

4 Ukraine's relations with Central and East European neighbours

Relations with Poland: from the declarative to the substantive

If harmonious relations with Russia were the priority in Ukraine's foreign and security policy in the years following independence in 1991, relations with Poland came a close second. It is worth reiterating the truism that 'among the central European counties, Poland is for political, historical and economic reasons clearly the most important to Ukraine'.[1] 'Historical reasons' refer to a series of turbulent episodes in relations between the two states, most recently in the aftermath of the Second World War.[2] The resurgence of such historical issues would be problematic for both parties, though more so for Ukraine as the more fractured of the two. As far as 'political and economic reasons' are concerned, stronger ties between Poland and Ukraine would help Kyiv avoid isolation. On the one hand, strong and harmonious ties between Kyiv and Warsaw were one of the key means by which Ukraine could cope with the political and economic pressures of being an ex-member of the Soviet Union and resist being drawn more deeply into the CIS. On the other hand, strong ties between Ukraine and Poland could help establish a foundation for Ukraine's political and economic future as a fully-fledged European state. Strong ties with Warsaw could help Kyiv redefine itself as a European state politically and economically. Politically, Poland could advise Ukraine on the adoption and consolidation of democratic forms of governance, the evolution of a civil society, the creation of a market economy, an appreciation of human rights, and establishing civilian authority over the military. In terms of economic issues, the relative size of Poland's economy could certainly contribute to Ukraine's efforts to overcome the dreadful Soviet economic legacy. Poland, as a geographically large and heavily populated state to the west, was Ukraine's 'natural' partner.[3]

Zbigniew Brzezinski stressed the importance of the bilateral relations between Ukraine and Poland in terms of their geopolitical context:

> Poland and Ukraine are regions, located between Germany and Russia, that have historically played a decisive role in European geopolitics. The extensive territory of Poland and Ukraine, their populations, great economic and military potential have been the source of clashes and secret pacts between Berlin and Moscow . . . If Poland and Ukraine become economically and politically

> bankrupt, they will create a political vacuum, which will encourage Russian and German interference. On the other hand, tight co-operative relations, that strengthen each others vitality and economic development, would caution Germany and Russia from the temptation, which has encouraged imperial ambitions in Eastern Europe in the past.[4]

Yet, in themselves, tight and co-operative relations between Warsaw and Kyiv were not enough to deal with their geopolitical predicament. While close relations between Ukraine and Poland were indeed likely to provide a bedrock of stability in a historically volatile part of the region, for these ties to represent more than the emergence of a new buffer zone in Central/Eastern Europe, it was believed in Kyiv that they needed to be embedded in the wider framework made up of subregional and regional institutions. As will be seen, tight and co-operative relations between Ukraine and Poland were expected by Kyiv to bring immediate benefits at the subregional level, namely much closer ties between Ukraine and the Central and East European institutions that had sprung up. In fact Kyiv, with Poland's help, was expectant of early membership of the key institutions such as the Central European Free Trade Area (CEFTA). In the longer term, it was further hoped by Kyiv that as Poland became integrated into regional institutions, Warsaw would perform an ambassadorial role on behalf of Ukraine. In this way, as Poland became ever more integrated with regional western security and economic structures, tight relations with Warsaw were seen by Kyiv as Ukraine's best strategy for avoiding ending up on the wrong side of a new European divide running from the Baltic to the Black Sea.

Two distinct periods have been identified in the development of Ukraine's relations with Poland. Up until 1994, while both actors were cognisant of the theoretical benefits that would accrue from 'tight and co-operative relations', each was driven by competing and incompatible demands. An examination of the substance behind the declarations reveals mutual ideologically based suspicions, domestic political and economic self-preoccupation, and the contradictory demands of wider integrative processes. As a result, between 1991 and 1994, relations were anything but tight and co-operative. It will be seen that change at the level of the political elite, the strengthening of ties between the two states, and the stimulating effects of subregional and regional integration had a positive impact on the extent to which the declarative became substantive from 1994 onwards.

1991–1994: unfulfilled declarations

On Ukrainian independence in 1991, Kyiv and Warsaw were on different political and economic trajectories. By 1991 a fervently nationalist Poland was well along the road to democracy and a full-blown market economy under the leadership of its first president, the arch anti-Communist Lech Walesa. As soon as it was able, Poland implemented rapid, immediate and profound economic and political change. The same could not be said for Ukraine. Ukraine was starting from a very different point, having to build a nation and a state simultaneously, two key features the

Poles, despite the Socialist years, could take for granted. Furthermore, the democratic election of the (up until 1991) arch Communist and former party ideologue Leonid Kravchuk as Ukrainian president in 1991 did not represent the same kind of break with the past in Ukraine that Walesa's election represented in Poland. Kravchuk's election reflected a fundamentally different value system on the part of the Ukrainians. The tried and trusted Kravchuk represented a degree of political continuity with the past Soviet system that would have been unthinkable in Poland. This continuity was equally evident in the economic system. In his years in power, Kravchuk failed to implement any meaningful reform, as the ossified Ukrainian economy first seized up and then collapsed, affected as it was by the hyperinflation, commodity shortages and currency devaluations that characterise the very worst declines. Without quite realising it at the time, in 1991 President Kravchuk was laying the foundations for the failure of his future foreign and security policy, which would come to have significant negative ramifications for Ukraine's relations with Poland. Indeed, the repercussions of the prolonged economic decline would come to haunt Kravchuk's successor, Leonid Kuchma, whose strategic objective of integration with the European Union would come to resemble little more than wishful thinking at the time of its proclamation in 1996.

Yet despite the incompatible political and economic ideologies, even prior to Ukraine's independence in 1991 there was a commitment on the part of influential Ukrainian and Polish figures to avoid the divisive mistakes of history. Certainly from the very earliest days of independence Poland was attributed a significant role in Ukraine's strategic planning, a role that went far beyond that allocated other CEES. President Kravchuk had high hopes for the relationship, arguing that 'the degree of co-operation with Poland will be higher than any country of the CIS, including Russia', a remarkable statement in light of the strength of Ukraine's economic, political and security ties with Russia.[5] In light of his pro-Russian orientation, the statement made by Prime Minister Kuchma in 1993 that 'from the point of view of economic interests, Poland is our number one state' was unexpected and indicative of the potential role Poland could play in Ukraine's foreign policy.[6] Primarily, these statements reflected hopes that Poland might serve as a counterbalance to what was perceived as Russia's overweening influence on Ukraine. President Kravchuk was convinced that Poland would serve as 'the gateway to the West' for Ukraine.[7] The feelings were reciprocated. The importance of an independent Ukraine to Poland was shown in the frequent quoting of Pilsudski's famous statement that 'without an independent Ukraine, there cannot be an independent Poland'.[8] What this in fact meant was that 'Poland favours an independent Ukraine because it serves as a buffer between Poland and Russia'.[9] Ukraine's role as a buffer explains why, according to Balmaceda, 'Ukraine's Central European neighbours – especially Poland and Hungary – under no circumstances would like to see Ukraine as a weak buffer between Russia and Europe'.[10] It is in this context that the statement made by Lech Walesa that 'it is impossible to imagine Europe without a democratic and independent Ukraine' makes most sense.[11]

The mutual esteem in which each party was apparently held was soon formalised in the signing of variety of accords and treaties. For example, the new Polish non-communist government formed links with the still communist Ukrainian SSR government as early as October 1990. The Declaration on Basic Principles and Directions of the Development of Ukrainian–Polish Relations was the first bilateral document signed between the two states and the first of any kind signed by a Ukrainian government in forty-six years. (It is of symbolic if incidental significance that the last bilateral document signed by Ukraine those forty-six years ago was in fact with Poland.)[12] The subsequent signing in May 1992 of the Treaty on Good Neighbourly and Friendly Relations and Co-operation[13] and in January 1993 of the Treaty on the Legal Regime on the Ukrainian–Polish National Boundaries, Co-operation and Mutual Support on Border Issues by the two states showed a more than satisfactory rate of progress and augured well for the future on important issues for both parties.[14] These successes, even if only at the level of protocol, are not to be underestimated.[15] Ukrainian–Polish relations had never been especially cordial. In the mid twentieth century in particular, they were disfigured by an ugly history of mutual detestation expressed in reciprocated atrocities. Furthermore, in the post-war years the mutual recriminations and accompanying vociferous claims to historical territories by the Diaspora were never fully resolved at the state level.[16] Thus on Ukrainian independence, there were real concerns on the part of the Poles and the Ukrainians that psychologically and socially unresolved territorial issues could explode into life. The success of the Treaty on Good Neighbourly and Friendly Relations lay in the fact that it addressed these issues directly. In renouncing mutual territorial claims, recognising the inviolability of borders, and guaranteeing the rights of each other's large national minorities, a significant move in the direction of resolving, or at least neutralising the impact of mutual and deeply held grievances was made.

However, away from the grandeur and formality of signing ceremonies and high-level talks, there were, from the earliest days of independence, grounds to suspect that relations were not developing swimmingly. For example, much was at the time made of the fact that Poland was the first country to recognise Ukraine's independence after the referendum in December 1991.[17] However, little mention was made of the fact that prior to the referendum, Poland 'while acknowledging Ukraine's free right to delineate its own external and internal situation, nevertheless reserved the right to formulate its final thoughts on relations with Ukraine up until the December referendum'.[18] There was hesitancy on the part of Warsaw toward Kyiv, which spoke volumes both for Poland's readiness to defer to Moscow's anticipated reaction to events as well as Warsaw's undefined policy toward Ukraine. As for the emphasis placed on the fact that Warsaw was the first to recognise Ukraine's independence, it is of note that Poland was far from being the first country to establish diplomatic links with Ukraine – that honour was reserved for Hungary, with Poland only finally establishing formal links on 4 January. This hesitancy seemed to reflect Poland's suspicions regarding the intentions of Ukraine. Indeed, it was not long before the Poles became concerned at the trajectory Ukrainian foreign and security policy had taken. Demonstrating the still fragile nature of Ukrainian–Polish ties, and underlining the importance of seemingly symbolic events, Warsaw was somewhat taken aback and made suspicious by the fact that the first official international visit by the president of Ukraine following independence was to Bonn in February 1992. The Poles were 'fearful of a German–Ukrainian encirclement'.[19] As a result, at a meeting of Ukrainian and Polish parliamentarians, ex-ministers and experts, great effort was exerted on the part of the Ukrainians to pacify the Poles by making clear that 'Poland is Ukraine's prime Western partner, and one cannot talk about any international peculiarities [sic] behind the back of Poland'.[20] To help eliminate such suspicions and give an impetus to the 'strategic partnership' between the two neighbours, a Ukrainian–Polish Presidential Consultative Committee was proposed by Polish President Lech Walesa and duly set up in 1993. (Ironically, the single most distinctive feature of the committee in the early years of its existence was that at one stage it failed to convene for over a year, although it would come into its own later.)

The most powerful indictment of the strategic relationship and the most obvious evidence of the lack of substance in Ukrainian–Polish relations was the insignificant development of economic relations between the two. By 1993 the glaring gap between word and deed was such that the normally diplomatic Ukrainian ambassador to Poland, Hennadiy Udovenko, was compelled to admit that 'it would be desirable if economic relations matched those of political relations. At the moment, however, such equivalence is missing'.[21] This refers to the fact that economic relations between the two states had not developed to the extent desired by the Ukrainians or to the extent necessary if Ukraine's economic dependence on Russia was to be reduced. This is in the main attributable to domestic economic problems in both of the states. With the collapse of the Soviet Union, a major market for Polish exports was decimated. Nevertheless, the Poles persisted with the painful Balcerowicz 'shock therapy' programme. While the economic decline in Ukraine had been even more precipitous, no meaningful reform was implemented until Kuchma's election in 1994.[22]

Overall, while the frequent high-level visits that took place between the two capitals between 1991 and 1994 officially resulted in harmonious political relations, in practice relations were hardly close and co-operative. This is attributable to three key factors. First, as has been noted by Garnett, Poland had three choices in terms of preventing the renewal of Russian hegemony: by turning to the West, by co-operating with Russia's neighbours, in particular Ukraine, and by co-operating with those forces in Russia that opposed the renewal of empire. Up till 1994, Poland had pursued only the first of those three options. It effectively had no Eastern policy, and certainly no coherent long-term policy on relations with Ukraine, as was noted above.[23] Second, this problem was exacerbated by the fact that 'since Ukraine became independent it has been equally neglected by the West', thereby reflecting the Russo-centric stance on the part of the West.[24] In this regard Poland was but 'following the leader'. Third, as will now be seen, matters were further compounded at the subregional level. From the very first days of its independence, to avoid the spectre of being locked *out* of a subregional and regional integration process to its West, in which it wished to participate, and being locked *into* an integration process to its East, which it wished to avoid participating in fully, the Ukrainians made a determined effort to take advantage of relations with Poland in pursuit of both of these objectives. However, the pressures placed on Ukraine and Poland at the subregional level by subregional and regional institutions between 1991 and 1994 made their respective subregional objectives incompatible. Indeed, the explicitness of the linkage between the development of bilateral relations, subregional and regional integration is striking.

Neither could Ukraine's domestic politics be ignored. The presidency of Leonid Kravchuk between 1991 and July 1994, when Leonid Kuchma replaced him, was a period characterised by a perplexing juxtaposition of national assertiveness and economic turmoil. While Kravchuk's new found nationalism provided the impetus for closer ties with the West, his failure to appreciate the need for economic reform proved to be his Achilles heel. The connection between domestic economic reform and international objectives was lost on him. As a result, throughout his presidency, the ossified economy of Ukraine in fact proved to be a major impediment to closer economic ties with an increasingly marketised Poland. This all changed with the election of Ukraine's second president, Leonid Kuchma, in July 1994.

1994 onwards: the declarative becomes substantive

The election of a reform-minded, though somewhat pro-Russian, Leonid Kuchma in July 1994 suggested that Russia rather than Poland would become the focus of Ukraine's international efforts. In fact, Kuchma was out to get the best from both worlds. By replacing Kravchuk's perception of Ukraine as a 'buffer', with a more pragmatic and economically viable and lucrative 'bridge', Kuchma underlined the bankruptcy of the former president's policy. While Poland as Ukraine's prime western neighbour would maintain the prominent position it held in the eyes of the previous administration, Russia would apparently come to be allocated its due weight. In reality, however, Poland continued to occupy a unique role in the view of the presidential administration. Kuchma regarded Poland as Ukraine's 'number one state' from an economic point of view.[25] Again there was evidence of the fact that larger goals were in mind. By 1996 Kuchma, continuing the policy of Kravchuk, was bold enough to proclaim the 'strategic goal of membership of the European Union'.[26] The new president's pragmatism was soon to be complemented by the election of the equally pragmatic Kwasniewski in Poland in autumn 1995. With these two leaders in power, there was now apparently a broad coincidence of political and economic ideology, despite the fact that Kuchma lacked reformist credentials.

In the light of the pro-Russian platform on which Kuchma stood in his election campaign, the growth in military co-operation between Ukraine and Poland was unexpected. In autumn 1995 a decision (strongly supported by the USA, which also volunteered some financing for the project at the time of its inception) was taken to create a joint Ukrainian–Polish battalion, consisting of the Przemyszl 14th Tank Brigade and the Ukrainian Mechanised Border Regiment.[27] After a protracted gestation it was finally brought into being in autumn 1997, when it held its first manoeuvres.[28] Further ambitions for the battalion included participation in peacekeeping duties under the aegis of either the UN or the OSCE. The event soon became politicised. Reflecting the continued inter-ethnic turbulence between Ukrainians and Poles at the popular level in this highly sensitive region, the Poles became highly concerned at the news that the shift of the Tank Brigade to another part of the *wojewodstwo* would leave Przemyszl effectively undefended (from the Ukrainians presumably).[29] Nevertheless, the brigade became a fixed military feature. There was also a pragmatic dimension to the military co-operation. This took the form of the Ukrainians being awarded a $150–200 million contract in March 1994 to maintain and renovate Poland's large stocks of Soviet-era weaponry, which included the T-72 tank (which made up 40 per cent of all Polish tanks) and some 600 Mig 21, Mig 29, Su 25 and Su 24MK aircraft.[30] This contract was particularly welcome for the stimulus it provided to the underemployed Ukrainian military industry. Significantly, it also made Ukraine the victor in a direct contest with the Russian military industry.

There was also significant growth in strategic co-operation between Ukraine and Poland. A particular factor in this regard was the emergence of the Caspian region as a rich source of hydrocarbons (for the West), as it highlighted the mutual and individual benefits that both Ukraine and Poland might derive if they were to co-operate on its transportation. There were a number of such benefits. First, the two states were in themselves likely to be major consumers of the oil transported, as they strove to reduce their dependence on Russian sources. Second, the joint transportation of hydrocarbons would strengthen bilateral ties and reverse the geopolitics of the past whereby 'transportation networks which evolved in the last few decades isolated Poland and Ukraine from each other'.[31] Third, as has been pointed out by Ukrainian analysts, 'the linking of transport, communication and energy networks into the pan-European networks is a prerequisite for the future integration of Ukraine into the European Union and will serve to prevent the emergence of a new line of division in Europe as Poland and Hungary enter the EU'.[32] Fourthly, each would benefit from the income the transportation of energy resources generated. Furthermore, the Ukrainian–Polish route offered a number of significant advantages over the others. According to Ukrainian estimates, a route through Ukraine and Poland offered by far the shortest routes of all the alternatives.[33] As was pointed out by the Polish president, 'the shortest route from the Near and Far East to Warsaw, Gdansk, Berlin, Hamburg and even Stockholm and London lies through Odesa, Illychivsk and Yuzniy'.[34] This in turn was estimated to reduce the costs of transportation by $20–30 per ton.[35] As a result of all of these factors, great efforts were placed into creating transport corridors between the Black Sea and Central and Western Europe, on the one hand, and the Baltic and Black Sea regions in the form of a Gdansk–Odesa link, on the other. There were to be two distinct segments to the network. In the first instance, a 670-kilometre link would be built from the Yuzniy marine terminal (located about 35 kilometres to the east of Odesa in Southern Ukraine) to the Brody pumping station based along on the 'Druzhba' oil pipeline in Western Ukraine. This Yuzniy–Brody pipeline, with a capacity of twelve million tons of oil, was due for completion in 1999. From Brody, the second stage of the pipeline was envisaged as linking the 'Yuzniy–Brody' pipeline with the Polish city of Plotsk or the Adamowa Zastava. From there it would service Poland, Germany and link up with Gdansk in northern Poland for transportation further north.[36] Indicative of the time (and cost) saving potential of such a pipeline as a link between Northern European states and Turkey was the new Gdansk–Odesa rail link, which cut container transportation time between Istanbul and Gdansk from sixteen days to about two and a half days.[37]

In the economic sphere, there was evidence of a growing interdependence. By 1994 Ukraine was becoming an important trading partner for Poland. Despite the slow start, economic ties had grown at an impressive rate (though they were still some way down on the potential trade that might be expected between two such heavily populated countries). Altogether, 6.6 million people passed through the Ukrainian–Polish border in 1994, swelling to 10.6 million by 1996.[38] In fact the sheer volume of individuals crossing the border from Ukraine placed Poland amongst the top ten of the most popular 'tourist' destinations in the world in 1996.[39] According to estimates, Ukrainian 'tourists' spent nearly $500 million in a burgeoning shuttle trade with Poland, and were second only to German tourists in terms of the total amount spent. Official trade also developed at a healthy rate though the totals involved were still small by absolute standards. In 1994, $358 million dollars worth of trade occurred between Ukraine and Poland, providing Ukraine with a $5.3 million surplus. By 1997 the overall figure had grown to $900 million, with Ukraine incurring a $140 million deficit.[40] In January 1998 the two presidents jointly opened the largest customs point in Europe between the two states.[41] A report by the Department of Economic Development in Zamost, on the Polish side of the Polish–Ukrainian border, concluded that trade with Ukraine was one of the most important stimuli to economic activity in the poorly developed regions which border on Ukraine.[42]

Furthermore, there was a continuation of the previous successful political ties between the two former enemies, culminating in the signing of a series of important documents in 1997. In a show of solidarity designed to reduce Ukraine's feeling of isolation *vis-à-vis* Russia and the CIS, Warsaw and Kyiv signed a 'Memorandum on the Liberalisation of Trade', in January 1997.[43] The document was more than symbolic. The memorandum was a highly significant development as, thanks to Poland, Ukraine had finally achieved a breakthrough in that it was an important first step toward creating a free trade area with Poland. This in turn had significance on a subregional level, to the extent that free trade areas with all CEFTA members were a precondition to joining the CEFTA. The signing of the symbolic 'Declaration on Agreement and Unity' between Ukraine and Poland not long after, on 21 May 1997, was yet another milestone and was designed to draw a line under the unfortunate past the two states shared. As Bronislaw Geremek, the Polish minister of foreign affairs, pointed out, 'the main problem becomes how an act founding new relations between Poland and Ukraine can simultaneously be an act expressing the obvious "strategic partnership", a concept that has been talked about on an official level in Poland and Ukraine for the last five years'.[44] Significantly, the signing of the declaration, as well as the memorandum, was interpreted as preparing the ground for Victor Chernomyrdin's visit to Kyiv a week later, and Boris Yeltsin's oft-postponed visit to Kyiv another two weeks later to sign the long-awaited Ukrainian–Russian Treaty.[45] The timing of both the Ukrainian–Polish declaration and the memorandum strongly suggests that it was part of a multi-pronged strategy to counter Russia's attempts to 'divide and conquer' the two CEES. Additionally, the two Ukrainian–Polish documents were clearly designed to send the signal to Brussels, in anticipation of the impending enlargement of NATO in July 1997, that these two former enemies were taking great strides to eliminate causes of disquiet between them. It was also a continuation of the longer-term strategy of preventing Ukraine's isolation as a buffer state between the Tashkent treaty states and the new NATO states. In a similar supportive vein, the Presidential Consultative Committee, meeting on 19–20 May 1997, examined the possibilities for the creation of a number of groups of three states in a form of 'triangular co-operation' involving Ukraine and Poland. Thus, Ukraine and Poland would be joined by the USA to form one triangle, and also by Germany, Lithuania and Belarus, respectively, to form three other 'triangles', though nothing has yet been formalised. Ukraine's partnerships with key regional actors were becoming increasingly institutionalised in Central and Eastern Europe. The idea was also mooted of Ukraine participating in the Weimar triangle, consisting of Poland, Germany and France, with observer status, though again this has not yet come to fruition.[46] By the end of 1997, ties between Ukraine and Poland were strong enough for Leszek Balcerowicz, the Polish economics minister, to boldly proclaim that 'the Polish Ministry on Foreign Affairs had reoriented itself from Russia toward Ukraine'.[47] This reorientation was also reflected in a new found Polish attitude toward Ukraine's integration with subregional structures.

Overall, after a hesitant start, Ukraine developed a fruitful but circumscribed working relationship with Poland. The two parties had managed to overcome potentially damaging historical episodes owing to the fact that both Kyiv and Warsaw had an eye firmly on the future, and their respective prospects for subregional and regional integration. As will be seen in the following chapter, despite their best endeavours, it was at the subregional and regional levels that Ukrainian–Polish relations were to meet with their greatest challenges.

Relations with Hungary

Kyiv's relations with Warsaw place Ukraine's relations with Hungary somewhat in the shade. Nevertheless, they are important in their own right for a number of reasons.

Hungary has been highly supportive of Ukraine's westward orientation. Hungary played a prominent role in the days leading up to Ukraine's full independence, paralleling that of Poland in some important respects. For a start, Hungary gained a high profile in Ukraine when, along with Poland, it reacted first to Ukraine's Declaration of Independence in July 1991. Indeed, on 3 December 1991, only two days after the referendum confirming Ukraine's status as a sovereign and independent state, Budapest established diplomatic relations with Kyiv. Only three days later, the foundation for a treaty on good neighbourliness and co-operation was laid. Hungary achieved the distinction of being the first country to open an embassy in Ukraine in March 1992.[48]

Of particular note is the political co-operation that exists between the two states, in particular in the sphere of ethnic minorities. It has been estimated that around 200,000 of the three and a half million Hungarians living outside Hungary reside in Transcarpathia in Western Ukraine. Such is the treatment of this minority that Ukraine's approach to national minorities has been held up as a model for the treatment of ethnic minorities in Europe. However, as Hungary moves ever closer to the EU, and is forced to adopt the Schengen Agreement, the visa regime demanded by the agreement will separate off the Hungarian minority in Ukraine from its brethren in Hungary. The fact that the cross-border trade that tends to benefit the Hungarian minority will probably cease is a particular worry as income rates in the region fall below the Ukrainian national average. Although a system is being considered whereby Hungarians resident abroad would have the right to passports, entitling them to travel to Hungary, but not the right to vote in elections or settle there, it is unlikely to be accepted by Brussels.[49]

Economic ties between the two countries are solid rather than spectacular: overall trade was $300 million in 1992, rising to $581.7 million in 1997.[50] More importantly, in preparation for CEFTA membership for Ukraine, one of the conditions of which is the signing of a free trade agreement with each of its members, by 1996 Kyiv was in deep discussions with Hungary on the signing of such an agreement (discussion were also well advanced with Poland, though not with Slovakia, with which discussions only started in earnest in 1996).[51] However, by 1999, agreements remained unsigned in all three cases, owing primarily to Ukraine's continued inability or reluctance to introduce meaningful economic reform. Certainly there is mutual trade dependence between the two. It has been estimated that between 25–30 per cent of Hungary's trade with the USSR was specifically with Ukraine. In particular, Hungary gets much of its energy via Ukraine, while the Ukrainian urban transportation system is effectively based on the buses produced by the Hungarian company *Ikarus*.[52]

On a subregional level, Ukraine and Hungary are competitors. For example, although in 1997 intra-CEFTA trade only accounted for 8 per cent of Hungary's total foreign trade, it was growing faster than was trade with the EU. However, this growth was at the expense of Russia, Ukraine and Moldova. To all intents and purposes, Ukraine was paying a price for remaining beyond CEFTA.[53]

On a military level, Ukraine's 103-kilometre border with Hungary has not been seen as a source of threat, and it would not be an exaggeration to suggest that Ukraine's bilateral relations with Hungary are amongst its most harmonious and trouble free.

Hungary's key role as far as Kyiv was concerned was as a member of the group moving westward, both as an invitee to NATO, and applicant to the European Union. In this regard it is particularly noteworthy that following his appointment as Ukraine's foreign minister in April 1998, Boris Tarasiuk's first visit abroad was to Budapest, apparently much to the chagrin of Moscow. The visit was unplanned and occurred at what could only be regarded as an inconvenient time for the Hungarians, facing as they were domestic elections. Yet, mindful of the need to supportive of Ukraine, Budapest went out of its way to accommodate Tarasiuk.[54] Such a move was a clear signal of Tarasiuk's priorities – the new Ukrainian foreign minister seemed not to be overly concerned by diplomatic niceties as far as the Russians were concerned. The visit was also driven by Ukraine's concern as to the ever-present threat of a new divide emerging between Ukraine and this particular western neighbour as it joined NATO and moved ever closer to the EU. To this end Ukraine needed a lot of reassurance on the part of Budapest that Kyiv was not going to be abandoned. During his visit in April 1998 Tarasiuk received that reassurance, although it was somewhat qualified.[55]

Relations with the Slovak Republic

The collapse of the Czechoslovakian Federation in 1993 was a positive development as far as Ukraine was concerned. With the Federation firmly focused on the West, and its membership of the Visegrad grouping as a means of joining the West, Ukraine was denied much attention from its small neighbour. The break-up of Czechoslovakia in 1993 changed the complexion of things considerably in that the leadership in Slovakia adopted a different stance to that of the leadership in the Czech Republic. Bratislava was much more eastward oriented than Prague. While this orientation was primarily toward Russia, it also included Ukraine. For example, in 1997 Slovakia's top ten destinations for exports included both Russia and Ukraine, in contrast to the Czech Republic's much lower exports to those countries.

These more intense ties between Ukraine and Slovakia, in contrast to those between Ukraine and the Czech Republic, can be explained by the structure of the Slovakian economy. For example, in 1993, 65 per cent of the former Czechoslovakia's arms industry was located in Slovakia, for which the market had collapsed when its largest customer, Russia, went into economic meltdown. At the same time, Russia was the source of most of the energy that powered Slovakia's energy intensive industries. In fact, Russia has provided up to 97.7 per cent of Slovakia's oil via Ukraine.

In turn, Slovakia was important to its eastern neighbours. Druzhba, the pipeline taking oil from Russia via Ukraine to the West (including the Czech Republic), passes through Slovakia.[56] For this reason, the Russians have described Slovakia as strategic territory, with the link to this strategic territory provided by Ukraine. Indeed, the energy aspects of relations between Slovakia, Ukraine and Russia demonstrate that while Slovakia is trying to manage a successful reorientation from a heavy dependence on its eastern neighbours toward its western neighbours, the interdependence between the trio nevertheless remains substantial.

There is a political dimension to these intense trade ties. For example, the natural gas agreement signed with Russia in May 1997, as a result of which Gazprom would remain the monopoly gas supplier for the next decade, was criticised by the Slovaks themselves on the grounds of the questionable benefits it brought Bratislava. As was argued by Alexander Duleba, from the Research Centre of the Slovak Society for Foreign Policy, 'Gazprom is setting up a joint venture on Slovak territory, it

[Gazprom] will in effect be negotiating prices with a company, half of which it owns'.[57] By tying Slovakia more closely to itself, Russia was increasing the reliance of the EU on itself – after all, Gazprom provided about one-third of European gas, a market that was set to rise by 75 per cent by 2010. Furthermore, by building underground gas storage tanks in Slovakia, Moscow would undermine the impact of Ukraine's ability to close off gas pipelines to the West in pursuit of political and economic advantage.

It is worth pointing out that despite this eastward orientation, CEFTA proved to be a much more important trading area for Slovakia than it did for the Czech Republic for example. In addition, by 1997 the largest percentage of both countries' exports were to the EU, a figure that had grown from 30 per cent in 1993 to 43 per cent in 1997 for Slovakia. Nevertheless, Ukraine was keen to take advantage of Slovakia's favourable trading position by promoting closer ties with Slovakia, perhaps in the form of a free trade zone as, for example, suggested by Russia in 1996. Such notions were rejected on the grounds that any subsequent increase in trade would be offset by a loss in trade with its CEFTA neighbours, most notably the Czech Republic. Furthermore, closer ties with Ukraine would have negative ramifications for Slovakia's goal of integration with the EU, in that membership would be precluded on the grounds of Ukraine's extensive tariff and non-tariff trade barriers by the standards of the WTO.

For geographical and geopolitical reasons, Ukraine's relations with Slovakia are to a large extent shaped by Slovakia's ties with Russia. As was pointed out by the US embassy in Bratislava in 1997:

> The Government of the Russian Federation has always made time for Slovakia be it in high level meetings in Moscow or through senior level visits to Bratislava. The Government of Slovakia, with important economic ties to Russia, has always seen itself as an East/West bridge; official Russian activities here have nurtured that feeling. Unlike its neighbours, the government of Slovakia fears capitalist/Western domination more than a return of 'Soviet' influence. Consequently, though the tangible above board benefits are few, we anticipate an ongoing strong relationship between Russia and Slovakia well into the next century.[58]

It is in part for these reasons, as well as unfavourable domestic political developments, that Slovakia was overlooked in the first wave of NATO enlargements in July 1997, and why its application to the EU was rejected twice, first in July 1997 and again in March of the following year, though ties have improved dramatically since the election of a new reformist Slovakian government. While this might normally be expected to provide a favourable set of circumstance for a rapprochement with Ukraine, even this is likely to be usurped by Russia, which will most probably seek to take advantage of Slovakia's marginalisation.

Overall, ties between Ukraine and Slovakia have since 1997 remained cordial, as the two states have moved toward their shared strategic goal of membership of the European Union, albeit along different trajectories. Turbulent times for relations between the two states clearly lie ahead, as Slovakia, with the more direct trajectory, moves more quickly towards membership of the European Union. As a result, Kyiv's relations with Bratislava are likely to be put under the same pressures as are Ukraine's relations with other EU contender states.

Relations with Romania

From the earliest days of Ukraine's independence, relations between Ukraine and Romania were soured by a territorial dispute. The issue concerned the formerly Romanian territories of Bukovina, Bessarabia, Hertza and Serpent's Island, which were occupied by Soviet forces during the Second World War (or soon after in the case of the island) and came to form a constituent part of post-Soviet Ukraine. However, from the first days of Ukrainian independence, Romania started to challenge Ukraine's right to these lands. While the issue was a substantial stumbling block in the way of the signing of a friendship and co-operation treaty between the two states, they were driven by competing objectives towards a final resolution of the dispute. Ukraine was primarily interested in the affirmation of its borders and consolidation of its fragile territorial integrity. Romania, on the other hand, was mesmerised by the prize of NATO membership, though at the cost of revoking any territorial claims against its neighbours. While this section of the chapter traces the evolution of relations between the two states, it does so in the context of NATO enlargement, as all other issues were addressed in its shadow. Relations between Ukraine and Romania are best understood when placed in the context of the integration process taking place on the continent. It will be seen that while NATO enlargement tangentially contributed to stability in Eastern Europe in the short to medium term, a long-term resolution that addresses the structural deficits of this volatile region has yet to be found.

The territorial dispute

Following independence in August 1991, it was of paramount importance to the government in Kyiv that friendship treaties be signed with all of Ukraine's immediate neighbours. In addition to confirming Ukraine's borders, such treaties were perceived as consolidating Ukraine's position in the international system and symbolised acceptance of the newly emerged state. However, with independence, Ukraine inherited a territorial dispute with Romania that precluded the signing of such a treaty and which had a number of far-reaching implications.[59] First, by questioning the ownership of various Ukrainian territories, Romania challenged the sovereignty of the newly emergent Ukrainian state. Second, with this territorial claim, Romania undermined the integrity of a state already divided along ethnic and linguistic lines. Third, there existed the possibility that any appeasement on the part of Kyiv would invite other such territorial challenges, especially on the part of Russia. The dispute revolved around the lands of Bukovina, Bessarabia, Hertza and Serpents Island, which, even prior to Ukrainian independence, had been a source of contention between Romania and the Soviet Union. Soviet forces occupied northern Bukovina, Bessarabia and Hertza in 1940, as provided for in the Ribbentrop–Molotov Pact. (The last of these three territories, the town of Hertza, was delineated for occupation by the Soviet Army when Molotov, the Soviet foreign minister, carelessly drew freehand a line on the map and inadvertently included the region.) Following occupation, the USSR added the central six districts of Bessarabia to the Moldovan Autonomous Soviet Socialist Republic, originally formed in 1924 on the eastern bank of the Dniester, to create the Moldovan Soviet Socialist Republic. The Ukrainian SSR was allocated northern Bukovina, which along with a section of northern Bessarabia, the region of Khotyn and the area around the unfortunate Hertza, were transformed into the Chernivetska *Oblast*; the remaining districts of southern Bessarabia along with the regions of Izmail and Ackerman were added to the Odesa *Oblast*. Although the Romanians reoccupied the territories in June 1941, by 1944 they were firmly in Soviet hands again, and formally recognised as such in the Paris Peace Treaty with Romania in February 1947. While the treaty included a basic territorial delimitation between the two states, it failed to provide for exact on site identification of the border. In order to clarify this murky situation, on 4 February 1948, the Protocol on the Clarification of the State Border between the USSR and Romania was signed, which also delineated as Soviet territory Serpents Island in the Danube Delta.[60] Located about 40 kilometres east of the Danube Delta, this 0.17 km^2 island-rock had, up until the end of the Second World War, little strategic significance, being in the unchallenged ownership of Romania. However, while the delimitation issue was dealt with satisfactorily in terms of land borders, with the result of the work of the Soviet–Romanian Commission on the Demarcation of Borders enshrined in the Treaty on the Regime of the Soviet–Romanian border of 1949 and subsequently ratified by both parliaments, insufficient attention was paid to marine border delimitation.[61] As will be seen below, this proved to be a troublesome oversight.

Relations since independence

There the matter effectively lay until the turmoil of independence in Ukraine provided a window of opportunity for the Romanians to start pressing their claim to the various disputed territories with renewed vigour, hope and assertiveness. When on 28 November 1991 the Romanian parliament urged the executive to regain the territories lost as a result of the Ribbentrop–Molotov Pact, the Romanian government responded the very next day with a statement affirming that

> the recognition of Ukraine's independence and the desire to develop mutually beneficial Romanian–Ukrainian relations do not entail the recognition of the inclusion in the territory of a newly independent Ukrainian state of northern Bukovina, the Hertza region, the Khotyn region or the region of southern Bessarabia, which were forcibly annexed by the USSR and thereafter incorporated into the territorial structure of Ukraine on the basis of the Ribbentrop–Molotov Pact.[62]

In addition, in the months leading up to the Ukrainian referendum on independence in December 1991, the Romanian parliament resolved not to recognise as binding the voting in the disputed areas.[63] If the aim of this resolution was to gauge the mood of voters in these regions, the 92.8 per cent of those who voted in the Chernivtsi Oblast and 85.4 per cent in the Odesa Oblast who voted in favour of Ukrainian independence, sent a clear message as to their views, despite the boycott of the referendum by some ethnic Romanians in parts of the Chernivtsi Oblast.

Although from 1991 to 1994 relations between the two states remained strained, in 1995 they deteriorated significantly, triggered especially by the aforementioned issue of Serpents Island. As a result of the discovery of substantial amounts of mineral resources on the continental shelf surrounding the island, in December 1995 Romania announced its intention to appeal to the International Court of Justice in the Hague regarding ownership of the island. This intention to pursue the matter, in conjunction with having declared as invalid agreements made on the territorial status of the island, was interpreted by Kyiv as a territorial claim on Ukraine.[64] Ukraine's response was to update the facilities of the military garrison there along with the creation of a number of specialised installations (e.g. a seismic station) all as part of a comprehensive programme for the strengthening of Ukraine's state border.[65]

Thus in the early days of independence Ukraine withstood some very serious challenges to its territorial integrity. The five issues (Bukovina, Hertza, Bessarabia, Serpents Island and the threat of mobilisation of the Romanian minority in Ukraine) were of such gravity that it was futile to talk about progress in the development of Ukrainian–Romanian relations; they were going from bad to worse. Ukraine was in no position to acquiesce on any of the points concerning the Romanians as any hint of weakness would have sent exactly the wrong signals to Ukraine's neighbours. On the other hand, the Romanian government, hampered by its small majority, was forced into responding to the demands of Romanian nationalists in parliament and pursuing an even more forceful line. Furthermore, the prospect of valuable minerals under the shelf around Serpents Island was a temptation too succulent to resist.

The catalyst to progress: NATO enlargement

The stimulus to progress proved to be the Romanian desire to be amongst the states invited to begin talks on membership with the transatlantic alliance at the Madrid summit in July 1997. Although Ukraine was not likely to be involved in the looming NATO enlargement process directly, Kyiv was in a favourable position to take advantage of the Romanian predicament. One of the criteria for NATO membership required that new members have no territorial disputes with any of its neighbours. Thus, relations with Kyiv desperately needed to be resolved by Bucharest if efforts at gaining NATO membership were to be meaningful. However, when the prime ministers of the two countries met in Izmail in Ukraine in March 1996, with the Madrid summit a still distant prospect, no progress was made on the friendship treaty. The main stumbling block remained the Romanian insistence that any treaty recognising the Ukrainian–Romanian border include a condemnation of the Ribbentrop–Molotov Pact with all of the associated implications of illegality in the transfer of territory from Romania to Ukraine. For its part, Kyiv was adamant in its refusal to get entrapped in the minefield of legalities associated with the denunciation of the act, fearful of the fact that any condemnation would leave Ukraine vulnerable to territorial claims. Instead, Kyiv retaliated by arguing that the USSR, rather than Ukraine, was party to the pact, adding that the pact itself was invalidated by the 1941 attack of one party on the other. Furthermore, it was argued by Kyiv that Ukrainian deputies had in fact already condemned the pact once before, as members of the USSR Congress of Peoples Deputies in 1989, which repudiated it in a resolution. The Ukrainian Commission on Foreign Affairs, while not denying or disputing the repercussions of the pact, responded to the Romanian demand by insisting that any reference to the Ribbentrop–Molotov Pact in any treaty be accompanied by a comment on Romanian territorial gains made at the expense of Ukraine in 1918 and those that resulted from agreements made between Antonescu and Hitler during the Second World War, something the Romanians balked at.[66] An alternative suggested by the Ukrainians, that of a general 'condemnation of the activities and crimes of totalitarian regimes, policy of force, etc.', was similarly rejected by Bucharest.[67]

The end to this impasse was provided by the defeat of President Iliescu of Romania in the elections in November 1996, after which it was very soon apparent that the new president, Emile Constantinescu, was willing to start making concessions in order to realise Romania's hopes of joining NATO (especially in the light of the now looming Madrid summit). Thus Emile Bistreanu, the ambassador of Romania to Ukraine, made clear that Serpents Island would no longer be subjected to any territorial claims, as Ukrainian ownership of the island, along with the borders which were delineated after the war, was recognised.[68] That this caused some pain in Bucharest was revealed by President Constantinescu himself, who, when visiting NATO headquarters, stated that 'northern Bukovina never belonged either to Ukraine or Russia, although the Romanians are prepared to make a "historical sacrifice" in order to enter NATO', something hardly likely to inspire the confidence of the Ukrainians.[69] With this apparent concession progress was becoming perceptible. However, the sticking points had changed: recognition of the Ukrainian–Romanian border had now become conditional on the satisfactory delimitation of both the continental shelf off the Black Sea coast and exclusive economic zones. The dropping of the condemnation of the Ribbentrop–Molotov Pact in the treaty was a critical concession on the part of the Romanians and is indicative of the price that Constantinescu was willing to pay in return for NATO membership, a decision on which was less than six months away. The signing of the Treaty on Good-Neighbourly Relations and Co-operation was now being made contingent on the successful conclusion of the Treaty on the Regime of State Borders, implying that the former ratifications were invalid, something which was unacceptable to Kyiv. Thus, while ownership of the island was not subject to debate, the legalities of the delimitation of the shelf surrounding the island were – something that the Ukrainians acknowledged and were sensitive to.[70] However, Kyiv was adamant that any such negotiations could only take place following the conclusion and ratification of a founding political treaty confirming the current Romanian–Ukrainian border and the repudiation of any territorial claims against Ukraine.[71]

An additional (and newly emerged) sticking point was the issue of Romanian minorities in Ukraine. While ostensibly this was to do with the existing discrepancy between Ukrainian and Romanian legislation with regard to citizenship, Kyiv suspected a more sinister motive behind Bucharest's manoeuvres.[72] This scepticism was exacerbated by what the Ukrainians saw as Romanian insistence that the Romanian minority in Ukraine be given collective rights in line with Recommendation 1201 of the Council of Europe. Ukrainian analysts have interpreted this recommendation as 'the right to autonomy of the Romanian ethnic minority in Ukraine'.[73] Inadvertently, the Ukrainians themselves did the groundwork for this right to autonomy. In Article 2 of the Declaration on the rights of Minorities of Ukraine, issued in October 1991, 'the Ukrainian Government guarantees all minorities the right to secure their traditional areas of habitation and warrants the existence of national–administrative units', i.e. limited territorial autonomy.[74] It is something of a truism to suggest that this represents a threat to a country as ethnically and linguistically divided as Ukraine.

The signing of the Good-Neighbourly Relations and Co-operation Treaty

Despite the above difficulties, there was a certain inevitability about the eventual signing of the Treaty on Good-Neighbourly Relations and Co-operation between the two states, especially if Bucharest was serious about NATO membership. The tactics adopted by the Ukrainians reflected the fact that they were conscious of the time constraints the Romanians were under: the Madrid NATO summit was now clearly visible in the distance. Bucharest desperately wished to avoid the possibility of conceding too much to Kyiv in pursuit of membership, without actually getting it: signing a treaty with Kyiv was a necessary but obviously not sufficient condition to obtain entry. The Romanians were, however, keenly aware that with a treaty signed, they only *might* gain an invitation; without a treaty they definitely would not be invited. The deadlock between the two sides was broken only on 28 April, the day before Romania presented its application to join NATO, at a meeting of the Black Sea Economic Co-operation Council (BSEC). At this meeting Presidents Kuchma and Constantinescu opened the way to an agreement on the text of the basic treaty in May 1997 after ten bruising rounds of negotiations. The treaty was finally signed on 2 June 1997 with less than five weeks to spare until the Madrid summit in July.

The Ukrainians had got their way (i.e. made the least concessions) in what can only be described as a piece of brinkmanship. There was no mention of the infamous 1939 Pact, only a reference in the preamble to the 'unfair acts of totalitarian and military–dictatorial regimes, which in the past negatively influenced relations between the Ukrainian and Romanian nations'. In addition, and crucially for Ukraine, existing territorial borders were affirmed (Article 2). Also, while Serpents Island was acknowledged as the territory of Ukraine, the delimitation of the continental shelf along with the exclusive economic zones in the Black Sea was deferred for a period of two years, following which, if no agreement could be reached, the matter was to be referred to the International Court of Justice in the Hague.[75] In the meantime, the Ukrainians agreed to refrain from stationing offensive weapons on the island.[76] (Significant, in the light of the multi-layered integration process, is Article 8, which referred to the development of Euroregions. Two were planned: 'Upper Prut' and 'Lower Danube'). Article 13, the largest in the treaty by some margin, provided extensive rights for the Romanian minority in Ukraine (and vice versa) in line with Recommendation 1201, though subject to the important proviso that 'the Recommendation refers to collective rights and does not require that either of the Parties confer relevant bodies the right to territorial autonomy based on ethnic criteria'.[77]

Overall, the signing of the treaty represented a major achievement for Ukraine. Despite the best efforts of the president and parliament, Romania found itself in a no-win situation: by failing to claim territories that it felt a historically and morally justified right to, it would have left itself open to the accusation by the domestic constituency that it had abandoned the ethnically Romanian inhabitants of these disputed lands. By claiming them, it laid itself open to the charge of troublemaking in a highly volatile part of the European continent, and, more seriously, would thereby prejudice its chances in the wider scheme of things. By contrast, Ukraine was in the luxurious position of being able to do no wrong: shielded by agreements, treaties and conventions, it was in legal though perhaps not moral terms invulnerable. The irony for the Romanians was that, in pursuit of their wider objectives they conceded to the Ukrainians without achieving those objectives – at least in the short term. However, when viewed in isolation, the treaty was a significant step forward: the ongoing territorial dispute was one of the very few in any part of Europe and its resolution contributed to the peacefulness and security of the region. Despite the fact that the Romanian government incurred the wrath of the nationalists, who argued that the treaty was rushed in pursuit of the elusive invitation to join NATO, it was highly unlikely that Ukrainian–Romanian relations would regress, as the Romanians had their eye firmly on the wider integration process. For Ukrainian foreign policy, the signing of a treaty with Romania represented a major accomplishment, removing as it did a hazard that not only undermined the territorial integrity of the new state but also threatened to escalate into what could have been an assault on most if not all azimuths. That the dispute did not evolve into a security threat speaks as eloquently for Ukrainian foreign policy as it does for the Ukrainian military forces, for which the Romanians were no match. However, if in the immediate term, relations between Ukraine and Romania appeared to be evolving successfully, it is pertinent to recall that the stimulus was extrinsic, rather than any inherent drive toward trouble-free relations, something that characterised Ukrainian–Polish relations, for example. The very circumstances under which the treaty was signed suggests that the relationship is reversible (especially if the Romanian nationalists were to get their way), dependent as it is on the continued successful evolution and openness of the regional integration process to which it was so closely tied.

Relations with Moldova

The development of relations with Moldova proved to be a considerably more complicated process than might have been expected when Ukraine and Moldova became independent in 1991. This forgotten corner of the Soviet empire was a veritable Pandora's box of trouble when it came to geopolitical disputes, a receptacle which was well and truly opened with Moldovan independence. Historically, there are three dimensions to the issues which emerged. First, its historical ties with Romania complicated Moldova's independence. Second, this complication was added to because of Moldova's former political relationship with Ukraine as an appendage of the Ukrainian SSR as an autonomous Soviet republic. Third, Moldova occupied a strategically valuable geopolitical location of interest to Moscow in the pre and post-Soviet periods. These three issues combined to form a volatile cocktail of problems on Ukraine's south-western border.

The historical, economic, ethnic and strategic context for Ukraine's relations with Moldova

Prior to independence, the Moldovan SSR was a relatively underdeveloped republic sandwiched between Romania and Ukraine. The river Prut formed Moldova's western border; while the Dniester formed much of Moldova's eastern border. Most significantly, the Moldovan SSR also incorporated a sliver of land about 225 kilometres long running along the left bank (if looking from north to south) of the Dniester; this sliver was known as Transdniester (or Prydniestrovye). The Moldovan SSR was recognised as formerly ethnic Romanian territory (known as Bessarabia in Romania); the same is not true of Transdniester, which has always been populated predominantly by Ukrainians and Russians. Indeed, in 1924, much of what is today known as Transdniester was formally incorporated into the Ukrainian SSR as the Moldovan Autonomous Socialist Soviet Republic (MASSR). Only when the Soviet Union annexed Bessarabia on 2 August 1940 were Bessarabia and Transdniester (MASSR) formally joined in what came to be known as the Moldovan Socialist Soviet Republic (MSSR). However, the 'join' continued to show throughout Moldova's existence as a Soviet republic.

In ethnic terms, on Moldovan independence, Ukrainians and Russians made up substantial minorities in Moldova (14 and 13 per cent respectively), but were concentrated in Transdniester where they made up 28.3 and 25.5 per cent of the population respectively; collectively they outnumbered the 40.1 per cent of Moldovans on the left bank.[78] Industry was as unequally dispersed as was the population in Moldova: 80 per cent of all Moldova's energy was produced in the Transdniester, along with 90 per cent of all steel and plastic and 40 per cent of food canning plants.[79] Transdniester was also the point of entry for fuel and raw material coming in from Russia, on which Moldova as a whole was heavily dependent.

Militarily important was the location of the headquarters and bulk of combat strength of the former Soviet 14th Army, in and around Tiraspol, 'the heart of the Russian-settled area of Moldova'.[80] In possession of an estimated 500,000 tons of military equipment, the 14th Army would prove to be a decisive force in subsequent events. Much of the reason for the army being there and for Moscow's interest in this relatively quiet and seemingly unimportant corner of Europe lay in its potential strategic significance especially during the Cold War. First, as part of the Odesa Military District, the Transdniester region was the launch pad for any operations in the Balkans, Greece and Turkey; the North African coast and Suez Canal were secondary strategic objectives.[81] However, since the collapse of the Soviet Union, the Army's significance had become distinctly regional. Thus by 1993, according to the Russian Association of Theories and Models in International Relations, the 14th Army's role was to be more in line with Russia's goals in the area, which were:

> To keep strategic positions in south-eastern Europe; to protect the interests of the Russian population there [as many as 500,000 people] and of other ethnic groups that consider Russia to be their historic homeland; to preserve co-operation with the Dniester [industrial] enterprises, several of which are unique, including some belonging to the military-industrial complex; to solve the [Dniester] conflict in order to ensure domestic stability . . . and to strengthen relations with near-abroad states that have Russian minorities; [and] . . . to establish more predictable and more stable relations with Romania, but at the same time to dam the growing Romanian nationalistic influence upon Moldova.[82]

In the event of a renewed union, or conflict in the Balkans, the Black Sea area and south-east coast of the Mediterranean, Moldova would become indispensable.[83] Whatever the circumstances, Moscow perceived a need for its troops in the region, as, according to General Lebed, 'the Dniester area is the key to the Balkans . . . if Russia withdraws from this little piece of land, it will lose that key and its influence in the region'.[84] With the above-mentioned ethnic divide, a partial and well-armed military presence and convoluted history, all the ingredients were present for the conflict which duly arose.

The Transdniestrian conflict

The problems first started just prior to Moldova's independence. In 1990, in the spirit of *glasnost*, and the atmosphere of thinking the unthinkable, Kishinev floated the idea of Moldova's reunification with Romania. More extreme elements in Moldova also suggested annexing the previously Romanian territories of northern Bukovina, southern Bessarabia from Ukraine.[85] These calls were accompanied by the reintroduction of the use of the Latin alphabet. The response of the Russian minority concentrated in Transdniester was swift and unambiguous: in August 1990 the Transdniester–Moldova Republic (TMR) was announced, with Igor Smirnov as its self-proclaimed president.[86] This drastic move was one with which the 14th Army would come to have considerable sympathy.

The Moldovan proclamation of independence in August 1991 and the subsequent Transdniestrian response threw into sharp focus three separate issues, each of which were pertinent to Moldova's relations with Ukraine: first, Romanian claims to Moldova; second, the role of the 14th Army and the threat it presented to Ukraine as well as Moldova; and third, the fast-diminishing prospects for Ukraine's claims to Moldovan territory.[87] In addition, the Moldovan imbroglio would serve to bring to the fore 'what appears to be a deeper-seated competition between Russia and Ukraine', both on a bilateral level and within the multilateral forum of the CIS.[88]

Moldovan independence elicited an immediate response on the part of the TMR, bolstered by the unofficial support of the 14th Army: by December 1991 Kishinev had effectively lost control of Transdniester. As the conflict became more militarised, Waters reported that:

> while perhaps in the initial turmoil Ukraine may have harboured hopes of recovering its former territory of Moldovan Transdniester, Kiev seems to have come to the view, as the Dniester insurrection escalated, that a Russian ultra nationalist, militarised enclave to the west of independent Ukraine presents it with a serious security problem.[89]

This latter aspect, rather than any efforts to claim former territories, was to characterise Kyiv's approach to the resolution of the conflict as it escalated. For example, when in March 1992 the fighting intensified, Kyiv, fearful that Moscow might use the crisis as an opportunity to destabilise the region as a means of putting pressure on the Ukrainians to back down on the issues of the BSF, Crimea and Sevastopol, issued a curt warning to Russia that it would not allow any violations of its borders. To show he meant business, on 18 March the Ukrainian president, Leonid Kravchuk, issued instructions for a 50-kilometre 'special regime' zone to be set up along the Ukrainian–Moldovan border in order to prevent incursions or infiltration by armed troops, or the smuggling of weapons into Ukraine.[90] The move was well judged in that it apparently anticipated Russia's attempts to get a tighter grip on the situation – on 1 April 1992, Yeltsin issued a decree subordinating the 14th Army to Russian command, a move countered by Kishinev claiming Moldovan jurisdiction.[91]

The underlying Ukrainian–Russian friction briefly surfaced as a result of inflammatory remarks made by the Russian vice-president, Aleksandr Rutskoi, who argued that Russia 'had to act to defend Russians throughout the former Soviet Union'.[92] Clearly aware that the remarks were aimed at Ukraine as much as they were at Moldova, Kyiv countered by, somewhat improbably, considering launching criminal proceedings against him. While up until that point the 14th Army mainly had a supporting role, as the conflict intensified, its units inevitably got more drawn in. The heaviest fighting occurred on 20 June 1992, when, in a move to pre-empt Transdniestrian forces occupying areas of the right bank, Moldovan forces attempted to gain control over the few remaining villages on the left bank that were still accessible. With the direct support of the 14th Army, the Transdniestrians successfully repelled the Moldovans, gaining the important right-bank city of Bendery in the process.

On 23 June, in a move designed to halt the fighting, and to prevent it from escalating into a fully blown conflagration and thereby further entrenching Russian forces in the region, the Ukrainian president, in a total reversal of former policy, floated the possibility of offering Transdniester the status of an autonomous republic within the Republic of Moldova. Soon after, on 3 July, the Moldovans effectively sued for peace with Moldovan President Snegur holding talks with President Yeltsin in Moscow, during which they agreed on steps for defusing the conflict starting with a cease-fire on 8 July. The signing by Snegur and Yeltsin, but not Smirnov, of the Agreement on the Regulation of the Transdniester Conflict on 21 July provided for the scheduling of a timetable for the withdrawal of the 14th Army and undefined special status for the TMR. In the words of Pavel Baev, the agreement resulted in

> a compromise deal, which had no analogies in the annals of peacekeeping . . . It envisaged the creation of a peacekeeping force comprising five (four of which were active and one in reserve) Russian battalions and three (two active and one in reserve) each from Moldova and Transdniester. The exclusion of the 14th Army from participation in this operation meant that one Russian army is keeping a peace that another has broken.[93]

The peacekeeping force was to be supervised by a joint control commission. In total, therefore, there were three main military forces present in Transdniester by the end of 1992: the peacekeeping force, the 14th Army, and the Transdniester forces.[94]

As well as signalling the end of the bloody confrontation, the agreement introduced onto the agenda a whole new issue, as unappealing to Kyiv as it was to Kishinev. This arose from an attempt by Moscow and Tiraspol to link the withdrawal of the 14th Army to the granting of special status to Transdniester, an interesting parallel situation to the one that existed between Ukraine and Russia with regard to Crimea and the BSF. Special status was understood as statehood; Tiraspol was not happy with the autonomy offered by Kishinev. According to an OSCE report, 'Transdniester leaders . . . successfully blocked the negotiations on the withdrawal of the Russian forces by making their agreement conditional upon their obtaining a status akin to that of a separate state'.[95] General Lebed, appointed commander of the 14th Army in June 1992, with the approbation of the Russian Ministry of Defence, though contrary to the wishes of the Kremlin, assisted the Transdniestrians in this. Lebed insisted that the Army remain in Transdniester for peacekeeping purposes, and because of the region's strategic role as 'the key to the Balkans'.[96] The Russian Ministry of Defence, taking advantage of the intransigence of the Transdniestrians and the insubordinate army generals, sought to make the resolution of the Transdniester problem dependent upon Moldova granting the 14th Army permanent residency status, whether as a peacekeeping force, or an outpost of the Russian Army.

Ukraine on the margins

Ukraine's role in the evolving imbroglio was marginal. This marginal status was in the main attributable to Ukraine's own problems, namely the economic meltdown taking place and Russian moves to claim the BSF, Crimea and Sevastopol. It was also partly attributable to the fact that Kyiv overestimated Russia's capacity to impose its will on events in Moldova. To an extent, the signing of a good neighbourliness, friendship and co-operation treaty between Ukraine and Moldova on 23 October 1992 symbolised the increasingly aligned stances adopted by the two states and compensated for Ukraine's marginality. Indeed, whether deliberately or not, the treaty was to provide a sound basis for co-operation between the two in pursuit of subregional integration. The treaty also contributed to their collusion in the slowing or hindering of CIS integration. Crucially, given the political context, the treaty prohibited 'the formation and transit of armed groups hostile to one of the sides on the territory of the other', a move designed to prevent Russian troops crossing the territory of Ukraine to reinforce its forces in Moldova.

In another morale boosting exercise for Moldova, Kyiv expressed its satisfaction with Ukrainian minority rights in Moldova after signing in March 1993 a whole host of agreements on issues ranging from minority rights to energy. At the same time, Kyiv announced that it would not 'accept the transit of goods produced in the TMR unless they were cleared by Moldova'.[97] The support was reciprocated by Moldova's ambassador to Ukraine, who was cited as saying that 'Ukrainian–Moldovan good neighbourly relations transcend the framework of merely state-to-state relations . . . as Ukraine provides an umbrella against those forces which want to bring down our independence and bring us into a neo-Soviet brotherhood'.[98] The coincidence of interests between the two former Soviet republics was becoming explicit, with the key goals of Moldova's foreign policy announced in January 1994. The key goals were much stronger ties with the EU, with which a partnership and co-operation agreement was initialled by Moldova in July 1994, and with NATO, with which the PfP was signed in March 1994. These objectives closely matched those of Ukraine and both objectives were at the expense of relations with Russia.[99] Similarly, Moldova sided with Ukraine in December 1992 by not signing the CIS Charter once it became clear to Kishinev that Kyiv was not going to sign.[100] Significantly in this regard, it was made clear to Kishinev by Moscow that any resolution of the Transdniestrian conflict was tied to Moldova's fuller compliance with and adherence to the demands of the CIS, in which Moldova was only a half-hearted participant.[101] Indeed, Moldova was punished with large increases in excise and customs taxes as a result of its failure to ratify CIS documents in August 1993, leading to an inability to pay its growing gas debt to Russia.[102] The pressure paid off as Moldova ratified its membership of the CIS and the Economic Union on 8 April 1994, after having failed to do this once earlier; nevertheless, Kishinev continued to voice objections to its political and military integration with the CIS.[103]

The impasse between Russia and Moldova

Kyiv's support for Kishinev must have been welcome as the Moldovans repeatedly and fruitlessly tried to thrash out a resolution to the Transdniestrian problem and enforce the withdrawal of the 14th Army with an intransigent Moscow throughout 1992–4. However, the talks broke down time after time during this period primarily because Moscow was seeking basing rights in Transdniester 'as a minimal objective and on both banks of the Dniester as a maximal objective', according to General Kondratev, the Russian deputy defence minister responsible for Russian peace-keepers, in return for a final resolution of the Transdniestrian situation.[104] In order to avoid either scenario, the Moldovan parliament put forward a draft law 'On the Special Status of the Territory on the Left Bank of the Nistru (Transnistria)'. The law provided for the use of Russian and Ukrainian as official languages in the area, a degree of political, economic and socio-cultural autonomy, and most importantly, the right to territorial self-determination in the event that the status of Moldova as an independent state was to change, i.e. if it was to unite with Romania. However, the Russian side was not impressed by the law and the ninth round of talks on 7–8 June 1994 failed to bring a resolution of the impasse. In turn, the Moldovan demand that the 14th Army start its withdrawal on 1 July 1994 was replaced with a new demand, specifically, that a withdrawal start on 31 December 1995.[105]

The breakthrough came at the tenth round of talks in August 1994 when Kishinev gave in to the linkage demanded by Russia. According to a joint press release, 'practical steps toward the withdrawal (of the 14th Army) . . . within the agreed time period will be synchronised with the political settlement of the Dniester conflict and the determination of the special status of the Dniester region of Moldova'.[106] The actual signing of the agreement on 21 October was subsequently overshadowed by a clause demanded by the Russians in the final moments of negotiation, which stated that the withdrawal would start not with the signing of the agreement, as the Moldovans insisted, but instead, with the 'entry into force' of the agreement, i.e. its ratification. In light of the fact that, in contrast to Moldova, the Russian Duma had not ratified the Russian–Moldovan treaty signed in 1990, this condition did not augur well for the early withdrawal of the 14th Army. So it proved. The invitation in talks on the 5 July 1995 for Ukraine to participate in future talks to help bring about a lasting solution to the crisis, while unlikely to be decisive, was significant and due primarily to the fact that it had 'a fair amount of influence in the region'.[107] The primary aim of this influence was to bring the two warring factions face to face to sign a joint memorandum in July 1996. In the event, the failure of the signing to take place was caused by the fact that the territorial integrity of Moldova was not affirmed in the memorandum – there was simply too much scope for Transdniester to continue to pursue sovereignty, as shown by the TMR's insistence on the right to establish interstate relations. Indeed, because the OSCE basic principles on Moldova's territorial integrity and sovereignty were not confirmed in the memorandum, the head of the OSCE in Moldova recommended against supporting it. In addition, the other parties had real qualms about it. For example, the main 'regulator' of the peace between the warring parties was to be the CIS, in which both

Kishinev and Kyiv had little faith, especially as this would legitimise the presence of a Russian force in the region. The Ukrainians continued to insist on a more prominent role for the OSCE instead.[108]

Ukraine's growing influence in the region was reflected in the decisive role it played in the formation of a subsequent version of the memorandum. The new version was signed on 8 May 1997 by the presidents of Moldova and the TMR, with Russia and Ukraine acting as guarantors, the OSCE as mediator (until September 1997), and with the CIS becoming the main organising structure following the implementation of the arrangements outlined in the memorandum.[109] Most importantly from the point of view of both Kishinev and Kyiv, Moldova's territorial integrity was affirmed with the Transdniester only granted 'special status'; the withdrawal of the 14th Army was once more confirmed. In line with this agreement on a withdrawal, and contrary to its earlier stance, Kyiv soon proved itself amenable to the removal of the 14th Army, and its 500,000 tons of material – taking up an estimated 11,233 railway carriages – across its territory.[110]

The effects of Ukraine's input were evident in a number of regards. First, the CIS was merely allocated a 'support' role in the memorandum, with primacy given to the OSCE. Second, Ukraine's role as guarantor challenged Russia's hitherto unique status. Third, the memorandum also opened the way for a tangible Ukrainian presence in the region, in the form of peacekeepers. However, the Russian Duma's subsequent claim that it had 'a basis on which to insist on the full membership of the TMR in the CIS' was ominous, as were other factors.[111] For example, by the time the memorandum was signed, the Russia–Moldovan Basic Treaty had remained unratified by the Russian Duma for seven years; similarly, the critical 'breakthrough' October 1994 Agreement also remained unratified, apparently at the request of Tiraspol.[112]

The support of the Russian Duma is a key factor explaining the lack of progress after the signing of the memorandum. For example, the president of the TMR, Smirnov, failed to attend a meeting with the Russian, Moldovan and Ukrainian presidents in Kishinev in October 1997. A letter demanding that the TMR be included 'in full scale political and economic CIS processes', was sent by the Duma in his stead.[113] Further provocative moves on the part of the TMR followed, mainly without the approbation of the Russian government, though probably with that of the parliament. The Transdniestrians blocked the removal of the 14th Army once it had in fact started in September 1997, when Tiraspol laid claim to what it regarded as its share of the army weaponry. Similarly, its decision in August 1997 to set up border signs was implemented in May 1998 when it in fact went a stage further by setting up new customs points in areas under the control of peacekeeping forces.[114]

Ukraine–Moldova: a growing alliance?

Ukraine's greater prominence in the peacekeeping process from 1995 onwards was paralleled by an intensification of ties between Kyiv and Moldova away from the Transdniestrian negotiating table on a bilateral level, and, as will be seen, on a subregional level, in terms of co-operation in the creation of a Euroregion and considerable co-operation within GUAM, as well as in terms of continued co-operation in CIS non-co-operation. As has been pointed out, the 'strong Ukrainian–Moldovan relations which emerged in 1997 reflect the more active position of Ukraine in the region and within the former Soviet Union'.[115] In particular, just before the signing of the above-mentioned memorandum, Kyiv and Kishinev signed a declaration laying the basis for the creation of a customs union between them in March 1997. However, Kuchma was careful not to snub the Transdniestrians and was particularly keen to renew economic ties with the heavily industrialised region. Crucially, both parties expressed willingness for Ukraine to make its presence felt in the region, in the form of a peacekeeping contingent, something which was agreed to by Kyiv but objected to by Moscow.[116] Furthermore, not only was that request reiterated by President Smirnov in his visit to Kyiv in June of that year, but a further intensification of ties were pursued. In particular, Smirnov, in recognition of the economic importance of Ukraine's neighbouring regions for the Transdniester economy, sought a liberalisation of ties between the two states, as allowed for by the memorandum, which permitted the region's economic independence within Moldova.[117] Clearly, Ukraine's regional influence was making itself felt in more ways than one.

Nevertheless, the stalemate continued. A multilateral summit held in Kyiv on 16 July 1999 to resolve disagreements between Moldova and Transdniester fell short of expectations. Although the summit, which brought together Moldovan President Luchinski and the leader of the Transdniester Republic, Igor Smirnov, in a meeting mediated by Ukraine, Russia and the OSCE, did not produce a final solution, it did provide a framework within which both sides could move towards a resolution of Transdniester's status within Moldova. Indeed, the joint declaration signed by both sides committed them to work towards reuniting in a single state. However, agreement could not be found on the form that the reunion was to take. The Moldovans pushed for the incorporation of the Transdniester region into Moldova as an autonomous republic. The Transdniestrians preferred that it should become an equal partner in a confederation. Nevertheless, both sides moved towards reconciliation, reaching agreement on the preservation of a common economic, political, legal and defence space. The key sticking point, as ever, remained the lack of common ground on the issue of Russian troops in the Transdniester region. While Russian Prime Minister Stepashin reiterated the commitment of Moscow to withdraw its troops, citing a withdrawal schedule as evidence, Smirnov remained intransigent.[118] In August 2000, William Hill, the head of the OSCE mission, suggested that the Russian contingent in Transdniester would be replaced 'in the distant future' by international peacekeepers.[119]

The signing of the memorandum and the subsequent gradual reconciliation between the two warring parties was a success attributable, at least in part, to the Ukrainians. It was also indicative of the change of locus of power that was taking place in parts of the CIS, in that while Ukraine was not an alternative to Russia as a source of such power, it was nevertheless a match in certain localised disputes, as in Moldova. As Garnett has pointed out 'it is now hard to envisage further efforts to regulate the Transdniester conflict without the input of Ukraine'.[120] While it would be a simplification to attribute Ukraine's ascendancy to Russia's decline, in hindsight both sides of the conflict perhaps exaggerated Russia's potential role.[121] Thus although Russia was clearly a decisive factor in halting the fighting between the protagonists and even maintaining an uneasy peace, it was incapable of imposing a final solution. It was precisely Russia's inability to impose its will on an assertive Moldova and an intransigent Transdniester that provided Ukraine with an opportunity to demonstrate a regional role.

In sum, on a bilateral level, the development of Kyiv's relations with neighbours along the Western azimuth between 1991 and 1999 was not a straightforward affair. As will now be seen, this lack of systematic progress at the bilateral level had negative as well as positive ramifications at the subregional and regional levels.

In theoretical terms, Ukraine as a newly independent state, the survival and security of which was far from consolidated, burdened with a history of occupation by territorially acquisitive neighbours, was at least initially concerned with any threats to its territorial integrity, as realists might predict. However, the threats failed to materialise – Romania's questioning of the legitimacy of the transfer of its former territory to Ukraine never amounted to a threat. As a result, along the Western azimuth, Ukraine could pursue a regionalist agenda from the very earliest days of its existence, the theoretical implications of which will be explored at the end of the following chapter.

5 The Western azimuth

Subregional and regional integration

In comparison to Ukraine's North-eastern azimuth, the Western azimuth held more promise and at the same time contained scope for greater disappointment. Along the North-eastern azimuth Ukraine was driven by one overriding objective: avoidance of subordination to Russia on a bilateral and regional level. Moscow made no secret of its desire for much stronger ties with Ukraine, and to this extent policy was transparent: it was uncomplicated by suspicions as to Russia's hidden agendas, as Moscow's agendum was there for all to see. Along the Western azimuth, Ukraine was denied such frank partners. In particular, it will be argued that Kyiv's efforts along the Western azimuth were complicated by the intricate nature of relations between the bilateral, subregional and regional levels. Ukraine believed that harmonious bilateral ties would provide a foundation for the attainment of subregional level objectives along the Western azimuth. In turn, bilateral relations were expected to facilitate the attainment of regional level objectives, and further, it was expected that membership of subregional institutions would help in joining regional institutions. In practice, things were rarely so straightforward, certainly up until 1994, and hardly more so since then. As will be seen, if anything, regional level developments led to deterioration in both Ukraine's bilateral ties and subregional prospects. Later, only once it had become clear that some of the CEES were to be invited to apply for membership of NATO, did the political fog lift temporarily, only to come down again once EU membership entered the agenda.

Ukraine's failed proposals for subregional security structures

Participation in subregional integration was one of the means with which Ukraine sought to deal with the Russian problem, especially in security terms in the early years following independence. Initial efforts designed to deal with the security vacuum that had emerged in Central and Eastern Europe were homegrown attempts at creating subregional security institutions. Within these potential security communities, owing to their size and geopolitical significance in any planning, Ukraine and Poland were destined to play central roles. Both Poland and Ukraine were crucial to any plans – it was meaningless to talk about any plan without the participation of either state. Two plans stand out – a Polish initiative in the shape of 'NATO-B' or 'NATO-*bis*', and the Ukrainian 'Zone of Stability and Security'.

The first of these, NATO-B, reflected concern about the security vacuum in the region, following the dissolution of the Warsaw Pact in April 1991. The proposal by Lech Walesa, the Polish president in 1992, also reflected increased assertiveness on the part of the Poles, and a desire to claim the role of regional leader. Finding itself in a security vacuum, with no chance of NATO membership, Warsaw, with the help of and under the patronage of NATO, suggested that an agreement be made between Central and East European states to give up territorial claims on one another, preclude the use of aggression in the resolution of bilateral difficulties, transfer control of weapons of mass destruction to NATO, and agree to joint action against any member in breach of the agreement.[1] The plan had two advantages. First, it would reduce the apprehension felt by the CEES in the face of a still-agitated Russia. Second, it would fill the security vacuum in the region. Polish analysts also believed that it would bring forward the dates of entry of some of these states into NATO. However, in reality it seems that the plan was driven by a hidden agenda. The proposal was intended to raise the profile of Poland as a regional actor and even leader, and Warsaw as a regional spokesperson. Warsaw believed Polish chances of entering NATO would in this way be enhanced. Warsaw was also demonstrating its credentials as a state displaying commitment to the stability of the region, willing to undertake responsibility for trying to ensure this stability within the framework of NATO, in the face of an outraged Moscow.[2]

However, the plan suffered from a number of predictable and insurmountable disadvantages. First, it elicited the ire of the Russians. Second, fellow CEES, in particular Czechoslovakia and Hungary – states with a very high chance of NATO membership in the first enlargement – were concerned by the fact that NATO-bis might be seen as precluding NATO enlargement at all. Third, Polish efforts at regional leadership appeared over-ambitious in the light of the economic plight of the country. It was also something which would inevitably upset neighbours whose experience of such leadership in the past was hardly remembered with fondness, i.e. Ukraine and Lithuania. For these and other reasons, the plan was stillborn.

The second effort at a subregional security institution was the Baltic to Black Sea Security Zone, proposed by Ukrainian President Kravchuk in May 1993. The notion of a nuclear-free zone of stability and security in the middle of Europe was hardly new, yet it soon became just another stillborn attempt to fill the security vacuum that had emerged in Central and Eastern Europe.

The proposal required the consensus of Ukraine, Poland, Estonia, Latvia, Lithuania, Belarus, Moldova, Austria, the Czech Republic, Slovakia, Bulgaria, Hungary and Romania to work. The plan was riddled with other faults. First, any alliance that so blatantly excluded Russia would inevitably come to be perceived by Moscow as a threat. Second, as with NATO-B, Poland, along with other CEES, was reluctant to become a member of an organisation that would hinder its chances of joining NATO. Yet, 'owing to Poland's weight in the region, Warsaw's involvement in the project was pivotal'; the fact that it was not forthcoming undermined the whole plan.[3] Third, despite its independence in 1991, Belarus was gradually moving back toward an alliance and eventual reunification with Russia, something that was the final nail in the coffin. The fact that subregional integration was again hindered by regional aspirations in general, and that relations between Ukraine and Poland were too weak to drive the plan forward, was almost incidental. As will be seen, neither were Ukraine's relations with Poland or other CEES helpful in terms of integration with less security-based subregional institutions.

Attempts to join politico-economic subregional structures

The Visegrad group and CEFTA

Ukraine's first effort at joining a specifically Central and East European subregional institution was an attempt in February 1992 to join the Visegrad group, a loose formation (created in 1991) consisting of Poland, Hungary and Czechoslovakia. Ostensibly the purpose of the organisation was to co-ordinate the efforts of the three countries in their interactions with European political and economic institutions, facilitate financial and trade flows amongst themselves, and collaborate on issues of security and ecology; in practice it was an attempt to escape from the influence still emanating from the East and to demonstrate their commitment to 'rejoining Europe'. Unfortunately for Ukraine, it also was to serve as a discriminating mechanism in that it created a clear line of differentiation between its members and those in the East. The purpose of this was twofold. First, it helped the CEES avoid the accusation of interference in what Russia would term its 'near abroad'. Second, it precluded the possibility of the backward state of the Ukrainian economy affecting their application for European Union membership.[4] For these reasons the February 1992 application was rejected.

Ultimately the competitiveness that led to the rejection of Ukraine's application undermined the effectiveness of the Visegrad group as a vehicle moving towards membership of the EU. This competitiveness was triggered in particular by the Czechs who, in 1993, rather than move forward as a member of the Visegrad group, tried to individualise their ties with the West and thereby enhance their chances of inclusion in the European regional integration process.

As far as Poland was concerned, such an individualised approach was unappealing. Because of its structural economic weaknesses, enormous debt, large and backward agricultural base, and sheer size, Warsaw believed that Poland would not have been a credible contender for membership of regional institutions if assessed on an individual basis. With competition between aspirants to the EU and NATO fierce, especially on the part of the Czech Republic, Poland was especially vulnerable to being left outside (along with Slovakia). Poland was thus an active proponent of the importance of subregional integration, as in the view of Pastusiak, 'Poland perceives the Visegrad Group as a form of co-operation which enables the development of trends for the integration of the countries of Central Europe and brings them closer to the West European structures of integration'.[5] By definition, such a stance did not extend to Ukraine. The contribution of the Poles to the rejection of Ukraine's application was clear. In particular, Polish Foreign

Minister Skubiszewski argued that the inclusion of Ukraine into the Visegrad group was impossible because of the 'different levels of economic and political development'.[6] The strategic partnership between Ukraine and Poland had failed to deliver the expected benefits in the political and economic spheres, despite Kyiv's efforts.[7]

The political orientation of Visegrad was soon complemented by the more economy-oriented Central European Free Trade Area (CEFTA); with time the latter effectively replaced the more politically motivated Visegrad group as a forum. CEFTA grew out of the free trade area established between Hungary, Poland and Czechoslovakia on 21 December 1991, after the collapse of the Soviet Union in August of that year. It was modelled on EFTA and hence to a large extent was already harmonised with the trade requirements of the EU; in fact the free trade area was an extension of trade preferences obtained by the member states on a bilateral basis with the EU. CEFTA was created to help co-ordinate trade between Poland, Hungary and Czechoslovakia, facilitate their interactions with European political and economic institutions, and demonstrate the willingness of its members to 'rejoin Europe'. Thus at no time did its members see CEFTA, or the Visegrad grouping, as an alternative to membership of the EU; rather it was a sort of a antechamber. It also functioned as a mechanism that helped discriminate its members from states to the East. This it did only too well: from early on it was clear that its entry criteria were harsh enough to preclude Ukraine's membership.[8]

In sum, up until 1994, the early hopes of Ukraine that membership of Central and East European subregional groupings would carry it along toward the regional institutions were dashed by an unhealthy competitiveness between the CEES. In addition, CEES were too concerned about their own prospects to be worried about Ukraine. Both of these factors negatively affected Ukraine's bilateral relations with CEES, in particular Poland. Despite the fact that bilateral relations with Poland were desirable, Warsaw was wary of getting too close to Kyiv politically and economically. This was because such closeness may have prejudiced Poland's own chances of being a member of the Central and East European bandwagon that was making its way, via subregional institutions, westwards. Up until 1994, as we have seen, Ukraine was effectively locked out of the subregional integration process, at least in part because of the lack of support of its 'strategic partner' – Poland. Despite Kyiv's hopes that Poland might serve as its ambassador in facilitating its participation in the subregional integration process, for good reason, Warsaw failed to do this in a quite overt fashion. Not only was there no incentive for Poland to have stronger ties with Ukraine. There was also the danger that strong ties with Ukraine might lead to Poland itself being locked out of not only the subregional process but also the regional process.

Relations with the remaining CEES were not of the same order of importance or relevance in the subregional process. Following the dissection of Czechoslovakia in 1993, the Czech Republic was relieved of the burden of the preoccupation of neighbouring on former Soviet republics. Prague (as well as Budapest) could focus its efforts on joining Western institutional structures: the implications for Ukraine of such a move did not really enter its reckoning. Slovakia was preoccupied with its own internal ructions. It was itself too weak and small to help Ukraine in its drive westward, though it did prove a useful economic trading partner. Clearly, poor relations with Romania were not very helpful in regard to Ukraine's subregional and regional goals. Even though Romania was not a key actor in the subregional or regional integration process, animosity between the two meant that they were hardly desirable partners in a subregional movement that was already riven with splits. Furthermore, it also raised the spectre of instability in this corner of Europe.

Ukraine's subregional prospects from 1994

From 1994 onwards, a substantial improvement in bilateral relations between Ukraine and the CEES in general (except Romania with whom relations only improved from 1997 onwards), and Poland in particular, was a prelude to an amelioration of Ukraine's subregional prospects. These advances in the bilateral and subregional spheres were helped by events at the regional level. As the West became ever more concerned with developments in Russia, especially the increasing proximity of Russia and Belarus, the ongoing conflict in Chechnya and political instability in Moscow, the Central East European region became more central to its strategy of dealing with Moscow. The reverberations of these concerns extended to Ukraine, especially in terms of its impact on Ukraine's relations with CEES and its prospects for subregional integration.

Any improvement at the bilateral level was welcome in Kyiv, as Ukraine's prospects for membership of the key subregional institutions, in particular CEFTA, were heavily dependent on Poland's patronage. However, as was discussed earlier, this Polish patronage took some time to appear, in that as long as Poland's own prospects of participation in the regional process, namely membership of NATO and the EU, were in doubt, as they very much were until 1994, Warsaw was economical in its efforts at helping Kyiv achieve its subregional objectives.

For example, as has been mentioned, Poland, along with other CEES (other than Romania which was happy merely to be included), was exasperated and horrified at being put into the same category as Ukraine in terms of membership of the Partnership for Peace programme at the beginning of 1994.[9] It was only when a differentiation was made between prospective NATO members, a group which was openly said to include Poland, Hungary and the Czech Republic, sometimes Slovakia, but not Romania, on the one hand, and those that would remain beyond the alliance, on the other, that a perceptible improvement was detected in efforts by CEES at helping Ukraine join subregional institutions. In other words, once CEES were assured of their place in regional institutions, as was the case in the second half of 1994, they became far more proactive. In October 1995 at a meeting of the leaders of the Central European Initiative (CEI) members in Warsaw, Hungary, the Czech Republic and in particular Poland came out in strong support of full Ukrainian membership of the organisation, obviously increasingly aware of the dangers for an isolated Ukraine, abandoned to its fate in the CIS.[10] In June 1996 Ukraine became a full member of the CEI.

The economic and political gap with the CEES was demonstrated by Ukraine's failure to gain membership of the key subregional institution, CEFTA. By 1995 Ukraine was still very isolated: in Brno in 1995 Slovenia was accepted as a member, and this status was by then being actively pursued by Bulgaria and Romania, while Turkey, Croatia and the Baltic states were looking to develop free trade with the CEFTA area. Ukraine was unable to participate in these discussions, much to the chagrin of Kuchma, who in June 1996 insisted that

> it is now not enough to acknowledge us as important partners, and it is time to make the next step – to support our political choice to integrate with Europe and link Ukraine to the club of Central and Eastern European states which are actively getting closer to the European and Western European Union.[11]

The signing in January 1997 of the Memorandum on the Liberalisation of Trade, between Ukraine and Poland was a welcome if belated move in the right direction as far as Kyiv was concerned.[12] Poland had become increasingly supportive of Ukraine's intention to join the Central European Free Trade Agreement and by late 1997 a plan of entry, involving the conclusion of bilateral free trade agreements with existing members (which would also facilitate Ukraine's entry into the World Trade Organisation, originally anticipated for mid-1997), had been established.[13]

However, the remaining criteria for CEFTA membership were still too stringent for Ukraine. Of the three criteria necessary for membership – a Europe or association agreement with the EU, membership of the WTO, and free trade agreements with all CEFTA states – only the last of these was becoming attainable thanks to the signing of the memorandum. Ukraine's chances of a Europe agreement were negligible; Ukraine was not classified as a market economy, one of the criteria for a Europe agreement. Furthermore, WTO membership was becoming increasingly unlikely as Ukraine reneged on its commitments to free trade. In the longer term, the real danger was that CEFTA would lose its appeal and significance to Ukraine as the CEES left it and joined the EU, thereby reducing the significance of CEFTA as a pre-entry economic forum for prospective members of the EU which Ukraine considered itself.

At this juncture it is worth noting that Ukraine's ties with Moldova were getting increasingly amicable, a development which was reflected at the subregional level in GUAM along the Southern azimuth, and not along the Western azimuth. Indeed, despite the signing of yet more 'confidence building' documents between Kishinev and Tiraspol in March 1998 in Odesa, Moldova was increasingly turning away from the CIS and Russia in search of a solution to its problems.[14] Specifically, the newly elected government in June 1998 was intent on 'turning Moldova 180 degrees away from the CIS' and, in the event of further failure as regards the Transdniestrian conflict, 'will turn for help to Western European countries, calling for economic sanctions against Transdniester'. This was something the Russians wished to avoid and the move restrained Russia in its dealings with Moldova.[15] A key part of this westward strategy involved joining GUAM, the members of which had their own ambitions along the Western azimuth, under the leadership of Kyiv, something that was a direct response to pressures on Kishinev from Moscow.

Overall, Ukraine's ambitions at the subregional level met with some, albeit limited success after 1994. Without a doubt, Poland was the most important potential actor in promoting Ukraine's chances at the subregional level. Poland was, however, by far the most vulnerable at the regional level when compared to both Hungary and the Czech Republic. Up until 1994/5, there was a real chance that it might itself be excluded from regional integration owing to its vulnerable geopolitical locus and economic weakness, poverty and size (though the probability of exclusion diminished very quickly as Poland's economy started to grow rapidly thereafter and once it became clear that NATO enlargement that did not include Poland was of marginal value). And even though its invitation to join NATO became increasingly likely after 1994, as did its chances of being invited to apply for EU membership, Ukraine was too weighty an economic and political problem for a still-enfeebled Poland to push for Ukraine's integration into subregional structures in all but the most symbolic way. Hungary was too preoccupied with Romania and Slovakia to do something similar, while Slovakia was itself too marginalised to help. Relations with Romania remained unresolved, especially regarding Serpents Island, even after the signing of a treaty in 1997.

Yet despite all of these problems, Ukraine, after 1994, came increasingly to acquire Central and East European credentials, even though it remained beyond the key institutional structure, CEFTA. On the one hand, this was due to the relations Ukraine itself came to form with the EU and NATO on a bilateral level. It was also in part to do with the fact that Ukraine's neighbours were encouraged to be more inclusive toward Ukraine. In particular, there is evidence to suggest that regional structures, in particular NATO though not the EU, actively supported subregional developments, as will now be examined.

Relations with Western regional institutions

As has been noted, membership of and/or closer ties with Western regional institutions represented end goals in Ukraine's foreign and security policy. The reasons were all too obvious. As a result of the demise of the bipolar international structure, the significance of the EU as a structural component of the change increased (after all, it was a vast and growing market, a source of investment and subsidies, and membership increasingly had security implications), as did its role as a beacon for countries emerging from the decomposing Soviet system. This was, however, especially true for NATO, the clear-cut victor in the drawn out confrontation with the Warsaw Pact. And while it is true that this has been argued to be a hollow victory to the extent that NATO may lose its *raison d'être*, the CEES did not subscribe to that view as they remained preoccupied with the threat that they believed Russia continued to represent. This was more than amply shown by the headlong rush by much of Eastern and Central Europe into economic and security integration with Europe. 'Europe', embodied in the form of the EU and NATO, had come to symbolise salvation in more ways than one.

Ukraine saw its salvation in a similar solution. As a result, Kyiv's main objective, despite the seemingly insurmountable barriers, was the political, economic and security benefits that accrue from membership of the EU and increasingly meaningful partnership with if not yet membership of NATO.

NATO

Up until 1994 Ukraine did not figure prominently in Western strategic planning or policy-making. This only changed in the 1993–4 period as NATO enlargement gained momentum, the Russian political scene deteriorated, a rapprochement between Moscow and Minsk took place, and the Russian assault on Chechnya reached its apogee.

As far as NATO enlargement was concerned, Ukraine's primary objective in the debate was to avoid ending up as the buffer between the West and Russia as they jostled for position. Originally this stance was cautious as Ukraine aimed to placate Russian sensibilities not by acquiescing to their objections but bearing them firmly in mind and insisting on their accommodation.[16] Most obviously, such accommodation meant the creation of a new security framework for the continent.[17]

However, there was a danger that this desire to join the North Atlantic alliance on the part of the CEES might damage Ukraine's bilateral relations with them. Worst of all, the rivalry within Visegrad/CEFTA in the race to enter NATO might damage ties between Ukraine and Poland. This was particularly true between 1991 and 1994 as the whole issue of NATO membership reverberated around Central and Eastern Europe. An example of the damage that this focus on NATO enlargement had on Poland's eastern policy was reflected in 'The Security Policy and Defence Strategy of Rzeczpospolita Polska' adopted in November 1992 for the period 1993–2000. The policy proclaimed that 'the strategic objective of Poland to the year 2000 is membership of NATO and the WEU' in contrast to the non-committal 'bilateral co-operation with Russia, Ukraine and Belarus'.[18] Warsaw rejected close ties with Ukraine or Russia or Belarus in order to avoid a slowdown in its progress westward. Indeed, the fact that the three former Soviet states were lumped together speaks volumes for the lack of importance Poland attributed to relations with Ukraine at the time. Poland was focused on joining NATO and would do what it had to in order to get in. The fact that this would place Ukraine in a predicament regarding Russia, in the sense that Ukraine would emerge as the no-man's land between Poland and Russia, did not seem to enter Warsaw's reckoning, something that might have been expected in light of the apparently 'strategic' relationship. Garnett has argued that the Poles 'postponed addressing these problems until after Poland and its Visegrad partners . . . enter NATO'.[19]

NATO at the time did try and help Ukraine out of its predicament. The stalling strategy devised by the alliance was the Partnership for Peace initiative, designed to placate Russia, and offered to the Visegrad group on 12 January 1994, customised to the needs of individual participants. Few were more enthusiastic participants than Ukraine; none were less keen than the CEES.

After signing up for the PfP, Ukraine became keen on joint exercises, in contrast to, for example, Russia, which, having joined reluctantly in June, was a noticeably less eager associate, slighted at its not being accorded the status 'due' a superpower. Ukraine also co-operated in the North Atlantic Co-operation Council and contributed to NATO-led peacekeeping operations in the former Yugoslavia as soon as it was able. The bitter irony was that the greater Ukraine's participation in the PfP the worse was the perception of the programme by the CEES – they did not want to be lumped into the same group as Ukraine, let alone Russia. Indeed, using less than diplomatic language the former deputy minister for Polish National Security argued 'that Poland and other states of the Visegrad group were reduced to a common denominator with the former Soviet bloc, a group to which we wanted to bade farewell'.[20]

In sum, the PfP programme was hardly universally approved. While the signing of the PfP by Ukraine in January 1994 was clearly a milestone in the improvement of Ukraine's geopolitical standing, this elevation of former Soviet republics was seen as a retrograde step in Warsaw, Prague and other CEES capitals (other than Bucharest, which saw PfP as its 'salvation'). They were horrified at being lumped into the same category as Kyiv and Moscow.[21] Indeed, Polish nationalists suggested that 'the idea of Partnership for Peace is an idea that Stalin himself would have been proud of'.[22] The PfP especially deflated the Poles, as they felt that their role as the *avant-garde* in the anti-Soviet crusade earned them a special accolade. The fact that the Poles had just been put on an equal footing with Ukraine was regarded by Warsaw as an 'inadequate step in the right direction'.[23]

Furthermore, PfP negatively impinged on prospects for subregional processes. Since the PfP failed to make an allowance for subregional groupings, some even regarded the subregional process doomed as a result.[24] For example, the PfP failed to specify any mechanism of co-operation with existing subregional groupings. Indeed, the contrary was true as again the individualised nature of the PfP exacerbated competitive tensions within the group, especially between the westernmost Visegrad members. The dissatisfaction of the CEES with PfP was such that a few months later a meaningful commitment to their inclusion in NATO enlargement was demanded.[25] As a result, President Clinton proclaimed in Warsaw in July 1994 that NATO expansion was 'no longer a question of whether, but when and how'. While on 30 September 1994 at a meeting of NATO defence ministers, the German minister of defence, Volker Ruhe, argued that 'We must at last say who is welcome to join NATO and who is not. I believe that the countries of the Visegrad Group should be the leading candidates for membership of the European Union and NATO'.[26] Ukraine was thus again placed in a predicament it had spent three years trying to avoid: with NATO enlargement threatening to take in its western neighbours, Ukraine was in danger of being left to face the economic, military and political pressures from Russia on its own.

Relations from 1994 onwards

Initially, the Ukrainians were not overtly opposed to the CEES entry into NATO, and Poland's in particular. They were, however, extremely concerned at the danger of Ukraine ending up in a buffer zone between the two military blocs, forced to remain beyond Western structures yet refusing to join CIS bodies. Furthermore, because it was not possible to predict the nature of Moscow's response to Polish membership, notwithstanding Yeltsin's original support for the idea, Kyiv was fearful that Ukraine might bear the brunt of Russia's wrath. This concern coincided with a growing Western interest in Ukraine. According to Zbigniew Brzezinski, along with the enlargement of NATO, 'the most effective means with which the West can impede Russia from becoming a expansionist state is decisive support for Ukraine's battle for economic stability and democracy'. While it is misleading to suggest that there was a consensus in the West about the approach that needed to be adopted towards Ukraine, the fact that Nicholas Burns, a representative of the US secretary of state, has argued that Ukraine is most likely to remain a key strategic priority for the US in the next century suggests that Ukraine was beginning to figure more prominently than hitherto.[27]

Ukrainian objections to Poland's entry into NATO were often vociferously expressed, leading to the occasional sharp exchange between the two 'strategic partners'.[28] It is perhaps worth pointing out that eminent Western analysts were in sympathy with the position of Ukraine. Zbigniew Brzezinski argued that if Poland was faced with the choice of either NATO membership or continued Ukrainian independence, Warsaw should choose the latter, presumably because of the danger of leaving Ukraine isolated.[29] However, despite the objections of the Ukrainians, Russians and others, the Poles, Czechs and Hungarians pressed ahead regardless, insisting on their right to membership of NATO.[30] The Slovaks were more uncertain in this regard, as were the hesitant Romanians. The Moldovans remained preoccupied with their internal turmoil.

Compounding the predicament of the Ukrainians was the fact that Poland's inclusion in NATO had the potential to sow additional seeds of discord between Kyiv and Warsaw, more so than between Kyiv and any other Central and East European capitals. The most dangerous issue as far as Kyiv was concerned was Poland's willingness as a member of the alliance to station nuclear weapons and foreign troops on its soil, despite Ukraine's objections.[31] On many occasions, the Ukrainians pressed their case.[32] The Poles remained intransigent, thereby demonstrating a lack of a coherent rational Eastern policy according to Garnett.[33] Indeed, Garnett suggested that 'Poland should declare that while it is prepared to be a full member of NATO, it sees no need under current military conditions to play host to nuclear weapons or foreign combat forces'.[34] The Poles nevertheless remained obstinate and eventually entered NATO without making such a declaration.

Ukraine adopted a twin track approach. First, it started to press for a more formal relationship with Brussels. On 1 June 1995 President Kuchma proposed a special partnership with NATO in the form of a Charter on a Distinctive Partnership.[35] In the context of the drive of the CEES westward, Ukraine saw tighter ties with NATO as critical to avoid ending up as a buffer state. Second, the Ukrainians took advantage of the expansion process to reinvigorate failing bilateral ties, in particular with Poland and Romania. Indeed, support for Poland in the NATO enlargement process appears to have been exchanged for Warsaw's support for Kyiv's efforts at participation in the wider integration process. This was hinted at by President Kwasniewski, who suggested that 'decisions will be made about the widening of NATO, therefore Poland needs to demonstrate a lot of activity not only in the European Union and NATO, but also regionally'.[36] The link between Poland's prospects for inclusion in NATO and more vigorous regional activity, something that above all related to Ukraine, was made explicit. In turn, Ukraine's stance toward Polish entry into NATO softened as progress was made on the charter, and as Ukraine joined European institutions.[37] Expressing this newfound stance, in a television interview while on a visit to Poland, President Kuchma voiced the view that Ukrainian neutrality did not preclude co-operation with NATO or any other European institution, arguing that NATO expansion is not perceived as a threat in Ukraine. Thus early suspicions of NATO enlargement and opposition to the issues of foreign troops and nuclear weapons being stationed on Polish soil came to be replaced with what might be called 'positive passivity' toward enlargement and acceptance of NATO assurance that there was no intention to station either troops or weapons on the soil of new entrants. The net result was that Kyiv's position on NATO enlargement shifted and it endorsed this process. This in turn eased Poland's accession into the alliance.[38]

The Poles were accommodating in return. The visit by the Polish president to Kyiv in May 1997 to sign the much heralded 'Declaration on Agreement and Unity' between Poland and Ukraine, in addition to the earlier memorandum on the liberalisation of trade in January, was designed to send a clear signal to NATO in anticipation of the upcoming 1997 summit as to the strength of the relationship between them.[39] In July 1997 Poland, Hungary, and the Czech Republic were invited to apply for membership at the NATO Madrid summit. At the same time, Ukraine signed a charter with NATO formalising its hitherto ever-warming ties and taking a step towards avoiding the isolation of finding itself between two military blocs, a position it so desperately feared.[40]

The signing of the charter was thus a significant achievement for Ukraine, and the government was delighted.[41] It had avoided isolation or, worse, being left to face Moscow on its own. Despite the fact that the charter lacked juridical force, which the Ukrainians yearned for, it was imbued with political significance.[42] The document concerns itself with a delineation of spheres of co-operation and partnership. Broadly, the charter is split into five sections. The first section provides a context for the Ukraine–NATO relationship, with a commitment to stronger and wider co-operation, and a distinctive relationship which promotes stability in Europe. The second section outlines the principles at the foundation of the relationship, such as recognition of the indivisibility of OSCE area states, and respect for the sovereignty, territorial integrity and political independence of states. The third section delineates areas for consultation and military co-operation, while the fourth section outlines the practical arrangements for co-operation and consultation. The fifth section refers to the security assurances provided to Ukraine by the five nuclear powers on the former's accession to the Non-Proliferation Treaty (NPT), and commits Ukraine and NATO to co-operation on CFE adaptation and crisis consultation mechanisms. For Sherr, the document represents further progress along the road of '*de facto* integration with NATO' with the military–political nature of the document reinforcing the ties evolving at the military–operational level.[43] In summary, 'the overwhelming benefit of the NATO–Ukraine relationship is the establishment of networks which both institutionalise and personalise the West's commitment to enhance what Horbulin has called Ukraine's "role in ensuring European political and economic stability." '[44]

A contrast with the Founding Act signed between Russia and NATO is also revealing of the nature of the document. For Russia, guided by the perception of itself as a major power and of NATO as an antagonist, the Founding Act is an instrument of control, designed to develop transparency between the two signatories; the document is in fact a corollary of arms control agreements and as such should contribute to the stabilisation of relations. In contrast, Ukraine is a regional power lacking any global ambitions. As such it is not antagonistic to NATO, and does not perceive the latter as such; in the main, Ukraine has excellent relations with NATO states. For reasons such as these, there was no need to incorporate confidence-building measures and transparency into the charter.[45]

The strength of Ukraine's relations with NATO was amply demonstrated, and put under their severest strain, as a result of NATO's actions in Kosovo in March 1999. The Ukrainian parliament, both left and right wing, was outraged at what it saw as an attack on a sovereign state, a Slavic one at that. While the left was incandescent at the principle of NATO undermining the sovereignty of a state, the right was fearful of the establishment of a precedent which Russia might take advantage of in relations with Ukraine. On 24 March a resolution urging the Ukrainian government to 'change the country's non-nuclear status' was approved overwhelmingly by parliament. The parliament also unequivocally condemned the actions of the Western alliance, with the left wing vociferously calling on the president to withdraw Ukraine from the PfP, as had Russia. The Communists, in particular, threatened to 're-examine' relations with Russia and pushed for the withdrawal of Ukraine's ambassadors to NATO. Despite the intense pressure, the president remained steadfast in his commitment to continued participation in PfP and tighter ties with NATO, reiterating that 'Ukraine needs military and other co-operation with NATO'.[46] He dismissed the proposal for renuclearisation. At the same time, the Foreign Ministry reassured the West 'that it was not parting ways with Europe'.[47]

Kyiv also rebuffed initiatives on the part of Minsk and Moscow for it to join forces with them in a joint stance against NATO. For example, at a meeting of the heads of the Commonwealth of Independent States in Moscow on 1 April, although Yeltsin called for a strategic partnership between Kyiv and Moscow, Russia was 'unable to wring sufficient concessions from Ukraine to stop the NATO bombing'.[48] The best Moscow could offer at the summit was an agreement to co-ordinate efforts to achieve a rapid cessation of hostilities.[49]

By the end of the first week of April, the anti-NATO drive in Ukraine had fizzled out. On 6 April an attempt (one of six) to muster a parliamentary majority to support a resolution to sever Ukraine's ties with NATO failed.[50] This was primarily due to the fact that the right wing of parliament, while temporarily prepared to side with the Left, was not prepared to sacrifice Ukraine's relations with NATO. Indeed, while the Left proposed the renuclearisation resolution as an anti-NATO move, the Right saw it as an anti-Russian step. The resilience of the president also helped explain the failure of parliament. The president was only too aware that breaking ties with NATO was a step he could ill-afford, threatening as it did not only isolation, but also the danger of being perceived as siding with Moscow.

However, indubitably, the NATO bombing presented Ukraine with a problem. First, there is little doubt that NATO's image as a stabilising influence had suffered in the eyes of the public. Second, the longer the bombing continued, the greater was the likelihood that Ukraine and Russia would eventually end up at loggerheads as regards the issue. Third, the NATO bombing had a more pernicious and less tangible long-term impact in that a worsening of relations with NATO represented a threat to Kuchma's multi-vectored foreign policy strategy.

Kyiv was helped out of its predicament by the relatively early cessation of the bombing following the capitulation of the Serbs. To tackle the damage its public image had suffered in Ukraine, NATO invited Ukrainian journalists to witness what had gone on in Kosovo, something which brought the media onto its side, much to Brussels' relief. Furthermore, the early cessation also meant that Ukraine's relations with Russia were saved from further deterioration, while Russia's financial dependence on the West spared Moscow further difficulties.

Overall, in the six years following independence, Ukraine's relationship with NATO underwent considerable change. The original commitment to neutrality and non-bloc status, which was in danger of leaving Ukraine in an uncomfortable limbo, was gradually replaced by a more positive stance toward the organisation, a stance which led to the institutionalisation of co-operation with NATO. Since the signing of the charter, Ukraine has remained amongst the more enthusiastic participants in the Partnership for Peace programme. The Kosovo crisis put the relationship between Kyiv and Brussels under severe strain. Nevertheless, a year on, the relationship seems to have prospered with few long-term repercussions.

The European Union

Membership of the EU represented the summit of Ukraine's ambitions in terms of foreign policy objectives. This was hardly surprising. In dramatic contrast to the North-eastern azimuth in general, and Russia in particular, the EU represented a potentially significant source of credits, finance and markets with which Russia simply could not compete. The policy of membership of the EU was initiated by Ukraine's first president, Leonid Kravchuk, and vigorously pursued by its second president, Leonid Kuchma, who in 1996 proclaimed membership as a strategic objective for Ukraine. However, while Ukraine's relations with NATO underwent a qualitative transformation, those with the EU were characterised by quantitative rather than qualitative improvements, and even they were highly circumscribed. As will now be seen, the dual strategy of developing direct ties with NATO, while taking advantage of close ties with prospective EU member states (especially Poland) and subregional institutions, was inadequate to drive Ukraine's relations with the EU forward.

Ties with the EU

Following the collapse of the Soviet Union (rendering obsolete the 1989 Trade and Co-operation Agreement with the European Union) an embryonic relationship began to form between Kyiv and Brussels, culminating in the Partnership and Co-operation Agreement (PCA), agreed on 23 March 1994 and signed by Kravchuk in June 1994, 'beating' Russia to the post by ten days. This relationship was consolidated by the approval of the EU's Common Position on Ukraine soon after in November 1994. The pledge to support Ukrainian independence and sovereignty, endorse Ukraine's democratic transformation and efforts to maintain its economic stability and integrate with the world economy, outlined in the EU Action Plan for Ukraine in December 1996, was a welcome statement of intent during what was a trying time for Ukraine, which in the context of continuing economic collapse was facing challenges from both Romania and Russia.

The plethora of bilateral committees that sprang up from the PCA, such as the EU-Ukraine Co-operation Council and all of its associated sub-committees, and the Parliamentary Co-operation Committee, suggested that the relationship was prospering. On the part of the Ukrainians, the formation of the National Strategy on Ukraine's integration into the EU, signed in June 1998, and the creation of the National Agency for Development of European Integration, together with the establishment of an EU department within the Foreign Ministry, all seemed to suggest that Ukraine was gradually putting together an infrastructure through which ties would come to be consolidated. Steps are currently underway for the establishment of a free trade zone, though as two leading Ukrainian economic commentators put it 'objective conditions make comprehensive negotiations on establishing a free trade zone premature . . . for Ukraine it would mean abolition of its rather high customs tariffs in exchange for abolition of comparatively moderate EU tariffs'.[51]

The establishment of formal ties was accompanied by desperately needed, though ultimately relative small-scale, economic assistance from the EU. Kyiv's anticipation that Ukraine's role in contributing to the demise of the Soviet Union and blocking role in the creation of a viable replacement would elicit a euphoric wave of support in the form of loans, aid and closer ties from a grateful West failed to materialise. The European response was mainly co-ordinated by the European Union on behalf of the G24/G7 in collaboration with the IMF and the World Bank. Independently, the European Union has been one of the principal international donors to Ukraine, with ECU 3.9 billion having been provided between 1991 and 1998 in technical and financial assistance. The TACIS programme represented over ECU 823 million of this, with ECU 105 million going to the nuclear safety programme and ECU 60.5 million to the EU/G7 Action Plan for the Chernobyl shutdown. It is estimated that between 1996 and 1999, ECU 538 million of TACIS funds were channelled to Ukraine through the Country Action Programme, the EU/G7 plan for Chernobyl and the Interstate, Nuclear Safety and Cross-border Co-operation Programmes.[52] In addition, the EU provided macroeconomic assistance for 1997 to support the IMF-led programme for stabilisation and economic reform. For a nation of 50 million, these were not large sums of money.

However, the grants, credits and loans that accompanied the establishment of formal ties have not prevented the emergence of damaging tensions between the two from early on. Much of this is attributable to actions by Kyiv. First, Ukraine has pursued actions which are contrary to the provisions of the PCA, as well as those of the rules of the WTO, with which PCA provisions were effectively harmonised. By introducing excessive and expensive certification on certain goods, of tariffs and certain excise duties, Ukraine was effectively reneging on its commitment to eliminate protectionist measures and progress toward the liberalisation of trade. The argument put forward by Kyiv that Ukraine's drastic and ongoing economic collapse, resulting in massive underemployment, and growing unemployment, necessitated protection of the few domestic producers that were still producing, was not accepted. The Ukrainian retort highlighted the quotas, restrictions and/or anti-dumping measures imposed on the few Ukrainian goods that were internationally competitive, in particular, textiles, steel products and chemicals.

It was clear that Kyiv got its strategy wrong. Above all, it fundamentally underestimated the implications of the demands of the PCA as well as the rules of the WTO, the membership of which was so fervently sought, but also the ramifications of rejecting the need to abide by laws and agreements which Ukraine voluntarily subjected itself to, or its 'legislative nihilism'.[53] As Sherr points out, 'Ukraine's political leaders have sometimes acted as if they could achieve integration by declaration, or simply by joining and participating in international organisational and political clubs rather than by undertaking concrete structural changes'.[54] Policy-makers, then, miscalculated the damage a reversal of liberalisation would do to Ukraine's wider objectives, namely membership of key international institutions such as the EU and the WTO. This in itself reflected flawed strategic reasoning, as 'accession to the WTO was . . . seen as a goal in itself, rather than as an element of comprehensive economic policy and development', something which Ukraine still sorely lacks.[55]

Second, Kyiv became increasingly convinced that the EU was not exactly welcoming Ukraine with open arms. For example, notwithstanding the limited economic value of the PCA, versions of which, after all, had been signed with a number of the other former Soviet republics, the ratification of the PCA was such a drawn out process, that in 1996 Kuchma felt compelled to castigate the member states of the EU over their slowness.[56] This complaint was voiced in spite of the Interim Agreement (IA), which was signed by Kuchma in June 1995, becoming effective on the 1 February 1996, on aspects of the agreement not requiring ratification by the parliaments of the European nations. In addition, the economic support provided by the EU was small in relative as well as absolute terms: Poland, a smaller and less problematic case, received ECU two billion of technical assistance compared to the ECU 823 million Ukraine received. The economic support was thus inadequate, especially when contrasted with Ukrainian expectations. In part this is attributable to the lack of progress in creating conditions for a market economy. However, much to the consternation of the Ukrainians, Kyiv also believes that Ukraine remains deliberately excluded from the European integration process and 'is not seen by the EU as a full and integral part of it', or in President Kuchma's words, 'nobody awaits us in the West'.[57]

At the root of these problems is a disparity of thinking, understanding and perception. Ostensibly, Ukraine's decision to pursue 'the strategic objective' of membership of the EU implied a two-tier set of goals. On one level, the objective of joining the EU represented a desire on the part of Ukraine to reverse its technological backwardness and non-competitiveness by gaining access to the foreign credits, investments, technologies and markets that come with membership of the EU. The alternative, a renewal of economic and political ties with Russia, is an anathema to strategists in Ukraine. The goal of membership of the EU reflects strategic thinking that is likely to shape Ukraine's socio-economic and geopolitical direction in the decades to come. On another level, the decision to pursue membership implied a willingness on the part of the Ukrainians to satisfy the more concrete political and economic requirements of EU membership. While Ukraine's commitment to the first-level objectives is beyond doubt, its willingness to adhere to the demands of the second set is distinctly more suspect. Specifically, while there are a few question marks over Ukraine's commitment to the ideals democracy, the rule of law, the promotion of human rights, and the protection of minority interests, Ukraine's relations with the EU continue to flounder, principally because of doubts concerning Kyiv's commitment to a functioning market economy: liberalisation of prices and trade remain still distant goals; barriers to market entry and disappearance are still prominent. Property rights, laws and contractual obligations remain far from transparent. Progress in the transformation of the financial sector is slow and interference by the state continues. All remain significant impediments to the full emergence of a market economy in Ukraine.[58] By 1999, it was clear that the Ukrainians had fundamentally failed to understand that the admirable and far-sighted objectives of the first level were inextricably linked to the achievement of the 'bread and butter' second-level objectives. In Kyiv, strategic thinking about the 'grand scheme of things' took precedence over the putting together of the nuts and bolts that would make such schemes work. There was a disparity between the desire to integrate, and the steps taken to bring about integration.

This misunderstanding of the link between the two levels camouflaged a further flaw: guided by a strong conviction of its geopolitical significance, for example, as a 'buffer against Russia', a commercial transit point, a country where 'East meets West', Kyiv failed to appreciate that 'its democratic development and economic performance matter more for the EU'.[59] There has been a decade-long lack of realisation on the part of Kyiv that geopolitical significance does not immediately translate into cash lump sums or painless integration into Western structures. There is only a budding awareness that there is a price to be paid for the benefits of belonging to them.

The role of the EU in Ukraine's bilateral ties and prospects for subregional integration

If Ukraine's relations with the EU were disappointing on a bilateral level, they were even more so in two other regards. First, the EU actively promoted measures, which contributed to the damaging of Ukraine's relations with Western neighbours. This was particularly so in relation to Ukraine's biggest trading partner in the West, Poland. Poland's growing proximity to EU structures imposed demands on Poland. Joining the Schengen Agreement and the imposition of a visa regime on Ukraine would mean the effective closure of its increasingly open and lucrative border with Ukraine, to the detriment of Poland's undeveloped border regions.[60] Furthermore, the imposition of EU external tariffs is hardly likely to be looked upon favourably by a Ukraine already irritated by what it sees as unfair treatment. Such measures are likely to exacerbate the existing differences in the degree of economic transformation that so distinguish Ukraine from Poland. Furthermore, as Poland and other CEES come ever to closer to joining the EU there is the fear that Ukraine might be denied the already limited funds trickling in from Brussels, further emphasising differences between them. In addition, as the CEES integrate, Ukraine is likely to face anti-dumping accusations as its non-competitive industries are exposed to the full blast of competition from more efficient producers. Furthermore, as the CEES prepare to access the EU, their relative interest in Ukraine is likely to tail off.[61]

The EU strategy of focusing on accession candidates from the CEES had further ramifications in that it fundamentally undermined a key dimension of Ukraine's strategy of integrating with European structures via bilateral relations with the CEES. Of the few areas in which Ukraine produced goods of world class competitiveness, most were in military production, much of it very high technology. In fact, Ukraine saw military–industrial co-operation with the states of Central and Eastern Europe, because of their strengthening ties with NATO, as a means of tying itself more closely to European structures. This strategy is seen as especially pertinent in light of the ongoing consolidation that is expected to take place in Europe as a means of avoiding Europe's technological dependence on the USA, something which Kyiv hoped would increase its appeal to the EU, especially in terms of its production of space technology and aeronautics.[62]

The second way in which the EU negatively affected Ukraine's regional objectives was by failing to place sufficient emphasis on subregional developments. For example, expectations as to the benefits of Euroregions in Ukrainian–Polish relations were not fulfilled. The first such region, the Carpathian Euroregion (with Poland, Ukraine, Hungary, and Slovakia as members and Romania as an observer) was created in 1993. It was known as the 'poorest Euroregion'. The initiative was acknowledged as having failed to provide the necessary stimulus for economic rejuvenation in these regions located far from administrative centres. By 1995 two of Hungary's four participating regions had withdrawn.[63] Of more direct interest to

Ukrainian–Polish relations was the Buh Euroregion created in 1996 and made up of the Volyn' oblast in Ukraine and four border provinces in Poland. However, by 1998, this Euroregion had singularly failed to deliver the investments that were hoped for. Worse was the fact that in the case of Ukraine and Poland the creation of the Euroregions exacerbated the ethnic tensions they were meant to eliminate. According to some sources, this was especially true on the Polish side. For example, civic leaders in Przemyszl were suspicious of Ukrainian intentions in the region, believing that the Ukrainians were planning to 'dominate' in the region.[64] On the other hand, Ukraine's attitude towards Euroregions was exposed when Polish proposals for other Euroregions on the Ukraine–Poland border were dismissed by the Ukrainian side.[65]

The extent to which the EU inadvertently undermined the development of the specifically Central and East European subregional institutions by not overtly encouraging the inclusion of new members was especially worrying for Kyiv as it set great store by these institutions.[66] In particular, the extent to which CEFTA would cease to be a viable institution as its members abandoned it for the EU was a major concern for Ukraine. In such a case, the alternatives for Kyiv remained very limited.

Overall, Ukraine's relations with EU were characterised by grand pronouncements. This is hardly surprising, as from the standpoint of Kyiv membership of the EU formed the cornerstone of its emergence into the wider world. Ties with the EU were a means of avoiding being sucked back into the economic and political orbit of Russia, and the backwardness that that entailed. In contrast, the EU offered the capital, technology and markets that could propel Ukraine rapidly towards modernity. Yet despite the pronouncements, after a decade of independence Ukraine remains nearly as far beyond EU structures as it was at the start. Indeed, Ukrainian expectations of some albeit vague and unspecified commitment on the part of the EU at the Helsinki summit in December 1999 went unfulfilled, something which was particularly distressing to Kyiv.[67] Clearly to a large extent this is attributable to Ukraine's own poor internal development. The lack of appreciation that economic reform (notwithstanding the dire state of the economy, and the hardship that further reform will impose) is a prerequisite for its future integration into the EU is causing a regression in relations with the EU. Kyiv's hopes that the Greek example would be followed in its case, when Athens was allowed into the EU for political rather than economic reasons, are forlorn. Ukraine is a considerably bigger and tougher problem from the perspective of Brussels. Indeed, the economic turmoil Ukraine went through in the summer of 1998 in response to the Russian economic crisis was a clear message to the EU that ties between the two states were such that by taking on Ukraine the EU would also bear a substantial Russian burden.

Compounding the problem, from the perspective of Brussels, is the fact that Ukraine is the source of a significant number of threats: Western capitals are already home to large and growing numbers of economic migrants from Ukraine (some legal; most illegal. It is estimated that currently there are 500,000 illegal immigrants in Ukraine, a figure that is likely to swell because of Ukraine's continued visa-free regime with GUUAM states, reaffirmed in September 2000).[68] In addition,

Ukraine's nuclear problem remains worrying for Brussels. Furthermore, as far as the EU is concerned, the geopolitical reasons for including Ukraine are not compelling. The alternatives for Europe are such that Ukraine is not an indispensable component in the developing architecture of Europe: a route through Turkey for Caspian hydrocarbons is a more than viable alternative. Ukraine's technology, without further inputs of research and development, is dating rapidly. Finally, Ukraine, by pilfering Russian gas going toward the West, has been instrumental in creating occasional gas shortages in the West: this unreliability on the part of Ukraine appears to be the motive behind the decision of key European gas companies to sign a memorandum of understanding in October 2000 to build a pipeline to further bypass Ukraine in the hydrocarbon transportation process.[69] Yet, despite all the negative signals emanating from Brussels, according to policy-shapers in Kyiv, Ukraine has no viable alternative to the Western option and membership of the EU, as the Russian azimuth is simply not appealing.[70] However, all of the available evidence suggests that Ukraine's objectives count for little in Brussels.

The impact of Ukraine's relations with states along the Western azimuth on relations with Russia and the CIS

The pressing objective for both Ukraine and the CEES in the early years following the collapse of the Soviet Union was how to deal with the security problem presented by Russia. Because the issues in their respective relations with Russia differed, the capitals of the CEES and Kyiv pursued independent, non co-ordinated and often incongruent policies. Inevitably, contradictory approaches would damage the development of bilateral relations between them, and their co-operation in subregional and regional integration.

As far as Kyiv was concerned, harmonious bilateral ties with CEES, especially with Poland, were highly desirable. Such ties were important if Kyiv was to deal with the immense pressure emanating from Russia for both stronger military and security ties with Ukraine, and Kyiv's participation in CIS structures. However, at the same time as Ukraine's relations with Russia started to hit new lows from 1992 onwards, especially as regards the BSF and Russian claims to Crimea, Poland, more so than the other Central and East European republics, was cultivating its own relations with Moscow, at the expense of Ukraine.

In 1991/2 Poland's chances of NATO membership were negligible. Thus Poland was forced to pursue an independent line regarding Russia, one that made its foreign and security policy incompatible with that of Ukraine. Irrespective of the damage to Poland's relations with Ukraine that such a stance would do, the Polish foreign minister, Andrzej Olechowski, made clear that the Poles 'would not do anything that would make it more difficult for Russia to become democratic and friendly' toward Poland.[71] Indeed, the intensity of Warsaw's ties with Moscow construed a significant impediment to the development of ties with Kyiv, as will be seen below. Despite domestic criticisms, in 1992 both the minister of defence, Janus Onyszkiewicz, and the head of the Department of National Security, Jerzy

Milewski, held to the line that co-operation with Russia was unavoidable and even indispensable in order to deal with Poland's geopolitical predicament. Working within a framework that presupposed that Russia was the dominant feature in Western strategic planning and that therefore Poland's chances of joining NATO were minimal, Polish strategists pursued a number of objectives. First, while keen to remove foreign troops from Polish soil, they were also cognisant of the need to guarantee supplies and maintain access to spare parts for the Soviet-era technology used by Polish forces. Second, it was deemed important to support the Russian market in its purchases of Polish military production. Third, and most directly impacting on relations with Ukraine, was the need to ensure the constant supply of Russian raw materials.[72] Fourth, was the desire of Poland to benefit from the transportation of gas from the huge Russian fields which met approximately 25 per cent of Western European energy needs in 1997, a figure which was projected to grow.[73] The temptation presented by the last issue was too strong to resist and is one of the clearest examples of Poland sticking to a Russia-first policy to the detriment of its relations with Kyiv. It is worth examining in some detail.

Ukraine, Poland and the transportation of Russian gas

One of the few effective weapons Kyiv could take advantage of in its ongoing political and economic struggle with Russia was Ukraine's virtual monopoly on the transportation of Russia gas to the West – the Ukrainian network carried some 90 per cent of the total.[74] This monopoly conferred on Ukraine a number of significant advantages. First, it provided an important source of income. Second, by fair means or foul, Ukraine was virtually guaranteed a supply of much needed, though often unaffordable, gas. Third, by threatening at times to cut off the pipeline in pursuit of political and economic advantage, Kyiv had at its disposal one of the few means of leverage against a much more generously endowed Russia. Fourth, by virtue of the fact that the Russians were highly dependent on the hard currency generated by the sale of raw materials to the West, any threat by Moscow to undermine Ukraine's independence by suspending oil and gas supplies was hardly realistic. For these reasons, the decision by Moscow in 1992 to build a new pipeline bypassing Ukraine, going instead through Belarus and Poland, was therefore from a geopolitical viewpoint predictable and understandable. The proposed 2,500-mile pipeline, running from the vast gas field on the Yamal peninsula, across Belarus to Kondratki on the Polish–Belarussian border and then across to Gorzyca on the German–Polish border, was a conspicuous effort to reduce Russian reliance on Ukraine. Joint ventures between Polish and Russian companies for the design and management of the pipeline were created in September 1992, while an agreement between Moscow and Warsaw on the actual construction of the pipeline was signed in August 1994. In the context of its rapidly deteriorating relations with Russia, Ukraine construed this step as a 'stab in the back'.[75] In one fell swoop, the Poles deprived the Ukrainians of one of their single most important strengths. Irrespective of Ukrainian concerns the project progressed, despite some difficulties and doubts.[76] By October 1996 various segments of the Polish route had been completed, leading to a contract being signed in that same month for the transportation of 65.7 billion cubic metres per annum by 2010.[77] (The pipeline was made operational at the beginning of 2000.) An attempt by the Poles to placate the Ukrainians by inviting them to participate in the construction of pipelines and compression pumps was unsuccessful. It was an overt attempt on the part of Poland to become a link between Europe, on the one hand, and Russian energy and Ukraine's machine building capacity, on the other.[78] In this way, not only would Poland have a guaranteed supply of energy (Poland at the time received 60 per cent of its natural gas from Russia) and gain from the income derived from the transit of energy across its territory, it would also become an indispensable part of the European energy transfer network.

In October 2000 Poland went some way toward redeeming itself in the eyes of Ukraine. On 18 October Russia's Gazprom signed a memorandum of understanding with major European gas companies to conduct a feasibility study into the building of a new section of the Yamal pipeline. The new section would be built passing south from Poland to Slovakia. In doing so, the pipeline would further reduce the amount of Russian gas traversing Ukrainian territory. Poland promptly announced that 'it would not support any gas supply scheme that would be to the detriment of Ukraine'.[79] While Poland's stance is, from the point of view of Kyiv, admirable, it is unlikely to be sustainable. First, in response to Poland's pronouncement, Moscow suggested it could examine the possibility of a pipeline crossing the Baltic, thereby bypassing Ukraine *and* Poland. Second, Poland is desirous of EU membership, and thus is likely to support any plan that links it to the union more closely. Third, Poland is itself in dire need of the revenue that such a pipeline might bring. On the other hand, as President Kuchma himself pointed out, 'it takes a lot of time [to proceed] from the project to its practical implementation'.[80] In any event, from Kyiv's point of view the real culprit is the EU.

On a smaller scale, similar ties were established between Hungary and Russia, as Gazprom bought segments of the Hungarian DKG-IST oil processing plant. In fact, because of the intensification of Russia's ties with Poland and Hungary in particular, it has been argued that 'it is reasonable to talk about the creation of a regional CEE financial–industrial Gazprom group'.[81] In the meantime, ties between Russia and Slovakia continued to be strong, with the latter acting as a key and enthusiastic transportation point for Russian materials.

Emergent tensions between Kyiv and Warsaw

Continuing the vein of Polish–Russian co-operation up until Ukraine's relations with Poland improved from 1994/5 onwards, and possibly even more alarming as far as the Ukrainians were concerned, was the proposal in 1992 on the part of the Polish minister of foreign affairs that Poland, in collaboration with Russia, take responsibility for the maintenance of peace on the territory of the former USSR.[82] This proposal was of concern for two reasons. First, it implied a lesser role for Ukraine in the region. Second, it smacked of a revival of the deeply unpopular 'Greater Poland'. Third, and even more disconcerting as far as the Ukrainians were concerned, was the growing if somewhat far-fetched perception that not only was Ukraine perceived by the Poles as a counterweight to Russia, but that Russia was seen as a counterweight to the military threat presented by a sovereign Ukraine.

Overall, the incompatibility of Moscow's respective relations with Kyiv and the Central and East European capitals, whether by accident or design, functioned as a strategy of *divide et impera* up until 1994. In particular, Ukraine's desperate desire to avoid integration with the CIS and ever closer ties with Russia meant that Kyiv's relationship with Warsaw suffered as the latter sought to turn its position regarding Russia to advantage. Russia was disruptive in Ukraine's efforts along its Western azimuth. Not only did Russia disrupt Ukraine's ties with Poland, its stance toward Ukraine also meant that NATO felt it had to tread carefully in its relations with Kyiv. Yet, as will now be seen, from 1994/5 relations between Ukraine and the CEES improved dramatically thanks to regional developments.

The impact of Ukraine's relations with states along the North-eastern azimuth on relations with states along the Western azimuth from 1994

If Russia played a divisive role in the Ukrainian–Polish/Central and Eastern Europe relationship prior to 1993–4, after 1994 Moscow's struggle to face up to the issues that were increasingly challenging it had a paradoxical result. After 1994, Russia inadvertently brought about a congruence of Ukraine–Polish/Central and East European interests. A number of causal factors stand out.

First, the continuation of the power struggle between the Yeltsin reformists and the parliamentary conservatives highlighted the potential for a rapid return to the past, something as unpalatable for Poland and the other CEES as it was for Ukraine. The military attack on the Russian parliament in October 1993 served as a stark reminder to leaders in both Warsaw and Kyiv that the reform process in Moscow was far from irreversible. The subsequent election of a left-oriented replacement parliament in December 1993 reinforced the neighbours' feelings of vulnerability. It became clear that Yeltsin remained their best hope. In the case of Ukraine, Yeltsin was outspoken in his condemnation of periodic claims by the Russian parliament to Crimea and Sevastopol. By 1993 these claims had grown increasingly vociferous, and despite his occasional temper tantrum toward Ukraine, he was arguably still the politician who was most tolerant of Ukrainian independence. Similarly, it was Yeltsin who in a joint declaration with Walesa in Warsaw on 25 August 1993 acquiesced to Poland's entry into NATO, accepting that such a move would not impede Moscow's relations with Warsaw. The attack on parliament served to remind both Kyiv and Warsaw how fragile their international status remained. A further reminder of the way things could still go was Russia's willingness to use force to resolve the 'Chechnya problem' in 1994.

Probably the most significant factor in stimulating an intensification of Ukrainian–Polish ties in particular was the gradual return of Belarus to the Russian fold from 1993 onwards. The tightening of the economic ties between Belarus and Russia that had been created with the establishment of the new rouble zone in

September 1993 was worrisome to Warsaw and Kyiv. Compounding this was Minsk's gradual abandonment of neutrality in favour of closer ties with Moscow, culminating in a comprehensive military agreement between the two on 11 March 1994. When during 1994, 'Belarus had returned', in the words of Taras Kuzio, 'to the status of a Russian gubernia, demanding a greater degree of integration than even the current Russian government was willing to provide', the signs looked ominous for both Poland and Ukraine.[83] Two 'joint' worries stand out. First, the desire by Russia to use Belarus as a significant military base presented a major threat to both Ukraine and Poland. Second, plans for regional structures such as the Baltic–Black Sea axis, something Russia was vociferously opposed to and which it warned the CEES against participating in, would be made obsolete at a stroke. The ever tighter ties between Moscow and Minsk, further intensified by the Belarussian referendum on the integration of Belarus and Russia in May 1995, culminated in the creation of a 'Community of Sovereign States' in April 1996, in anticipation of impending NATO enlargement.[84] The response of Ukraine and Poland was to co-ordinate their positions on Belarus. For example, the presidents of Ukraine, Poland and Lithuania overtly criticised the closeness between Minsk and Moscow at the OSCE summit in Lisbon at the end of 1996, much to the dismay of Russia.

Predictably, Russia perceived the PfP, the enlargement of NATO and the formalisation of Ukraine's ties with NATO through the same prism as it viewed all of NATO's activities in the region, namely as the Western alliance starting to impinge on Russia's traditional stamping grounds. Yet, in part, it was this narrow Russian perception of events to its west that reinforced that which it wished to avoid. By failing to develop more normal ties with the CEES and Ukraine between 1994 and 1996, Russia itself intensified the focus on the security vacuum on the continent. This had the opposite effect from that intended. And as NATO's encroachment gained at the expense of Russia's proposals for *de facto* neutral and weakly armed CEES, Primakov expressed the view that

> If NATO, at the time created to repel global threats, comes to engulf the territory of the Warsaw Pact, from our point of view, the geopolitical situation will deteriorate. Why? Because intentions change. But opportunities are a constant. Obviously I do not believe that NATO will attack us. However, on a hypothetical level a situation might emerge in which we will be forced to act in a way which is not in our best interests.[85]

Belatedly, to preclude such a situation emerging, and end the *impasse* in ties with Ukraine at a time when Kyiv's ties with Brussels were improving, Moscow, as we have seen, hurriedly signed the Friendship and Co-operation Treaty with Ukraine days prior to Ukraine signing a charter with NATO in 1997. This is a good demonstration of Russia's relative impotence, NATO's potency and the relative effectiveness of Ukraine's foreign policy stratagems.

Conclusion to Part III

Between 1991 and 1998, Ukraine's relations along the Western azimuth underwent a noticeable transformation. Relations with the CEES represented an avenue of real opportunity for Kyiv. The establishment of bilateral ties with Poland, in particular, was a key means for Ukraine to reduce its overwhelming economic reliance on Russia. And, while the progress in economic terms was not as fruitful as Kyiv (or Warsaw) might have hoped, this was to some extent compensated for by the eventual emergence of extremely harmonious political ties. It is noteworthy that the stimulus to the improvement of ties noted from 1994 onward was provided by extrinsic factors: relations between the two of them, despite the proclamations, were never quite dynamic enough.

Relations with Hungary and Slovakia were never expected to be as fulfilling, and as a result there were fewer disappointments. Thus, while both proved to be important trading partners, neither matched the 'strategic' importance of Poland to Ukraine. Yet harmonious relations with them were clearly doing Ukraine no harm.

The contrast to the above posed by relations with Romania was sharp. The removal of the territorial dispute between them came as no small relief to Kyiv. And though the matter was not fully resolved, even its temporary resolution made Kyiv feel less vulnerable both on its exposed south-western flank, and in general terms, as the potential for precedent-setting was there for all to see. The albeit temporary resolution of the crisis was driven by the demands of the regional integration process.

In a similar vein, even the partial and temporary resolution of the Moldovan problem brought some respite to the region. Russia's relative impotence to impose its solution was a relief in itself since it also opened the way for Ukraine to play a regional role. Ukraine's increased regional prominence not only bolstered Kyiv's relations with Kishinev, but set in train a partnership that would come to serve them well in the formation of GUUAM, a key subregional organisation within the CIS.

On a bilateral level, Ukraine's policy along its Western azimuth was a success: relations were established with all neighbours – even its most troublesome – and significant points of contention were removed or postponed. The establishment of harmonious relations with the CEES was, naturally, especially welcome in the context of the frequently poor state of Ukraine's relations with Russia. As such the Western azimuth brought Ukraine a much needed sense of achievement, and bolstered its sometimes fraught independent status. However, bilateral relations were merely one stage in a multi-stage process. Above all, Kyiv hoped that by developing ties with its Western neighbours, it would participate in the development of subregional and regional institutions. Not only was eventual membership of Western institutional structures desirable *per se*, but it was also welcome in terms of the potential relief it could bring Kyiv as it sought to resist pressure emanating from its Eastern azimuth.

However, Ukraine not only currently remains beyond key subregional structures. It is difficult to envisage Kyiv satisfying the criteria for entry into, for example, CEFTA in the next few years. It has been argued that the many benefits of subregional institutions include the fact that they fill a political vacuum and restart regional economic co-operation.[86] Yet to a very large extent Ukraine was prevented from helping fill the political vacuum and restart economic co-operation at the subregional level. From the point of view of Kyiv, much of the blame in this regard must be attributable to regional institutions, in particular the EU.[87] By not encouraging subregional institutions to develop inclusiveness toward stragglers such as Ukraine, there is the widespread belief in Kyiv that the EU is in danger of driving Ukraine back into the economic embrace of Russia.[88]

There is the additional danger that once the CEES enter NATO, CEFTA, the key subregional organisation, will lose much of its appeal and attraction, leaving Ukraine floundering in isolation once more. Furthermore, the EU's demands on aspirants such as Poland are likely to drive a wedge in economic and political relations with Ukraine in the absence of some mechanism designed to soften the impact of Poland's transition. Such EU demands have already led to a hardening of the CEES' stance toward Ukraine, leading it to remain isolated and beyond subregional organisations.

Notwithstanding the fact that Kyiv has failed to fulfil its share of the bargain as regard institutional reform, a critical failure on the part of Ukraine, it is nevertheless difficult to establish exactly what Brussels' objectives toward Kyiv precisely are. On the one hand, the EU has been willing to establish a dialogue with Ukraine as evidenced by the PCA and the albeit limited flow of funds from Brussels to Kyiv. On the other hand, it is clear that 'the EU can be faulted for a lack of enthusiasm at working level and a lack of strategic vision at the top'.[89] The lack of acknowledgement and acceptance of Ukraine's aspirations to membership of the EU at the 1999 Helsinki Conference not only provided more evidence for this contention but also intensified the disillusionment that had set in following a similar failure at the London Conference in 1998. The prioritisation by the EU of Russia as a partner has also not helped in Ukraine–EU relations.

There is a view that part of the problem also lays in the fact that the EU as an institution that germinated from the ideological conflict that was the Cold War, has not undergone significant ideological change with the end of that conflict. The mechanisms of the EU were 'devised by governments whose aim was to contain the encroachments of the East rather than enlarge the domain of the West'.[90] In this regard, the EU contrasts with NATO, an institution that has purposefully sought to eliminate the boundaries between the insiders and outsiders. In sum, it is

> not surprising, therefore, Ukraine has been increasingly finding itself subject to two distinct, if not contradictory, vectors of Western policy: that pursued by NATO and that pursued by the European Union. With anxiety and surprise, knowledgeable Ukrainians are coming to the conclusion that the latter vector operates according to principles which are rather distinct from NATO's and which Ukraine may have limited ability to influence.[91]

A contrasting view is that the divergence between the stances adopted by the two regional institutions reflect their different functional perspectives. NATO's forthcomingness is attributable to its geopolitical perspective, namely the need to deal with Russia. The EU's attitude toward Ukraine is guided by the very practical issues of economic compatibility and manageability, areas in which Ukraine continues to provide major cause for concern.[92]

It is evident that Ukraine's efforts along the Western azimuth on bilateral, subregional and regional levels were impelled by Kyiv's concerns as to the security threats it perceived as emanating from the North-eastern azimuth. While it is clear that it failed to achieve key goals (i.e. membership of CEFTA and at least a form of recognition that the EU was open to Ukraine's eventual membership), many other key objectives were attained. Above all, by the end of the decade the 'strategic' relationship with Poland was delivering tangible benefits. Furthermore, harmonious bilateral relations had been established with its most troublesome neighbour, Romania, and the Moldovan problem was relegated from that of a potential region of conflict to an area that required ongoing attention. Subregionally, Ukraine was gaining the credentials of a CEES, though the lack of membership of key subregional and regional institutions still jars in Kyiv. Furthermore, the signing of the charter with NATO in 1997 and the ongoing co-operation with the alliance suggest that ten years after independence Ukraine had indeed achieved a degree of success in preserving its security and enlarging its freedom of manoeuvre by so doing, especially in light of the numerous internal and external obstacles it faced.

Ukraine's early efforts to create subregional security structures bolster the realist view that the formation of alliances is a natural strategy of weaker states in the presence of stronger foes. However, realist theory can take less comfort from the vigour with which Ukraine pursued membership of non-security subregional and regional institutions along the Western azimuth. While the theory of structural interdependence does provide some insight into Ukraine's willingness to pursue integration along the Western azimuth (the low salience of force and the lowly position of military concerns in the hierarchy of issues were clearly functional in this regard), ultimately it reveals little about Ukraine's stance towards institutions to its West. Much the same can be said about globalisation theory which struggles to provide meaningful commentary on Ukraine's policy choices in its regional behaviour along the Western azimuth.

Neoliberal institutionalism is considerably more successful in its explanatory power, offering an insight into the rationale behind Ukraine's pursuit of membership of subregional as well as regional institutions. Faced with states that had at one time or another been hostile to it (and with which the resolution of hostilities had never been achieved on a bilateral inter-state and sub-state levels), Ukraine sought membership of subregional institutions (in particular CEFTA) in which many of these CEES participated in order to benefit from the security enhancing transparency and opportunity for communication that these institutions provided. The fact that the objectives underlying the existence of subregional institutions (i.e. closer ties with and ultimately membership of regional institutions) meant that member states pursued the harmonisation of democratic and economic laws and principles with the regional institutions (in particular the EU) indicated that Ukraine's pursuit of membership of subregional institutions was synonymous with its pursuit of membership of the EU.

The advantages of subregionalism, claimed by 'subregional' regionalists, were not lost on Kyiv. Subregional institutions potentially offered Ukraine a means of avoiding ending up on the wrong side of a new division in Europe and, thanks to collectivism, of carrying greater weight than it might individually. Yet, for a variety of reasons, Ukraine could not exploit these advantages, as a result of which Kyiv's strategy of EU membership via membership of key subregional institutions in Central and Eastern Europe met with limited success. The prime reason was that regional institutions, and in particular the EU, were not overly supportive of the subregional process. As a result subregionalism in the region was racked with competitiveness between members states and an over-concern for the damage that the 'slowest-moving' member would do to other, 'faster-moving' members' prospects.[93] This problem was further exacerbated by the contradictions inherent in treating members of subregional institutions as a group, 'but also treating the Central and Eastern European states individually in terms of their relationships with and prospects for membership of NATO and the EU. As a consequence, the Visegrad group's relations with NATO and the EU created both incentives and disincentives for regional co-operation' and the net loser was Ukraine.[94] For these reasons, Ukraine's chances of membership of subregional institutions were circumscribed before it had even embarked on the strategy. In sum, Ukraine simply could not single-handedly surmount the inherent flaws of subregionalism recognised by 'subregional regionalists'.

New Wave regionalists extend the argument of subregional integration in Central and Eastern Europe in a number of ways. First, they recognise that 'PTAs might form . . . because they usually have greater aggregate market power and thus more bargaining power than their constituent members'.[95] This was certainly at least partly true in the case of CEFTA, the members of which wished to enhance their negotiating position in pursuit of their unambiguous aim of EU membership.[96] (Although it has to be said that the welfare benefits from the increase in trade, harmonisation of rules, standards and economic policy, and the growth of economic co-operation at the expense of irrational competition were neither lost on member states nor prospective members states such as Ukraine.) Yet, it was precisely Ukraine's inability to implement economic reform that precluded it from CEFTA membership and benefiting from a common negotiating position.

Second, by making provision for the relationship between the political and economic, New Wave regionalists help explain Ukraine's failure at the subregional level, certainly as regards CEFTA membership. Ukraine's reluctance to implement essential economic reform, compatible with requirements for CEFTA membership (and also with the PCA), was the result of Kyiv's over-focus on the political at the expense of the economic.[97] Admittedly, Ukraine suffered inordinately from the 'COMECON syndrome' – 'centralism, the prevalence of political over economic motives, an inefficient economic mechanism, a lack of mutual trust, and [the] one-sidedness of relations (biased towards the Soviet Union)'.[98] Yet even within these constraints, Kyiv's progress on the reform necessary for membership of CEFTA was lamentable, precisely because of the priority of the political over economic factors within Ukraine. This was not only a matter of external or international politics. By catering for a narrow domestic constituency of industrialists and oligarchs eager to exploit lax regulations, consecutive Ukrainian governments and presidents demonstrated their preparedness to subordinate the general societal welfare that derives from economic reform to self-serving politics. If it is true that 'whether a country chooses to enter a regional trade agreement is determined by how much influence different interest groups exert and how much the government is concerned about voters' welfare', it is evident that in Ukraine some interest groups exert huge pressure, and the governments have not been very concerned with voter's welfare, with the honourable exception of the short-lived government of Viktor Yushchenko between autumn 1999 and spring 2000.[99]

Kyiv's constructivistic emphasis on its Central European identity was complementary to the politico-economic bent of the above theories as it set out to participate in the community formation taking place on its western borders, and which it saw as incomplete in the absence of itself. This effort to reconnect, which drew heavily on positive, though rare, 'European' experiences alongside moves to relegate divisive historical episodes to the history books, was indicative of Ukraine's desire to reconstitute itself as a member of a European family.

A key feature of this constructivism was also the emphasis placed by the leadership on the link between Ukraine's ongoing democratisation and its return to Europe. Ukraine's post-independence leadership was quick to realise that the latter could not occur without the former, and by extension that Ukraine's regional objectives could not be attained without the implementation of democratic reform. This link was evident at the bilateral level with Poland especially keen on 'Europeanising' and democratising Ukraine. However, it was even more in evidence at the subregional level where 'while cross-border co-operation cannot easily be measured, a strong case can be made that it contributes to the development of democracy within and stable relations between the states concerned' (though in Central and Eastern Europe the mechanism for such co-operation were Euroregions rather than, for example, CEFTA).[100] However, at the regional level, institutions have made the link between regionalism and democracy explicit with the EU, indicating 'that various Eastern European countries must consolidate democratic reforms as one precondition for membership'.[101] Indeed, this message was reiterated most forcefully by Brussels for Kyiv's exclusive attention following the 1999 presidential elections, after the scale of corruption on the part of the incumbent and eventual winner, Leonid Kuchma, had become clear. (The same message, in the form of a 'last warning', was once again sent to Kyiv by Brussels following the albeit unproven implication of the Ukrainian president in the murder in 2000 of a young Ukrainian journalist critical of the regime.) Although New Wave theorists steer clear of 'suggesting that the desire to gain access to a PTA has been a primary force driving democratisation in Eastern Europe', it is evident that the EU has encouraged Ukraine to make such a link.[102]

Part IV

The Southern azimuth

Over the centuries it could be argued that Ukraine paid an enormous price in terms of its East–West predicament: subordination to Russia, and sometimes Poland, left scars which are still visible centuries later. With independence in 1991, this predicament re-emerged in a dramatic way. On Ukraine's independence, its ethnic, linguistic, religious and political splits appeared glaring. Movement towards the West threatened secession in Eastern Ukraine, while tighter ties with the East threatened instability in Western Ukraine. While Ukraine tried to balance these pressures by implementing an often measured foreign and security policy, it simultaneously pursued one other avenue. The Southern azimuth was a key means for Ukraine to escape from these East–West pressures. According to Ukraine's foreign policy experts, 'the most positive changes, compared to other directions, are taking place in the process of Ukraine's integration into the Black Sea region'.[1] Such positive changes included the discovery of energy resources, the development of transportation routes, a reduced role for Russia, and challenges to its dominance by subregional institutions and regional institutions. All of these things meant that the Southern azimuth has represented a field of considerable opportunity for Ukraine.

6 Relations with Black Sea littoral neighbours

Kyiv, as did Moscow before it, regards Ukraine's 1,632-kilometre coastline on the Black Sea as one of its main geostrategic assets.[1] There are a number of reasons for this. First, the Black Sea is an important trading area.[2] Second, the Black Sea provides an outlet for industry on the Dunai, Dniester and Dnipro rivers.[3] Third, the temperate climate of the Black Sea gives Ukraine's ports an all-year-round usability. Indeed, with the 'loss' of Ukraine in 1991, Russia was deprived of access to a significant proportion of its few warm-water ports, the most important strategically of which was Sevastopol, home of the Black Sea Fleet (BSF). Fourth, Ukraine's Black Sea continental shelf is a potentially very rich source of hydrocarbons.[4] As will be seen below, Ukraine's claim to outright ownership of this submerged wealth did not go unchallenged, most notably by Russia and Romania. Fifth, because of the access provided to the Middle East, the Mediterranean–Black Sea region, along with the Straits of Gibraltar, has been identified by the US Department of Defense as one of the eight strategic regions regarded as containing significant chokepoints.[5] Sixth, following the post-Soviet rediscovery of Caspian hydrocarbons, the Black Sea came to be spoken of as a transit route in bringing these resources to market in Europe.[6] From very early on, Ukraine hoped and planned to become an integral segment of that route. This was not a forlorn expectation. As Balmaceda has pointed out

> As the emergence of Ukraine as an independent state has changed the geopolitical map of Europe, it has also highlighted the importance of Ukraine's links with its western and southern neighbours across the Carpathian Mountains and the Black Sea. These geopolitical factors have also affected the issue of energy resources and their transport.[7]

Ukraine based its hopes on the fact that the transit of oil via its territory represented the shortest route between the oil-rich, cash-poor Caspian region and energy-hungry Western and Northern Europe. Inevitably, Ukraine's ambition put Kyiv into conflict with other regional states as they jostled for advantage in pursuit of the *grand prix*.

Clearly, there is an interconnectedness between many of the above-mentioned points, which, in many subtle and less than subtle ways, has the potential to damage

Ukraine's status as a Black Sea power, its relations with other littoral states (in particular Russia) and its participation in subregional and regional developments. For example, Ukraine paid a heavy psychological price for Russia's desperation to hang on to the vast military infrastructure in Sevastopol. The eventual agreement between Russia and Ukraine, signed in 1997, legitimising the stationing of Russian troops in Crimea, which was explicitly forbidden by the Ukrainian constitution, was seen as undermining the sovereignty of Ukraine. However, if the Black Sea is a zone of potential conflict, it is also a region of great opportunity for Ukraine. So even though Kyiv would be hard pressed to replicate Moscow's traditional regional role – Ukraine's utter dependence on Russian energy resources see to that – Ukraine is nevertheless striving to become a major regional player, spurred on by a desperate need to diversify its energy sources and benefit financially from the transportation of Caspian oil and gas.

Ukraine's Black Sea role lends itself to three levels of analysis. It will start by examining Ukraine's bilateral ties with the littoral states. Kyiv has made enormous strides in making its relative political weight felt. The focus of Ukrainian foreign policy was on becoming an accepted Black Sea state with recognised borders, co-operating on a bilateral as well as multilateral level with other regional states in an attempt to ensure the stability of the sea, tempering Russian regional power and influencing the direction in which Caspian oil would flow. This section will explore how these various issue-areas impacted on Ukraine's bilateral relations with its Black Sea neighbours, and the means Kyiv used to resolve, or not as the case may be, any problems encountered. It will then be argued that Kyiv's efforts at the bilateral level formed part of a concerted effort to pursue objectives at the subregional and regional levels. Thus, the section will also examine the extent to which Ukraine's bilateral ties with regional neighbours impacted on its membership of, and participation in, the two main Black Sea subregional groupings, the institutionalised Black Sea Economic Co-operation forum (BSEC) and the non-institutionalised grouping of GUUAM. The interaction between these two levels reflects the primary focus of Ukraine's strategic foreign and security policy planning with respect to this region. Third, while the link between bilateral ties and regional-level institutions will be touched on where appropriate, the section will analyse the relationship between subregional and regional institutions. Kyiv sees the BSEC as a vehicle that may in some way contribute towards Ukraine's ambition of integrating with the pre-eminent regional institution, the European Union (EU). In a parallel vein, Ukraine's role in the informal GUUAM is an effort to provide alternative leadership to that of Russia for disaffected members of the CIS. Furthermore, Ukraine's ambitions within GUUAM appear to be directly linked to the issue of transporting Caspian hydrocarbons, something which policy-makers in Kyiv hoped might contribute in some vague and unspecified way to closer ties between Ukraine and the EU. Throughout, it will be argued that while efforts at each of the above mentioned three levels form part of a coherent foreign and security policy, significant domestic and international impediments existed that prevented the achievement of important regional policy objectives. The chapter will start by examining Ukraine's bilateral relations with other Black Sea states, followed by an analysis of the single biggest issue that affected those relations, namely the politics surrounding potential transportation routes for Caspian oil.

Relations with Black Sea littoral states

Ukraine 'shares' the Black Sea with five other states: Russia, Georgia, Turkey, Bulgaria and Romania. Traditionally, Russia and Turkey have been the two main protagonists for control over the sea and the access afforded to the oceans of the world. Between the seventeenth and nineteenth centuries, in a two-pronged assault, Russia painfully and gradually wrestled control of the sea out of the hands of Turkey. On water this was achieved first by expelling the Turks from the Azov Sea, then at the end of the eighteenth century by taking control of the Kerch straits. On land the annexation of the northern Black Sea coast and the Crimean peninsula gave Russia strategic control over the sea. Ukrainian independence in 1991 signified a momentous reversal of Russia's centuries-long campaign, and was followed by an inevitable diminution of Russian influence in the region. Following the 'retreat' of Russia, a vacuum appeared which Ukraine tried to fill. As this inevitably meant that Ukraine's ambitions clashed with those of its neighbours, which nurtured similar ambitions to fill the vacuum, the maintenance of harmonious relations with Black Sea states was at the forefront of Ukraine's foreign and security policy. Relations with each of those states will now be examined.

Russia

Ukraine's location on the Black Sea has been a major factor explaining Russia's sense of loss of empire following the collapse of the Soviet Union. This sense of loss has been considerably exacerbated by Kyiv's determination to plough a lone, independent-of-Russia furrow on the international scene.

The sheer vigour with which Moscow fought to keep control over the BSF and its associated infrastructure amply demonstrated the psychological importance of the region to the Russia, something that had inevitable political ramifications. The involuntary 'loss' of Crimea, let alone Sevastopol, was a burden that weighed heavily in Russian domestic politics and was a frequent reference point for Russian politicians seeking to win quick political points. Despite the fact that Ukraine and Russia signed a friendship, co-operation and partnership treaty in 1997, which was eventually ratified in February 1999, a number of Russian political figures came out against ratification of the treaty as it wound its way through the Russian Duma at the end of 1998 and beginning of 1999. One of the most vociferous opponents of the treaty was the mayor of Moscow, Yuri Luzkhov, who argued that 'ratification of the treaty would in effect separate Crimea and Sevastopol from Russia forever'.[8]

The political significance of Ukraine's southern border is, as might be expected, associated with the military–strategic importance of Crimea, and in particular, of Sevastopol, 'the city of Russia's military glory' as it is often referred to. The radar station in Sevastopol forms an integral component of Russia's early warning system against missile attack. Also, Sevastopol is the base of the Black Sea Fleet, and the vast infrastructure that goes with it.[9] The loss of Sevastopol, and by extension the fleet, would have represented a heavy blow to Russia on its south-western flank. Ukrainian independence threatened to deprive Russia of some of its most important warm-water outlets, most notably Sevastopol, leaving Moscow with only two major ports, Novorossiysk and Tuapse, on the distant north-eastern corner of the Black Sea.

Loss of access to Ukraine's Black Sea ports also imposed economic costs on Russia. Ukraine's ports were a small but significant outlet for Russian crude oil as it found its way westward. In part due to the transit costs incurred, only 0.2 MMBD (millions of barrels per day) were exported from Odesa on the Black Sea in 1997, a figure down by nearly 50 per cent from the 1990 figure of 0.36 MMBD.[10] However, in the long term, the economic costs of 'losing' Ukraine were considerably greater. Soon after independence, Ukraine started to insist on the delineation of the Black Sea and the Sea of Azov continental shelves. While the delineation of the seas was of itself important to a country keen to guard its territorial integrity, delineation would also confer the right to ownership of the significant hydrocarbon resources that were believed to lie under the waters of the seas. Balmaceda notes that despite the signing of the Ukraine–Russia Treaty in 1997 and the commitment that border delimitation would be defined and enshrined in law,

> Russia's foot-dragging over the demarcation of its borders with Ukraine has delayed the exploration of new fields: drilling cannot begin in the Black Sea shelf until ownership is legalised, which in turn requires the clarification of the Ukrainian-Russian border. . . . If they were to be fully exploited together with deposits in the Crimean area . . . [they] could make Ukraine into a net exporter of energy.[11]

Kyiv's confrontation with Moscow over the Black Sea 'issues' had direct implications for Ukraine's long-term economic prospects. Indeed, it was only because of Ukraine's decision to start the delineation process unilaterally that a recalcitrant Russia agreed to co-operate.

As we have seen, holding on to the BSF and by extension Sevastopol was a key tactic in Moscow's strategy of slowing and at some stage in the future reversing the decline of Russia's influence in the Black Sea region. In this light, the eventual signing of the Ukrainian–Russia treaty on the Black Sea Fleet and Sevastopol in 1997 can be seen as a major foreign policy success for Moscow and must in part be regarded as a blow to the prestige of Ukraine. However, harmonious bilateral relations with other influential regional neighbours tempered the impact of the setback for Ukraine.

Turkey

Even before Ukrainian independence in 1991, relations between the Ukrainian SSR and Turkey were noteworthy for their warmth. As early as 1989, when it was clear that the Soviet Union was in decline, a protocol was signed between the two states on economic development and trade. Ten days before the Ukrainian referendum on independence in 1991, Ankara announced its intention to establish consular relations with Kyiv.[12] In May 1992, during President Kravchuk's visit to Ankara, a treaty on friendship and good-neighbourly relations was signed.[13] These early developments were indicative of the mutual importance of each of the states for one another and they soon led to economic, political and even strategic co-operation.

As two of the larger states on the Black Sea, Ukraine and Turkey were natural trading partners and following Ukrainian independence trade grew quickly. Between 1993 and 1995, Ukrainian exports to Turkey rose from $185 million to $442 million, with a trade surplus of $167 million and $381 million respectively accruing to the Ukrainians. By 1996, trade turnover was estimated to have reached the $1 billion mark, if shuttle trade was included.[14]

Even political issues with the potential to damage relations were dealt with amicably. For example, as was pointed out by Turkey's president on the fiftieth anniversary of the deportation of the Tartars by Stalin, 'our Tartar brethren . . . are a great branch of the Turkish nation, and they are the strongest bridge of the friendship between Turkey and Ukraine'.[15] Although, whilst on a visit to Ukraine in May 1994, Turkish President Demirel 'advised' Ukraine to allow any Turks of Crimean origin (the figure could be as high as 600,000) to return to their homeland, he did temper this advice, and demonstrated Turkey's potential moderating role in the region, with a call to the Crimean Tartars to act with caution. There was striking co-operation on the Tartar issue, with both presidents calling on the international community, and in particular the G7, to support Ukrainian and Turkish efforts to provide accommodation for homeless Tartars, a problem with which Ukraine has nevertheless continued to struggle virtually single-handedly.[16]

The level of strategic co-operation over oil and gas pipeline development in particular indicated that both parties were keen to pursue common benefits, to contribute to the marginalisation of Russia in the region, and to delay any regional Russian resurgence. One of the means for such a Russian resurgence was for Russia to become the main route for the transportation of Caspian oil, regaining its stranglehold over energy supplies as well as benefiting from the transportation fees. In this light, as will be examined in greater detail below, the agreement of both parties to build complementary pipeline systems for the transportation of Caspian oil was a key step forward.

Overall, good ties with Turkey were strategically vital for Kyiv. Ukraine was too weak to constrain Moscow's regional ambitions independently and to pursue its own; much the same could be said for Turkey. Ukrainian–Turkish co-operation in the Black Sea region was a means of dealing with this predicament. Furthermore, Ankara intended to extend the role of the Black Sea region as a factor in NATO strategic thinking. In James Sherr's words, 'Turkey has developed its relationship with Ukraine . . . conscious that it will add a north–south dimension to a NATO–Ukraine relationship still largely seen in east–west terms'.[17]

Romania

As we have seen, all aspects of Ukraine's relations with Romania were from the beginning overshadowed by controversy over territory. While the main dispute was over the former Romanian territories of Bessarabia and Bukovina incorporated into South-Western Ukraine in 1940, matters were further exacerbated in 1995 by Romania's proclamations regarding Serpents Island in the Black Sea.[18] While Ukraine's ownership of the island itself was not disputed by Bucharest, ownership of the continental shelf surrounding the island was, after it had emerged that substantial amounts of mineral resources were contained therein. In December 1995 the Romanian government announced that it would appeal to the International Court of Justice in the Hague, challenging Ukraine's rights to the continental shelf. Inevitably, given the context of Ukraine's deteriorating relationship with Russia, especially regarding the issue of Sevastopol and the BSF, the announcement was interpreted by Kyiv as a territorial claim on Ukraine.[19] However, as noted in Chapter 4, Bucharest's ambition of being one of the states invited to apply for NATO membership, a decision which was due to be announced in July 1997, placed significant constraints on the lengths to which Romania was prepared to go in areas where it might damage relations with Kyiv. The subsequent signing of a bilateral treaty in June 1997 provided space for the two sides to agree to disagree.[20] Serpents Island was formally recognised as the territory of Ukraine, and the actual delimitation of the continental shelf around the island was to be subject to negotiation for two years. If no agreement followed, the whole issue was to be referred to the International Court of Justice in the Hague. In the interests of co-operation, the Ukrainians agreed to halt and refrain from placing offensive weapons on island.[21] Crucially, as part of the treaty, both parties also agreed to refrain from geological exploration in the area under contention.[22]

However, if the Black Sea proved to be a source of friction between the two states, it also provided an opportunity for co-operation. In February 1998, the Ukrainian ambassador to Romania, Alexander Chalyi, suggested that 'Romania can benefit from important advantages as regards the Ukrainian project pertaining to the transportation of the Caspian sea oil. We are neighbouring countries who can and must participate jointly in shipment of Caspian Sea petroleum'.[23] This newfound warmth toward Bucharest was more than an attempt to take advantage of Romania's strengths in oil transportation, specifically the large capacity of the port at Constanta. This approach suggests willingness on the part of Kyiv to demonstrate a degree of regional leadership and contribute to the stability of the Black Sea region by co-operating with its neighbours and avoiding needless competition in a volatile part of Europe.

At around the same time as Ukrainian–Romanian relations were becoming turbulent, a curious but minor territorial spat blew up between Kyiv and Kishinev. It emerged during the process of demarcating and delimiting borders between the two states, a process that was related to the transportation of oil. As things stood in terms of borders between the two states, the Moldovan border fell some 1,800 metres short of the mouth of the river Prut as it joins the Danube in the region of the town of Dzurdzuleszti. As a result, Moldova is not accessible to tankers coming in from the Black Sea. However, in the interests of obtaining oil supplies from a source other than Russia, such access was indispensable. To this end the Moldovans requested of the Ukrainians access to a 400-metre length of the bank of the Danube. Both parties agreed to submit this question to a joint delimitation committee. However, in the summer of 1997 the Moldovan side commissioned a Moldovan–Greek consortium to start building an oil terminal (much of the $38 million cost of which was provided for by a $25.5 million credit from the European Bank for Reconstruction and Development [EBRD]) with a 2.1 million ton capacity. Because the proposed building was to go up on the state boundary, the Ukrainians reinforced the state border, arguing that the building presented a significant ecological risk to Europe's largest wetlands, a few kilometres upstream from the proposed terminal, and should be halted.[24] It is likely that the Ukrainians were concerned about the impact that such an oil terminal might have on their own plans for the transportation of Caspian oil. A resolution to the problem was found when the three neighbours in the region of the dispute (Ukraine, Moldova and Romania) agreed to the setting up of a Euroregion with an oil terminal as its focus.

Overall, however, territorial disputes dwarfed all other issues in Ukrainian–Romanian relations. As far as Serpents Island was concerned, this was hardly surprising in light of what was at stake. And yet, the very same temptation brought about by the income to be derived from hydrocarbon extraction and transportation, contained the seeds of reconciliation between Ukraine and Romania.

Georgia

As former constituent parts of the Soviet Union, Georgia and Ukraine shared a political extraction that was to determine their geopolitical outlook, especially their perception of Moscow. The latter helped to shape their respective and often complementary regional ambitions. In turn, there can be little doubt that Russia's policy toward the 'near abroad' served to stimulate ties between the two smaller former Soviet republics. Between 1991 and 1997, Ukraine's relations with Georgia were driven, as one Ukrainian commentator expressed it, 'from the romantic stage to that of concrete pragmatism'.[25]

The closeness of these relations was demonstrated by Ukraine's willingness to become involved in an issue that had poisoned relations between Russia and Georgia soon after the collapse of the Soviet Union, namely Moscow's support for Abkhazian separatists within Georgia. Russia's encouragement of Abkhazian separatism was directly related to Moscow's effort to reduce the growing appeal of Georgia as a transit route for the main Caspian oil. A conflict on Georgian territory close to any proposed pipeline was bound to jeopardise Georgia's chances and could tip the balance in favour of a route across Russia. Tbilisi turned to Kyiv for support. In 1996 ties were formalised in a series of agreements demonstrating the newfound assertiveness of the two states, particularly in Ukraine's support for the Georgian initiative 'For a Peaceful Caucasus' (effectively aimed directly against Russia).[26] However, by 1997 it was clear that a stronger strand was developing to link the two states, and that relations had progressed beyond mere bilateral relations to co-operation in regional developments. Indeed, Ukraine and Georgia started to co-ordinate and co-operate on policy on a number of issues, to the extent that it was difficult to interpret them as *not* aimed against Russia. A good example of this was the fuss made by both parties as to the success of the ferry between Poti and Odesa, which in the words of a Ukrainian newspaper helped 'Georgia break through its geographical blockade' and reduce its reliance on the Russian rail network.[27] More significant was the meeting between Kuchma and Shevardnadze at which Georgia invited Ukrainian peacekeepers in to replace Russian 'peacekeepers' in the Abkhazia conflict once the Russian mandate ran out on 31 March 1998.[28] Russian blunders contributed to the further intensification of ties between Kyiv and Tbilisi. In particular, Ukraine was able to take advantage of Russia's dismissive attitude toward the claims of former republics to their proportional inheritance of the wealth of the USSR following the collapse of the Soviet Union. For example, Russia's rejection of Georgian claims to what Tbilisi regarded as its share of the BSF, anchored at the Georgian ports of Poti and Batumi, contrasted with Kyiv's willingness to act on behalf of Tbilisi in Ukraine's bilateral discussions with Russia on the subject of the BSF. This intervention was interpreted by Tbilisi as a friendly and symbolic gesture on the part of Kyiv. It was indicative of Ukraine's keen appreciation of the need to promote conciliation in the short term if Ukraine was to fulfil its regional leadership potential in the longer term.

Overall, the development of ties between Ukraine and Georgia reflected the coincidence of the respective goals of both states, namely those of counteracting Russian influence and developing independent strands of power that would consolidate their respective independence. Georgian willingness to co-operate with Ukraine was undoubtedly associated, as one journalist in Kyiv expressed it, with the 'expectation that with time Ukraine would inevitably become the leader of the Eastern European region', and by extension serve as a link with Western Europe.[29] Furthermore, the development of ties between Tbilisi and Kyiv bolstered, as we shall see, Ukraine's leadership of the key subregional institution within the CIS, GUUAM, a grouping that was intended to facilitate the transportation of Caspian hydrocarbons across the territory of member states.

Bulgaria

Ukraine's ties with Bulgaria, as a Black Sea littoral state, have not been characterised by either significant affinity or hostility. This is primarily because of the geographical distance between the two and Bulgaria's marginal economic significance in the region. Nevertheless, Bulgaria is a potential competitor in the transportation of Caspian oil. Most of the traffic coming from Iran via Georgia to Europe passes through Burgas in Bulgaria on its way to the West.[30]

Overall, it can be seen that a number of issues either unite or divide Ukraine from its regional neighbours. As a former Soviet state, Ukraine had a natural affinity with Georgia as an ally against Moscow. Both could consolidate their independence by reducing their dependence on Russian energy networks. Furthermore, Ukraine,

Turkey and Georgia are united by a common objective, namely to participate in the transportation of Caspian oil, something which would help them become more tightly integrated with European structures as well as providing welcome income. This ambition put them into direct competition with Russia in an area where it had so long enjoyed a dominant position. In addition to the confrontation with Moscow, Kyiv was also challenged by Bucharest. While formerly Ukraine's status as a Soviet republic protected it from Romanian challenges to its territorial waters, independence elicited a fresh bout of claims, tempered only by wider systemic developments and the prospect of participating in the transportation of Caspian oil. In the following section, the politics surrounding the transportation of the hydrocarbons will be examined in greater detail, since Caspian oil is clearly the key factor in Kyiv's relations with the other Black Sea states.

The politics of transporting Caspian hydrocarbons

Ukraine occupies a location directly between Northern Europe and the oil and gas reserves of the Caspian Sea. By emphasising its position on this diagonal axis, i.e. between Berlin and Baku, as opposed to its more traditionally perceived position between East and West, Kyiv has attempted to take on a role in which it acts not so much as a weak border-land or buffer state but more as a state which can exploit its advantages as a link between a Northern Europe constantly seeking new and reliable energy supplies and the newly rediscovered Transcaucasian hydrocarbon sources.

The plan to transport Caspian oil via Ukraine was part of grander scheme for a transport corridor – in effect a renewal of the 'Silk Road' – put forward by Georgia in 1993. The 'Silk Road' plan had the backing of the European Union and was envisaged as linking Europe with the Caucasus, the Middle East, and eventually the Far East.[31] While such a corridor was ostensibly designed to facilitate trade, at its heart was the trade associated with the transportation of Caspian hydrocarbons. By the second Pan-European Transportation conference, on Crete in 1994, the notion of a Silk Road had become more concrete, with nine transport routes proposed. Of these nine, four traversed Ukraine, with one in particular intended to link up directly with the Caspian region.[32]

It had long been known that the Caspian region was a significant source of hydrocarbons. Although the Soviets had been adept at exploiting the onshore energy resources of Azerbaijan, the sea remained effectively unexplored and offshore resources remained intact because of a lack of deep-sea technology. It was only with the collapse of the Soviet Union that these energy resources became accessible to Western companies. The six different hydrocarbon basins that were discovered under the waters of the Caspian Sea, in addition to those that existed onshore, were estimated to contain between 15 and 29 billion barrels of oil and 236–337 trillion cubic feet of natural gas, though the figures are subject to some disagreement.[33] The key was getting these resources to market and therein lay the opportunity for Ukraine.

There were very practical benefits for Ukraine. For example, Kyiv hoped to bring some desperately needed employment to workers on a much under-utilised pipeline network (extending to some 4,000 kilometres), with six major oil refineries working at far below capacity.[34] Kyiv also anticipated benefiting financially from the transportation of the oil across its territory, in particular, in terms of the lucrative transit fees (estimated at some $300 million per annum) that the oil would generate as it wound its way toward the West. The income would then be used to offset the cost of imported oil.[35]

There were a series of 'strategic' advantages that would accrue to Kyiv if Caspian hydrocarbons were to traverse its territory. Caspian oil represented a way out of a predicament that had proved to be Ukraine's single biggest handicap since the first days of independence. The oil represented a means of reducing Ukraine's almost total reliance on Russian oil (between 1991 and 1998 it was variously estimated that Ukraine imported between 70 and 95 per cent of its oil from Russia).[36] Caspian oil also provided a means of escape from the energy blackmail that Kyiv felt it had been subjected to. Ukraine was highly vulnerable to any Russian moves involving energy – as we have seen Moscow was not averse to stopping or slowing energy flows to Ukraine. Efforts by Kyiv at energy import diversification had been unsuccessful, especially those attempts which involved importing Iranian oil, which in turn brought the opposition of the United States.[37] The alternative energy source provided by Caspian oil provided a means out of this predicament. Finally, there was also a more serious, less immediate, and longer-term practical consideration that Caspian oil would help address: Russian production was expected to fall between 2000 and 2005. As production fell, the Russians were likely to redirect the sale of oil to markets capable of paying in hard foreign currency.[38] In the even longer term, according to Ukrainian sources, Kyiv faced the possibility that in twenty years time, Russian oil could run out altogether.[39] This also in part explains Russia's determination to ensure that Caspian oil traversed its own territory.

In addition to the practical and strategic advantages of transporting Caspian oil, Ukraine hoped to benefit in terms of its subregional and regional objectives. By becoming part of the Caspian transportation network, Ukraine, it was hoped, would become more tightly integrated with and hence increasingly indispensable to the European energy infrastructure.[40] At the subregional level, this could bind Ukraine more tightly to the other states involved in the transportation, particularly Poland. In turn, it was believed in Kyiv that this subregional advantage could confer advantage at the regional level, namely facilitate Ukraine's eventual integration with the European Union and NATO, along the lines described in Chapter 5.

However, for these advantages to be exploited, much depended on the specific route chosen. There were a number of competing routes, some attractive to Kyiv, some less attractive. Each of these three key options will now be examined.

Proposed transit routes

The oil was expected to flow in two different waves: 'early' and 'main' oil. 'Early' oil was planned to flow along the existing Baku–Novorossiysk and Baku–Supsa pipelines at the rate of 100,000 barrels per day respectively. Ukraine could play no role in the transportation of 'early' oil. Of interest to Kyiv was the transportation of the 'main' oil, i.e. the vast quantities believed to lie under the Caspian itself.[41] Ukraine's two main competitors in its proposals for bringing Caspian oil to market were Russia and Turkey. As one commentator has put it, 'for Russian politicians in search of a grand cause, re-establishing the empire and paying for it with Eurasian oil revenues is a winning proposition'.[42] For Turkey, Caspian hydrocarbons were a matter of usurping Russia's traditional regional role, and preventing the 're-establishment of the empire'. The Turkish option suited Kyiv.

Option one: the Russian option

The Russian option consisted of a proposal for a 1,500-kilometre pipeline which would link the Tengiz oil field, on the Kazakh side of the Caspian Sea, with the Black Sea port of Novorossiysk; it would supplement the existing pipeline carrying 'early' oil from Baku to Novorossiysk.[43] The new pipeline was to have an initial capacity of 500,000 barrels per day, rising to 1.34 million per day, and was to be operational by the year 2000.[44] From Novorossiysk, it was proposed that the oil be transported by tanker through the Bosphorus to markets in the West. The plan had some significant drawbacks.

For some time Turkey has been exploiting concern about the growing amounts of oil being transported from Russia's Black Sea ports via the narrow Bosphorus straits on to markets in the West. Despite the collapse of exports in 1991 (in 1990 0.679 MMBD and 0.187 MMBD were exported via Novorossiysk and Tuapse respectively), by 1994 the amounts exported had reached their previous peaks, and by 1997 a total of 1.06 MMBD, some 30 per cent of total Russian oil production, was exported from Russia through the Bosphorus.[45] Ostensibly fearful of the environmental catastrophe that such large exports might cause in the event of a collision in the narrow straits, and much to the consternation of Moscow, Turkey took it upon itself in May 1994 to unilaterally introduce amendments to the 1936 Montreux convention,[46] which regulated the flow of maritime traffic through the Bosphorus.[47] In particular, the Turks announced a 200-metre limit on the size of oil tankers traversing the strait, a major blow to Russian ambitions to transport oil from Novorossiysk, as the enforced use of smaller vessels would drive the costs of transportation up. Furthermore, in the longer term Ankara envisaged that oil tankers would be prohibited from passing through altogether. While the decision was made ostensibly on environmental grounds, it was interpreted by the Russians (and indeed others) as aimed against them, with the objective of reducing their capacity to act as a link in the transit of Caspian oil. The Russian response was to denounce Turkey's right to act unilaterally on the issue, and accuse Ankara of using safety and environmental concerns as a camouflage to disguise its own pipeline initiatives and regional ambitions.[48] Although the Turks subsequently failed to enforce the new measures stringently, the battle lines nevertheless appear to have been drawn.

The Russian option had a second drawback. The United States did not favour a renewed Russian monopoly over energy provision in the region; this will be discussed in more detail below. Moreover, the sheer expense of the Russian pipeline in the context of the abnormally low price of oil meant that by mid 1998, the prospects for the option looked dim.[49]

Option two: the Ukrainian option

The most straightforward option from the point of view of Kyiv, and the least likely to be realised, was transporting oil by tankers from a Georgian port, most probably Supsa, after the arrival of the oil from Baku, to a terminal to be built near Odesa, which would then pump the oil westward.[50] This option was the least likely to be implemented for the simple reason that both Turkey and Russia were competing for the very same oil. Ukraine, without the kind of backing afforded Turkey by the West or the geopolitical weight of Russia, was not in a position to impose its preference. However, Kyiv was willing to combine its proposal with Turkey's. In other words, Ukraine was willing to take its Caspian oil via Samsun on Turkey's northern Black Sea coast, rather than directly from Georgia. The Turkish option and its Ukrainian subset will now be examined.

Option three: the Turkish option(s)

There were two Turkish options: Baku–Samsun in northern Turkey on the Black Sea and Baku–Ceyhan in southern Turkey, on the Mediterranean. From the beginning, the Baku–Samsun route was the less desirable option, as it depended on the narrow and congested Bosphorus to bring the oil to market. As a result, Western interest focused on the Baku–Ceyhan route. This option involved the transportation of oil by a new 1,700-kilometre pipeline from Baku to the port at Ceyhan, on Turkey's Mediterranean south coast.[51] Much of the appeal of the route for the Western multinationals extracting the oil was based on technical aspects that gave it an advantage over the Novorossiysk route. Ceyhan was a modern port with four times the processing capacity of the Russian port. More significantly, the Ceyhan route could utilise 300,000-ton dead-weight tankers, something that lowered the transportation costs dramatically, compared to the Novorossiysk route, which was unable to use such huge tankers – they simply could not squeeze through the Bosphorus. Turkey's unilateral revisions to the Montreux treaty mentioned above, only exacerbated Russia's predicament.

From the point of view of Kyiv, the single biggest disadvantage of the Baku–Ceyhan route was that Ceyhan was too remote. However, Kyiv could benefit from the Baku–Ceyhan option. To do so, it was necessary to overcome the obvious technical obstacle of transporting oil across the harsh terrain of Anatolian Turkey northwards to the port of Samsun, from where the oil could relatively easily be transported across the Black Sea to Ukrainian ports. In apparent anticipation of this problem, as far back as 1993, the Ukrainians suggested the building of a 600-kilometre long, 1,200-millimetre diameter reversible pipeline linking Samsun and Ceyhan via Anatolia. The reversibility of the pipeline was a significant technical feature which reflected both Kyiv's and Ankara's desire to preserve flexibility. A reversible pipeline between Samsun and Ceyhan meant that if the Baku–Samsun route was by any chance chosen, not only would Ukraine get its oil from Samsun, but also the port facilities at Ceyhan could still be utilised after delivery there by the reversible pipeline, the commitment to an ecologically Bosphorus preserved, and the costs of a lengthy new Baku–Ceyhan pipeline avoided. If instead the oil was delivered via the Baku–Ceyhan route, the Ukrainians would still get their oil from Samsun, after its arrival there from Ceyhan via the pipeline. Furthermore, the reversibility of the pipeline also meant that it could take Middle Eastern oil to Europe, something in which some of the Middle East powers had expressed an interest.[52] Pipeline reversibility was a shrewd feature, as it played on concerns in the United States about the dangers of energy and transportation power being concentrated in the hands of Iran by giving Middle Eastern oil an alternative route to the politically vulnerable Strait of Hormuz.[53] The proposed pipeline was also the shortest route between the Caspian Sea and Europe. On his visit to Odesa in May 1997, the Polish president, Alexander Kwasniewski, propagated the notion of a Baltic–Black Sea corridor by emphasising the fact that 'the shortest route from the Near and Far East to Warsaw, Gdansk, Berlin, Hamburg and even Stockholm and London lies through Odesa, Illychivsk and Yuzniy'.[54] It was also, as a result, the cheapest route.[55] However, there was much work to do at the Ukrainian end of things if Kyiv was to become an integral segment of the route.

Since August 1994, Kyiv had planned to take oil from Samsun, irrespective of the means by which it arrived there. More specifically, it was anticipated that oil would be poured into tankers at Samsun and transported to a new oil terminal to be built at Yuzniy, located 35 kilometres to the east of Odesa. The terminal was to have an initial throughput capacity of 12 million tons, expandable to 58 million tons. The total projected cost of the terminal was $216 million, sponsored by UkrNaftoTerm, a Ukrainian state enterprise, with the EBRD guaranteeing a loan for $101 million.[56] A separate state-owned company, UkrTransNafta[57] (Ukrainian Oil Transportation), was created[58] with the specific objective of constructing a 667-kilometre 'Yuzniy' pipeline[59] link between the Yuzniy terminal to the Brody pumping station on the Druzhba oil pipeline in Western Ukraine. From Brody, the 'Yuzniy' pipeline would be extended to the city of Plotsk or the Adamowa Zastava in eastern Poland. This link with Poland was important in the wider context of things, as noted by President Kuchma, who argued that 'One of the most important elements in the creation of a Europe–Caucasus–Asia transport corridor, is the resolution of oil routes. One of these could become the Ukrainian–Polish route'.[60] From Poland, it was planned that the oil could then be dispersed to Slovakia, the Czech Republic, Hungary, Austria, Germany (via the Leuna refinery) and the Baltic Sea region (via Gdansk).

In light of all the above-mentioned advantages of oil going through Ukraine, the Azeri rejection of the Ukrainian option in May 1997 on the grounds that it was not commercially viable was a severe disappointment.[61] The Azeri intervention was understandable. Despite the plethora of benefits that could potentially accrue to Kyiv, the whole enterprise was plagued by extensive procrastination at the Ukrainian end. Progress on the Yuzniy terminal was effectively non-existent between 1993 and 1997, something which had as much to do with clandestine features of Ukrainian domestic politics as anything else, while work on the Yuzniy–Brody pipeline could be best described as dawdling. Events beyond Ukraine were moving at a faster rate.

The Azeri comment elicited a flurry of activity on the part of Kyiv. Soon after, in June 1997, following four years of negotiation, the long-awaited agreement on the building of a pipeline between Ceyhan and Samsun was signed by Kyiv and Ankara.[62] Also, progress was made with the laying of the Yuzniy pipeline in Ukraine: by June 1998 about 256 kilometres had been constructed, rising to 351 kilometres by September 1998, giving some idea of the pace at which work had started to proceed after the very slow start.[63] Nevertheless, plans to have the terminal operational toward the end of 1998 were wildly optimistic, as by the middle of 1998 it was reported that 'there was little news . . . on the ground, where at some forgotten time they managed to put foundations for seven of the ten planned reservoirs, silence reigns'.[64] Much of this has to do with domestic politics in Ukraine, funding shortages (although following the creation of UkrTransNafta in May 1997 this became less of a problem), and even bribes required by minor officials.[65] The leisurely approach that characterised Ukraine's contribution was as much of an impediment to the achievement of Kyiv's objectives as were events beyond its control: by 1998, other factors were working against the Turkish option, and by extension, the Ukrainian segment. First, the Azerbaijan International Oil Consortium (AIOC), the builder of the pipeline, was showing a distinct preference for the cheapest route, something the Baku–Ceyhan route most certainly was not (although the Turks accused BP, the leading member of the consortium, of exaggerating the cost). By late 1998 it was increasingly being argued by the AIOC that, based on the production projections of Azeri oil, the Baku–Ceyhan route was beginning to look commercially unviable. While the route needed to carry 1 million barrels of crude per day to be viable, Azeri oil was expected to peak at about 800,000 barrels per day.[66] By the end of 1998, owing to the Asian economic collapse, oil had reached its lowest price for twenty-five years (though by mid 2000 the situation had changed considerably).[67] As a result, by December 1998, much to the consternation of Kyiv, and contrary to the wishes of the US government, according to *The Economist* the 'prospects for building a . . . pipeline from Baku in Azerbaijan to Ceyhan in Southern Turkey rarely looked so doubtful'.[68] Nevertheless, despite the fact that the US government was prevented from directly subsidising the Turkish option, in January 1999 a US official argued that

> During the past twelve months, companies and regional governments have realised the importance of some broader considerations. These include long-term energy security . . . and the attractiveness of large-diameter pipeline to a port like Ceyhan, which is able to handle exports from both sides of the Caspian . . . [making the] Baku–Ceyhan the optimal route for Caspian oil exports.[69]

Overall, by late 2000, it was still unclear which route was the likeliest option.[70] Baku–Ceyhan, while the preferred choice of the US, still failed to find favour with others on cost and strategic grounds.[71] What was clear, however, was that Ukraine had its own preferred option. The Russian option was likely to damage Ukraine's regional standing, while the Turkish option was likely to reinforce Ukraine's growing regional profile. However, the advantage of oil going via Ukraine into Europe goes much beyond oil – the wider context will be considered in the following chapter.

As, along the Southern azimuth, Ukraine's co-operation with littoral neighbours, particularly Georgia and Turkey, in pursuit of a common strategy in the transportation of oil was inextricably linked to its regional agenda, the theoretical implications of these bilateral and regional objectives will be explored at the end of the following chapter.

7 The Southern azimuth

Subregional and regional integration

From the perspective of Kyiv, Caspian oil was also a means to an end. Kyiv was motivated by something more alluring than the consolidation of Ukrainian independence through ensuring energy supplies and the financial benefits. The transportation of Caspian oil across Ukrainian territory could make the single biggest contribution to Ukraine's eventual integration – a term used somewhat loosely by Ukrainian analysts – with European subregional and, by extension, regional structures.[1] From the Ukrainian point of view, Caspian oil was the fuel that propelled the development of Black Sea subregional institutions. For Kyiv, membership of subregional institutions would raise Ukraine's subregional profile, highlight its geopolitical weight, and in turn attract the kind of international financial resources and political attention Kyiv felt the state was entitled to, help counteract the overweening influence of Russia, and fill the security vacuum that Russian weakness had exposed. These are the objectives which explain Ukraine's desire to play a vigorous and active role in key subregional institutions, the BSEC and G(U)UAM. This section will examine the extent to which Ukraine's role within these institutions has helped Kyiv achieve its objectives.

Subregional institutions in Black Sea politics

BSEC

With the collapse of the Soviet Union, the Black Sea had effectively became a free-for-all region in which, for the first time in decades, there was an opportunity for regional dominance by any state ready to challenge an emasculated Russia. There were two competitors that were realistic contenders for Russia's mantle: Ukraine and Turkey. While Ukraine's relative military might and economic potential put it in contention, it was the weakest of the three – its economic collapse and energy dependence on Russia put paid to any immediate ambitions of single-handed regional leadership. Furthermore, any regional authority Ukraine aspired to was significantly undermined by the dispute over the ownership of the BSF as well as Russia's ongoing claims to Crimea/Sevastopol; any unfavourable resolution of the issues from Ukraine's point of view would reinforce Kyiv's relative weakness in relation to Moscow in the Black Sea. Yet the fact that between 1991 and 1997

Russia was unable to unilaterally impose a settlement regarding the BSF and Crimea/Sevastopol underlined Moscow's waning power and influence, which, in turn, raised Ukraine's profile.

While Ukraine bickered with Russia, Turkey staked its claim. Energised by one of the strongest – a relative term – economies in the region, bolstered by the confidence of membership of NATO and emboldened by the fact that it was an albeit unwelcome contender for European Union membership, Turkey could aspire realistically to regional leadership.

Turkish aspirations to regional dominance were reflected in Ankara's initiative in creating the Black Sea Economic Co-operation Forum (BSEC) in June 1992.[2] While ostensibly the organisation was to facilitate ties between Black Sea states and provide a common regional platform on which member states could voice their views about regional issues, arguably the BSEC was developed as a vehicle via which Turkey could exert its influence. Yet as will be seen, in many respects the co-operation of Kyiv was essential if Ankara was to succeed.

On an economic level, the BSEC was to function as Turkey's tool. This was in line with Ankara's self-perception as the regional economic powerhouse, capable of influencing capital and technology flows to the former Eastern bloc countries, and even acting as the funnel through which any US financial influence spread throughout the region. Admittedly, the 'as and when' of the flow of funds for the regeneration of the region (i.e. the creation of a transportation network in general, and for the transportation of Caspian oil in particular) were uncertain. However, as the West's only ally in the region, that Turkey would be the viaduct through which funds would flow was unquestioned, at least in Ankara. As one Turkish commentator expressed it, 'lacking sufficient resources itself, Turkey persuaded the West to provide financial aid . . . to support Turkey's economic and cultural mission' in a region that extends beyond the Black Sea region.[3] Needless to say, devoid of its own funds, Kyiv welcomed such an input.

Politically, there were determined efforts on the part of both Ankara and Kyiv for the BSEC to take on a more meaningful status. This was shown by their efforts to establish a BSEC parliamentary assembly at a time when Ukraine was vehemently opposing the establishment of an equivalent CIS body because of its implied supranational nature. Turkey had far-reaching political objectives, specifically that of playing 'a strategic role in international politics through co-operation with surrounding countries – Balkan Co-operation in the west, the Economic Co-operation Organisation with Iran and Pakistan in the east, and the BSEC in the north', something which was not necessarily contrary to Ukrainian interests.[4] (Iran and Pakistan were both states with which Ukraine had been cultivating ties. For example, Kyiv had only just been persuaded by Washington not to sell power station turbines to Teheran in 1997. In the same year, the $800 million deal to sell Ukrainian tanks to Islamabad – with prospects of more sales to come – was hailed in Kyiv as the deal of the century.)

The Ukrainians, with the support of the Turks, have been keen to pursue solutions to military–security issues within the framework of the BSEC. Thus Kyiv, encouraged by Ankara, put forward security proposals for the Black Sea region, including banning the offensive capabilities of Black Sea navies, reducing the number of naval exercises in the sea, signing non-aggression treaties between Black Sea states, declaring the inviolability of borders, giving advance notice of naval activities and not admitting members who either utilise their naval forces against other BSEC members or allow the use of their territory by others for aggressive acts. These proposals formed part of a larger strategy adopted by the two states in tandem, namely one aimed at the denuclearisation and demilitarisation of the Black Sea.[5] An increased Turkish and NATO presence in the Black Sea accompanied these initiatives.[6]

Additionally, co-operation between Kyiv and Ankara within the BSEC served 'strategic' objectives – in particular, the marginalisation of Russia, a prerequisite for both Turkey's and Ukraine's regional ambitions. Indeed, the very existence of the BSEC was testimony to the extent to which Russian (and CIS) interests were neglected, and even counteracted. The formation of subregional groupings beyond the CIS, yet including CIS members, was not a welcome development from the point of view of Moscow, as it was clear evidence of a loss of control over a geo-economically attractive region. Yet, in this case, the rationale underlying the formation was explicit: many BSEC states 'depend on outside sources of energy [i.e. Russia]' and were, as a result, 'interested in strengthening long-term interaction with those BSEC countries which possess significant resources of energy for providing sustainable energy supplies'.[7]

The 'strategic' nature of the BSEC is suggested by the sheer political diversity and geographical dispersion of BSEC member states. They include former Soviet states, actual and prospective EU member states, NATO members and non-members, European and non-European states, and indeed Black Sea and non-Black Sea states. The geographical dispersal of member states, a trail spreading from the Balkans to the Transcaucasus, provided strong hints as to the rationale of the organisation as a link between the European Union and the Caspian hydrocarbon resources.[8] Among this diversity, the influence of Russia was heavily diluted.

Above all, the BSEC as a link in the transportation of Caspian oil was expected to facilitate Turkey's entry into the EU and, as Kyiv hoped, contribute to its own closer ties and even eventual integration. Turkey made a great deal of its geopolitical location, arguing that 'without turning its back on the EC, Turkey is also able to develop ties with Central Asia as well as with the Middle East, the Balkans and Western Europe'.[9] As far as Ankara was concerned, there was the potential for a link between the geographical dispersion of members of the BSEC, the issue of the transportation of Caspian oil, and Turkey's eventual integration with the European Union. As has been argued, the 'formation of the BSEC Project . . . can be viewed as a link in this larger European chain'.[10]

However, as was mentioned above, the BSEC served Ukrainian interests equally well in a number of crucial regards. Primarily, membership of the BSEC became yet another means by which Ukraine could demonstrate its pro-Western geopolitical preference and thereby underline its commitment to a 'return to Europe', despite the fact that as the century drew to a close the latter was an increasingly remote prospect at least in institutional terms. Influenced by Turkish rhetoric,

Kyiv also perceived the BSEC as a potential link with the European Union. Other initiatives, such as the signing of an agreement between three BSEC members – Ukraine, Romania and Moldova – on the creation of a free economic zone between Reni (in the Odesa *oblast* of Ukraine), Galac (in Romania) and Dzurdzuleszti (in Moldova) in late 1998, need to be seen in this light.[11] That this was done with an eye on collaboration in the transportation of Caspian oil, on the one hand, and European integration, on the other, was supported by two facts. First, an oil terminal was being built in the Dzurdzuleszti.[12] Second, the Ukrainian–Romanian–Moldovan grouping was based on the Lower Danube Euroregion: there was a desire in Ukraine, as one newspaper expressed it, to 'take advantage of the Caspian transport corridor, to incorporate the Euro-region investors and breath some life into the region'.[13]

Additionally, the BSEC became a device with which Ukraine could demonstrate opposition to any strengthening of the CIS. A good example of this stance was the approach adopted by Ukraine toward the issue of ecological damage in the Black Sea. Ukraine was conspicuous by its absence at a meeting of members of the CIS in Moscow in February 1992 at which participants put their names to an inter-republican agreement on co-operation in the area of ecology. Ukraine also only participated as an observer at a follow-up meeting in Minsk in July 1992, where it was agreed that member states were to fund an inter-state ecological fund at the rate of 0.05 per cent of their GNP. Ukraine's omission from these agreements was all the more surprising in the light of the sheer extent of contamination of the Black Sea.[14] This reluctance to participate in CIS structures was in sharp contrast to Ukraine's willingness to co-operate with Turkey, within the framework of the BSEC, in regard to ecological damage. In particular, the Declaration on Principals and Goals of Relations signed between the two states in fact made explicit reference to both states' desire to co-operate on environmental protection, in line with the first ever BSEC summit declaration, and work toward the creation of an environmental convention. A similar disparity existed between Kyiv's enthusiastic attitude toward the establishment of a BSEC parliamentary assembly and its reluctance to be involved in an equivalent CIS body.[15] In contrast, with Turkey pushing hard for EU membership, and keen to promote a Black Sea zone as one of the means of participating in the integration process in Europe, it was clear to Kyiv that Ukraine's regional objectives were more likely to be promoted by participation in initiatives motivated by Ankara than by backing Moscow's ones.

Overall, while Ukraine was far from dominant within the BSEC, the spoken and unspoken objectives of the institution matched its own. To this extent, the BSEC contributed to the consolidation of Ukraine as a Black Sea power.

GUUAM

At the same time as the BSEC was evolving, another parallel, complementary and also competing grouping was taking shape. GUUAM (an acronym made up of the initials of its member states) started to emerge in 1996 as an informal, non-institutionalised, consultative grouping initially made up of Georgia, Ukraine and Azerbaijan, subsequently joined by Moldova and later still Uzbekistan.[16]

Although the alignment was originally triggered by the shared concerns of states negatively affected by proposals by Russia for revisions to the Conventional Forces in Europe Treaty (Moscow made proposals which would have damaged the existing configuration of forces in the other former Soviet republics to its own benefit), the group came to be consolidated by a number of common features. First, each participant had been affected by separatist tendencies. The fact that these separatist tendencies were the result of a second commonality, namely the direct or indirect interference of Moscow, served only to reinforce the bond. Third, the four states were united by a collective interest in a general transportation corridor between Europe and Asia, and specifically, the transportation of Caspian oil using a pipeline that bypassed Russia. For example, such a pipeline was described by the *Financial Times* as 'the jugular vein for Azerbaijan's oil and its independence from Russia'; it might be added that the belief that what applied to Azerbaijan applied equally to Ukraine, Moldova and Georgia, was widespread.[17] Fourth, in their desire to transport Caspian oil, the states were put into direct confrontation with Russia, which itself had set great store on involvement in the transportation. The four GUAM states were united not only by shared experiences, but also by the desire to diminish Russian influence in their part of the world so that their own interests could prosper. Stimulated by such commonalties, bilateral relations between the four states went from strength to strength, contributing to GUAM's importance as a multilateral formation.

That a new regional formation was in the offing was hinted at by a series of closely packed bilateral and multilateral meetings. In October 1996, a meeting took place between President Kuchma and President Aliyev of Azerbaijan at the Lisbon OSCE conference to discuss, amongst other things, Ukraine's potential role in the transportation of Caspian oil. This meeting was followed by Ukrainian Prime Minister Lazarenko's visit to Tbilisi in November 1996, continuing the theme. Soon after, following a conference in Odesa at the end of 1996, an agreement was signed between Ukraine, Azerbaijan and Georgia to create a transport corridor between Europe and Asia.[18] Coincidentally, in the following days Xavier Solana, the NATO General Secretary, undertook a tour of the Caucasian region.[19] Following the agreement on the transport corridor, Eduard Shevardnadze made a surprise visit to Kyiv on 18 February 1997. While he was ostensibly there to sign a number of minor bilateral agreements, two particular issues were discussed, one of which was the possibility of Ukraine, as was mentioned earlier, displacing Russia as a peace-keeper in Georgia – a hint as to Ukraine's growing significance within GUAM; the other issue was, inevitably, the matter of Caspian hydrocarbons.[20] A week later, Shevardnadze was in Baku, where, motivated by these very same hydro-carbons, a 'strategic' partnership was signed between Georgia and Azerbaijan.[21] The formation of tangible ties between member states represented an intensification of the emerging multilateralism of the region, a process in which Ukraine was heavily involved.[22] The first fruit of such co-operation was the announcement by the Azeris that Georgia had been chosen as the route for the main oil.[23]

This suited Ukraine's interests. First, oil from Supsa or Poti directly to Odesa had become a real possibility. Second, it was evident that Russia was therefore not the route of the main oil. Third, the decision would reinforce ties between Georgia and Ukraine. Georgia was a close ally of Ukraine and would be the automatic choice of Tbilisi if Georgia were to run into trouble with Russia, despite Shevardnadze's reassurance soon after the announcement that 'the project was not meant to impinge on Russian interests'.[24] However, a subsequent assassination attempt on the former Soviet foreign minister in February 1998 (which itself followed a previous attempt in August 1995), in which Russian forces were apparently implicated, testified all too clearly to the fact that Russian interests were to be taken seriously.

Azerbaijan's invitation to Georgia stimulated the efforts of the leaders of GUAM member states to endow it with a more tangible form. Shevardnadze stated that Azeri President Aliyev's visit to Ukraine would strengthen the evolving ties between the states, 'especially bearing in mind that the Ukrainian side is ready for serious co-operation in that direction'.[25] Specifically, 'serious co-operation' meant a more prominent security role for Ukraine. Although the subsequent visit of President Aliyev to Kyiv between 24 and 25 March 1997 focused on the transportation of the Caspian hydrocarbons, Aliyev touched on a far more sensitive issue. Paralleling the request made by Georgia earlier, Aliyev discussed the possible involvement of Ukrainian observers and/or peacekeepers in the Nagorno–Karabakh ethnic conflict.[26] The Georgian/Azeri invitations were indicative of the fact that Ukraine was being offered a more central role than had been anticipated by Kyiv. In response, and cognisant of the implications such a role was likely to have for Ukraine's reputation in the region, Kyiv acquiesced to these requests,[27] a decision which was reiterated after the conference in Baku on oil transportation at the beginning of September 1998.[28] Reflecting the apparent disregard in which Russian opinion was by then held, Russian protests at the intensification of ties were dismissed by Aliyev who argued that 'any such far-fetched protests would have no basis, as Azerbaijan is acting in accordance with its rights as a sovereign state'.[29] A seal was subsequently put on the visit by the signing of a strategic partnership between Ukraine and Azerbaijan, similar to those signed between Azerbaijan and Georgia, and Ukraine and Georgia earlier.[30] GUAM was taking on a tangible form. The fact that this was a structure under the leadership of Kyiv was demonstrated at a meeting of the OSCE in Austria in October 1997, when the Ukrainian ambassador acted as a representative for all the GUAM states. Aware of the dangerous ramifications of these developments for its own regional status, Russia adopted a more subtle stance toward the states of the 'near abroad' in an attempt to reverse the undermining of the CIS: it conceded that Ukrainian peacekeepers were acceptable in the region, albeit under the aegis of the CIS. This, of course, was something Kyiv was vehemently opposed to.[31]

Instead, there was growing talk of co-ordinating GUAM's security policy in the Partnership for Peace framework (specifically in terms of sixteen plus the four GUAM members), first mooted during Kuchma's visit to Georgia in October 1997.[32] Anton Buteyko, the Ukrainian deputy foreign minister, and then acting head of the Department of Foreign Affairs of the GUAM states, complained that 'members of the PfP programme are not giving enough attention to these conflicts, which are slowly smouldering'.[33] Furthermore, the potential security role for GUAM and indeed its prospective institutionalisation, was subsequently reinforced by a proposal to set up a GUAM peacekeeping battalion.[34]

Even more pernicious from Moscow's point of view was the idea which emerged at this time, that Turkey might become a member of GUAM.[35] Any Turkish alliance with GUAM would indicate the creation of an unparalleled alignment of interests of BSEC and GUAM states, unlikely to be looked upon favourably by Moscow. Furthermore, Ankara's participation in GUAM would introduce an East–West dimension, if only by dint of Turkey's membership of NATO and ties with the EU, into the heart of the CIS. Indeed, a hint as to the effects that close co-operation between GUAM and Turkey might have was provided by the conference in September 1998, organised under the auspices of the European Union, to discuss the issue of Europe–Caucasus–Asia transport corridors. While the Ukrainians, Georgians, Azeris and Turks were sufficiently satisfied with proceedings to sign a multilateral agreement on a number of issues pertaining to the creation of a transportation corridor, namely the legal framework, ecological issues, etc., the Russians failed to put their signature to the document, citing the fact that 'the Russian side did not participate in its formulation'.[36]

Russia's presence at the conference was in effect that of an observer, with Moscow unable to influence proceedings. Taking account also the progress made on the development of competing transportation routes, and the closer ties developing between the states that made up GUAM, the conclusion that Russia was effectively marginalised is inescapable. The conference also indicated that the coalition of forces gathered against Russia was not only growing in numbers, but also growing in strength. This was most clearly shown in April 1999, when Georgia, Azerbaijan and Uzbekistan, all reluctant signatories to the CIS Collective Security Treaty, failed to sign a protocol prolonging the validity of the treaty following its expiry on 20 April 1999. Then, in a move steeped in symbolic meaning, on 24 April 1999, during NATO's fiftieth anniversary summit in Washington, Uzbekistan announced that it was joining GUAM. The significance of the event was multifaceted. First, Uzbekistan's effective defection exposed the inadequacy of Moscow's policies in the 'near abroad'. The inability of Moscow to ensure the continuation of the three states' continued participation in the Tashkent treaty was a clear reflection of its deteriorating position. Second, Ukraine's position was reinforced. By exempting themselves from Tashkent treaty commitments, Azerbaijan, Georgia and Uzbekistan sided with Ukraine as a non-participant in the Collective Security Treaty. Third, the fact that the announcement was made in Washington at the NATO summit was the clearest possible indication of the Western orientation that the member states had adopted. Moscow's ambitions for the CIS were publicly rebuffed by the states. The message was reinforced with the pronouncement of their intention to intensify their co-operation with the Partnership for Peace programme, in contrast to Russia's avowed non-participation. After the summit and following the example set by Azerbaijan earlier, Georgia made clear its goal of membership of NATO.

After a period of quiescence, in September 2000 in New York, GUUAM re-emerged onto the international stage with an announcement by the presidents of the member states (other than Uzbekistan, the president of which sent a representative). First, an agreement had been made to initiate negotiations on the creation of a free trade area between member states, something which was highlighted as being in marked contrast to the failure to achieve the same within the CIS. Second, a commitment to visa-free travel between member states was reiterated, again, something which put into sharp relief Moscow's decision in May 2000 to abandon the CIS agreement on visa-free travel. Third, it was expressly hoped that both moves would encourage not only other CIS states to join GUUAM, but also non-CIS states (in particular Romania).[37]

Overall, using its geographical location and geopolitical significance as a fulcrum, Kyiv was able to lever Ukraine into a favourable position with regard to the key states which hoped to be involved in the transportation of Caspian oil, i.e. Turkey, Azerbaijan and Georgia, and by extension into the two key subregional institutions analysed above. As a result, by the end of 1998, Ukraine found itself in a potentially highly advantageous position within the two institutions. Though urging caution, Olcott *et al.* argue that 'it would be wrong . . . to exaggerate the significance or influence of GUUAM' for a plethora of reasons, including the poverty of and competition between member states and Russia's 'hold' over them.[38] However, as we shall see, GUUAM has played an important role, in a wider context, in forwarding Ukraine's goals at the regional level.

Regional institutions in Black Sea politics

The benefits derived from the establishment of strong bilateral ties with Black Sea littoral states and Ukraine's firm entrenchment within the two subregional institutions extended to the regional level. Thanks to tighter bilateral ties and participation in subregional processes, Kyiv could now counteract Russian pressure to become further integrated with the CIS. From the point of view of the Ukrainians, there was a certain geographical inevitability about Ukraine's tighter links with Europe, especially in light of Ukraine's geographical location between Europe and the energy resources of the Middle East and the Caucasus. The eminent Ukrainian analyst, Serhiy Pyrozkov, argued that Ukraine's geographical location would help realise Ukraine's aspirations to get 'more tightly integrated with the countries of the EU and other European international organisations' on '"a vertical level" thus linking northern regions of Europe with *Perednaya* [i.e. the nearest part of] Asia and North Africa'.[39] The following section will examine the western and north-eastern regional dimensions in terms of Ukraine's Black Sea regional policy.

CIS

From the moment of its inception, the CIS failed to function as a post-Soviet institution of the type envisaged by Moscow, especially in terms of integrating Ukraine. On the one hand, the tendency for CIS structures to benefit Moscow repelled Ukraine.[40] So, while the CIS was a framework within which Kyiv participated, Ukraine did so as little more than an observer. The CIS, or Russia for that matter, had little power to enforce either compliance, or indeed insist on full membership for Ukraine. On the other hand, the lure of factors beyond Russia's control, such as investment and income to be derived from transportation of oil, were too great for Kyiv to resist. In pursuit of Western investment and greater freedom from CIS structures, Kyiv took advantage of the strength of the bilateral relations it had built up and its role within the various Black Sea subregional organisations to attempt to undermine the CIS by at least questioning the purpose of its existence. For example, not only were Ukraine and Azerbaijan highly supportive of each other's policy stances within the CIS, they were at the forefront of the growing scepticism about the effectiveness of the institution, its future, and the need for a replacement.[41] Indeed, driven by the belief that the CIS was designed to serve the needs of Moscow, they questioned its very purpose. Thus, any challenges by Ukraine to Russia's all-pervading authority within the CIS through the formation of strategic alliances with other post-Soviet states was deemed by commentators in Kyiv to be treading on dangerous territory as it was believed that 'such strategic collaboration, if it is to be without consequences, was only possible with one member of the CIS', i.e. Russia: apparently 'the very thought of such partnerships was even more painful than the fact of their existence'.[42] By precluding the development of ties beyond the 'one member of CIS', Russia was precisely trying to prevent the evolution of a structure such as GUUAM. Yet develop it did. As has been discussed, the signing of bilateral 'strategic' ties between Georgia, Ukraine and Azerbaijan and the tangible framework which began to grow up around GUUAM suggested that a creeping deterioration was taking place within the CIS. Indeed, with time the GUUAM states became highly co-ordinated in terms of their stance on and within the CIS, to the detriment of its functioning. Such co-ordinated moves were of course interpreted by Russia as anti-Russian in nature, but Moscow's essential helplessness was amply demonstrated by its response, which was described by a Ukrainian newspaper as 'nothing more than a stream of abuse'.[43]

The role of Ukraine within GUUAM was of course intended to have far-reaching implications for the CIS and Russia's role within it. First, it has been argued that Ukraine used GUUAM as a vehicle to replace Russia as a leader of states within the CIS.[44] Ukraine was the only country within the CIS capable of at least partially counteracting the effects of Russian influence in the Caucasus. When member GUUAM states Georgia and Azerbaijan invited the Ukrainians to participate in peacekeeping activities, it was to supplant Moscow's forces not to complement them. With this invitation, the extent to which Russia's traditional role as regional leader had been eroded was made plain. Furthermore, in light of the fact that the entire rationale underlying the proposals for a GUUAM battalion, mentioned above, was the protection of the Georgian segment of the pipeline, it was clear that with Kyiv's input, Moscow's all important ace – its monopoly over energy supplies – was in danger of being neutralised by GUUAM.[45] It was growing increasingly true in the words of a Ukrainian newspaper that 'Russia has no friends on the Black Sea, especially after the fall of the communists in Bulgaria'.[46] Second, with

Ukraine's involvement, the potential of GUUAM to provide an alternative to the CIS as a post-Soviet institution linking regional members was real. Ukraine's relative military, political and economic weight conferred on GUUAM some gravitas with which to provide competition to the CIS as a forum for a group of post-Soviet states. Furthermore, while the CIS was perceived as the tool of Moscow in pursuit of the re-animation of its empire, GUUAM was a forum set up in the interests of its member states. The same could not be said of the CIS.

In sum, the encroachment of BSEC onto previously sacrosanct territory and the evolution of GUUAM, a non-cooperative subregional grouping within the CIS, was a painful experience for Moscow. Moreover, as will now be seen, Moscow's predicament was compounded by the fact that Western actors were encroaching on the 'near abroad'. However, to Kyiv's consternation, not only did Ukraine remain something of a bystander in these developments, its efforts at the subregional level brought it few tangible benefits.

NATO and the EU

With the collapse of the Soviet Union, Western actors inevitably became more involved in Russia's 'near abroad'. For example, as the extent of Russia's inability to affect Caspian developments, especially decisions regarding transportation routes, was becoming clear at the beginning of 1997, Xavier Solana, General Secretary of NATO, visited Moldova and afterwards the Caucasian region. Soon after, representatives of NATO and the ex-Soviet Central Asian republics gathered in Kyrgyzstan to discuss the possibility of co-operation.[47] Despite the symbolic nature of these events, the fact that these visits took place around the time that Aslan Maskhadov was sworn in as Chechnya's president was an unwelcome confluence of events in the eyes of the Russian leadership. More seriously from the point of view of Moscow, was that in that same year invitations were issued to Poland, Hungary and the Czech Republic to apply for NATO membership.[48] Soon after these events, Ukraine consolidated its reputation as one of the most enthusiastic participants in the Partnership for Peace programme by staging the 'Sea Breeze' NATO manoeuvres in the Black Sea, and signing a charter with the transatlantic alliance in mid 1997. Ukraine's willingness to get involved in Georgia's problem with Abkhazia by agreeing to send peacekeepers there, within the framework of the PfP, further demonstrated the confidence Kyiv had in the Western alliance.[49] However, despite the flourishing ties between GUUAM states, the option of oil crossing Ukraine on its way to Europe was deemed as flawed by the United States and was, as a result, rejected by an American official who scoffed that 'we don't see them [i.e. non-Baku–Ceyhan routes] as practical and we don't see who would finance them. Baku–Ceyhan is the way to go'.[50] There were a number of reasons for this rejection of alternatives. Even eight years after independence, Ukraine's destiny was far from certain. Three possible scenarios involving Ukraine can be envisaged. The first scenario envisages that if Ukraine's relations with Russia were to remain those of an independent sovereign state, the choice of the Ukrainian route would be more than justified, as it was the shortest and also the most cost effective.

The second scenario suggests that any need for US/NATO involvement to protect the pipeline in the event of a conflict between Ukraine and Russia was a considerably less appealing option than that requiring involvement in the event of Kurdish insurrection should the Turkish route be chosen.[51] The third scenario suggests that if Kyiv's relations with Moscow were to revert back to their former Soviet-era status the entire rationale for selecting the Ukrainian route, i.e. a reduction in the Russian monopoly on energy provision, would become undermined. The odds for US support for a Ukrainian pipeline were not good.

In contrast, Turkey, a NATO member, has been sponsored by the USA in its efforts to ensure that Caspian oil traverses Turkish territory. The institutionalisation of US interest in the region took the form of the project referred to in 'The 1997 Law on the Silk Road Strategy'.[52] At the root of policy, devised by the Senatorial Committee on International Relations, under the guidance of a sub-committee on Western and Southern Asian Affairs, was a desire to marginalise the influence of Iran in a profoundly Islamic region, parts of which, such as Afghanistan, were succumbing to Islamic fundamentalism.[53] Behind this policy was the objective of keeping Caspian oil reserves and its transportation out of Iranian control, and within the influence and control of the Western world. The Turkish/NATO route was the key means by which Washington could control the flow of Caspian oil and hang onto the power that went with it, notwithstanding Turkish efforts to build stronger bonds with Iran and other Muslim states. Such a route would also bolster Turkey's role in NATO.[54]

According to some sources, 'the political decision in favour of the route from Baku to Ceyhan on Turkey's Mediterranean coast was made some time ago, and in late 1998 was reconfirmed in the Ankara Declaration, signed by the US energy secretary, and the presidents of Azerbaijan, Turkey, Georgia, Kazakhstan and Uzbekistan', though this was subject to the approval of the Azerbaijan International Oil Consortium (AIOC), which was paying for the pipeline.[55] Although USA support for the Baku–Ceyhan pipeline was holding firm by late 1998, the route was losing its appeal, ostensibly on ground of cost.[56] For political reasons, the USA could not offer direct financial support to build the Baku–Ceyhan route; nevertheless Washington was behind the array of incentives laid down before the AIOC, the main builders of the pipeline.[57]

Ties between Ukraine and the European Union on Black Sea issues were quite tenuous. The $101 million loan the EBRD was prepared to make the Ukrainians for the building of the terminal at Yuzniy was significant though primarily symbolic,[58] as was the visit of Peter Schuterle, the General Secretary of the European Energy Charter, to examine the building of the Odesa–Brody pipeline in the middle of 1998.[59] Similarly, the EU has been linked to the activities of GUUAM by a very thin strand, the most obvious example of which was the fact that the September 1998 Baku conference on the Caspian transport corridor was organised under the auspices of the European Commission.

Despite Turkey's ambition that the BSEC serve as an institution that might complement the EU and, so Ankara hopes, reinforce the chances of Turkey's entry into the EU, ties between the two organisations have yet to take on a tangible form.

So far, relations extend to the fact that Greece, an EU member, belongs to the BSEC. In turn, the EBRD has shown some interest in supporting the creation of a Black Sea Trade and Development Bank, with headquarters in Thessalonica in Greece, in other words, within the orbit of the EU.[60]

By the end of 2000 it was still unclear via which route the hydrocarbons were going to be transported. Despite the price of oil surging throughout 2000, thereby making Baku–Ceyhan a more viable alternative, the option has been labelled a 'strategic and economic disaster' for the US.[61] In light of the agreement signed in October 2000 between the EU and Russia for the latter to increase by as much as 100 per cent its hydrocarbon supplies to the former, preferably by a route bypassing Ukraine and marginalising it yet further, the Baku–Ceyhan route was becoming a urgent necessity rather than a luxury for Ukraine's future energy security.[62]

Conclusion to Part IV

The Southern azimuth was of critical importance to Ukraine: it was a potential link to the West and at the same time an avenue along which it could undermine Russia's energy hold over it. Yet it is clear that such objectives were over-ambitious in light of Ukraine's limited capacity to impose its will. First, Ukraine was far from the key player in the region. Both Turkey and Russia were the chief competitors in the battle for transporting Caspian oil and ensuring any pipeline traversed its territory. Ukraine was always going to be placed third in such a competition. Second, Ukraine did not have the wherewithal to entice any of the consortia to build a key pipeline across its territory. The best it could offer was an adjunct to the Turkish option. Third, Ukraine's competitors offered more appealing alternatives for economic and geopolitical reasons. Fourth, Ukraine did not have the support of the US in regard to the transportation of Caspian oil, although it could benefit from Washington's support for the Baku–Ceyhan option.

Yet the Southern azimuth was a source of success especially in terms of the achievement of objectives along the North-eastern azimuth. The establishment of bilateral ties with Black Sea neighbours was a contributing factor to the evolution of subregional institutions, in particular GUUAM. Although this has been dismissed as a talking shop, such a view misreads the significance of the emergence and subsequent growth of the institution. The very fact that such a body developed within the CIS, and was made up of CIS member states, demonstrates not only the inadequacy of the Commonwealth as an integrating body, and the willingness of its members to search for an alternative institution that is more customised to their group needs, but above all the relative weakness of the Commonwealth. In addition, GUUAM facilitated Ukraine in its goal of avoiding further integration within the CIS. The Southern azimuth at least in part contributed to Ukraine's success in avoiding too close ties along the North-eastern azimuth.

However, Ukraine's efforts along the Southern azimuth failed to facilitate the achievement of goals along the Western azimuth. Kyiv's focus on energy transportation and hopeful references to Ukraine's geopolitical significance to Europe, that is its location between Northern Europe and the energy resources of the Caucasus and Middle East, was not misconceived. But Ukraine failed to achieve these over-optimistic goals and fulfil the latent potential of its geopolitical location, and instead exposed its relative political and economic weaknesses and its inability to recognise that EU membership necessitates above all institutional change, reform, economic planning, and the eradication of corruption.

In theoretical terms, Southern azimuth subregional and regional developments pose some interesting challenges to theories of regionalism, while at the same time offer support for some often-stated claims. For example, it is evident that Ukraine's pursuit of Black Sea alliances, especially its key contribution to the creation and maintenance of GUUAM, testified to Ukraine's willingness to balance Russia, albeit tentatively, despite protestations by Kyiv to the contrary. In realist terms, Russia, as a declining hegemon, elicited an alliance-forming response on the part of former underlings. Furthermore, because 'for Russia, the Commonwealth was the institutional framework for continued hegemony over the former Soviet regions', the creation of a subregional alliance by the GUUAM states was a means of undermining Russian efforts to re-create this hegemony.[63] Along the Southern azimuth, the formation of subregional alliances was indeed the response of weak states in the 'near abroad' of the strong.

Similarly, the ever-denser network of political, economic and even military co-operation that characterised the development of GUUAM, despite predictions of its imminent demise, endorses the neoliberal institutionalist explanation of regionalism. However, as a theory which suggests that institutions are collective solutions to problems which emanate from increasing interdependence (an interdependence which grew as the GUUAM states adopted a more-or-less common strategy in pursuit of energy independence from Russia), along the Southern azimuth neoliberal institutionalism struggles to provide a plausible explanation for the growth of interdependence where there was a dearth of interdependence to start with.

However, subregional developments along the Southern azimuth pose interesting questions for 'subregional regionalism'. First, Southern subregional institutions were qualitatively different from Western subregional institutions and therefore it is difficult to talk about a generic subregional institution, as subregional theorists are prone to. Compared to Visegrad/ CEFTA, the BSEC, for example, was 'more likely to have longer-term roles because [it] include[s] former Soviet states, above all Russia, unlikely to join NATO or the EU'.[64] (This likely longevity applies equally to GUUAM, which has over time become increasingly institutionalised.) This difference highlights the transitory nature of subregional institutions along the Western azimuth, which had an altogether different brief to Southern institutions in terms of function, scope and long-term institutional objectives. (In a similar vein, as will become evident, it is difficult to talk about a generic subregional institution along the Southern azimuth. The BSEC and GUUAM also differ extensively on these same criteria.)

Second, Southern subregional institutions were affected by different flaws to those affecting Western subregional institutions. The membership of the BSEC in particular was more extensive, considerably more heterogeneous, and overall (probably) more pauperised that was CEFTA/Visegrad, something which considerably limited the scope of what it was able to achieve.[65] Arguably, the BSEC, as does GUUAM, also lacks some of the prerequisites for a successful subregional institution identified by subregional regionalists, such as a common historic sense or identity.[66]

Third, the BSEC was less institutionally focused than was either Visegrad or CEFTA. For example, in contrast to Russia,

> Bulgaria and Romania view the BSEC largely from a political point of view: as a complementary and helpful instrument for their future integration into European institutions. . . . A similar approach is taken by Ukraine. Membership of the BSEC corresponds to Ukraine's general approach of gradual integration into Europe using *inter alia* the possibilities offered by subregional groups. Consequently, Kyiv also considers the BSEC a necessary component of European integration.[67]

The discrepancy between member states on their view of the purpose of a particular subregional institution could only but impact on what that institution was able to achieve. In this regard, the coincidence of views as to the purpose of CEFTA (i.e. harmonisation of rules, regulations, laws and policies between member states and with those of the EU in pursuit of membership of the latter), for example, contrasts sharply with the BSEC which served the very different needs of member states.

Above all, Southern-tier subregional institutions struggled for support from regional institutions, one of the prerequisites for successful subregionalism, demonstrating once again the extent to which subregional regionalism, to be successful, needs to be 'sponsored' by a regional institution. As has been noted, 'subregions and subregional arrangements that are geographically distant from "richer" co-operation arrangements, such as the EU, are obviously in a more difficult situation'.[68] For example, the BSEC was at best 'encouraged' by symbolic gestures, and at worst, cold-shouldered by the EU.[69] GUUAM was an institutional orphan regarding western and north-eastern regional institutions: NATO and the EU kept it well and truly at arms length, despite the ambitions of some of the former Soviet republics for closer ties if not membership of the latter two. The CIS was downright hostile towards it. Somewhat ironically, GUUAM has continued to evolve despite this lack of support. Realists rather than subregional regionalists provide a clearer explanation as to why this is so.

Despite the ostensibly economic focus of the BSEC, impediments to the development of the institution have been created by 'political tensions' within the region, highlighting once more the importance of the link made by New Wave regionalists between economics and politics.[70] As a result of these tensions, although moves have been made toward a BSEC common energy market, the 'BSEC still lacks a clear priority or unifying core for its activities (for example, a free trade agreement or a customs union)'.[71] As has been noted, 'economic development – international investment, pipeline construction, and the rebuilding of infrastructure

– will not be free to follow its own non-zero-sum logic until fundamental political problems have been resolved'.[72] In contrast, with the political underpinnings in place, the economic dimension of the ostensibly political GUUAM appears to be growing, as evidenced by the proposal for a free trade area between member states.

8 Conclusion

In 1991, following the proclamation of independence, Ukraine found itself facing an unforeseen opportunity – the chance to reorient its primary geopolitical and geoeconomic ties from East to West. A decision to reorient from East to West was not as straightforward as might have been expected by observers at both 'ends' of the continent. Russia had for centuries been a friendly, even 'brotherly', state. Notwithstanding the sometimes enforced linguistic and cultural Russification of Ukraine, the two states did not share a history besmirched by mutually inflicted atrocities, as was the case, for example, between Ukraine and Poland. On the contrary, Ukrainians and Russians shared a collective history of hardship and misfortune, whether that be the costs of industrialisation and collectivisation or the demographic losses which were the price of victory for the USSR in the Second World War. In a great many respects, there was more linking than separating the two states: the choice for Ukraine of remaining oriented toward the 'East' might have seemed self-evident and the obvious one to make.

The fact that this choice was not made was highly indicative of the profoundly changed geopolitical context Ukraine found itself in. First, it was unclear to Kyiv when again it was likely to find itself in a position of autonomously deciding on its own geopolitical fate. This was an opportunity seemingly too good to miss, especially in the light of the fact that ties with Russia had turned Ukraine into very much of a backwater. Second, by 1991, economic power had seemingly displaced military power, and Europe represented one of the three poles of economic power in the world, along with Japan and the USA. Furthermore, the West's victory in the Cold War was comprehensive: it was moral, economic, social, political and technological. The East's defeat was total: moral bankruptcy, economic collapse, military decrepitude, political civil war and social breakdown. Thus the West was a lure for Ukraine with which the East simply could not compete, other than on emotional, social and historical terms. Because the ties of loyalty to Moscow of decision-makers in Kyiv were by 1991 so stretched by the prosperity that the West offered, the dilemma of choosing to reorient Ukraine from East to West was not as great as Moscow might have expected, or as Brussels might at times have wished. It hardly needed an economist to calculate that for Ukraine modernity and thus the future lay in the West, while backwardness and retardation awaited in the East.

However, the Western azimuth was not immediately accessible to Ukraine. That is, it was an option, but only up to an all too limited point. There were at least two reasons for this. First, Russia, the vanquished, was hardly likely to 'let Ukraine go' without a fight or some opposition. There is little doubt that Russia would be prepared to go a long way to prevent such a reorientation, at the very least by exploiting Ukraine's economic dependence on it. The second problem facing Ukraine in the implementation of a decision to turn westward was that few in the West were really prepared to countenance Ukrainian membership of its key institutions. Furthermore, Europe was not willing to side with Ukraine if it were forced to make a choice between Ukraine and Russia. Russia was the preferred partner for Europe. This book has explored how Ukraine came to terms with this predicament.

The North-eastern azimuth

In the early days of independence, Ukraine was above all motivated by a desire to avoid any form of reintegration into the post-Soviet space. Indeed, the greater the pressure emanating from Russia on Ukraine to reintegrate, the more resistant did Kyiv become. Russia's motivation to bring about this reintegration was powerful: the deeply interwoven ideological, economic, political, ethnic and military ties were such that Moscow was unlikely to have too much difficulty in mobilising its forces to bring about a desired outcome, or so Kyiv believed. Thus the outcome predicted by hegemonic stability theory, namely, that Russia – the hegemon – was perceived as willing, if not actually able, to impose its version of security and stability on the region, was confirmed. At least up until 1994, Russia remained the hegemon, albeit a declining one, which strained to maintain its pre-eminent position in the regional power play, especially in terms of its 'hold' over Ukraine. It is the fear of Russian hegemony which explains Ukraine's somewhat crude efforts in 1992/3 to establish what it promoted as a collective security system verging on a collective defence in the middle of Europe, but which Moscow perceived as efforts to balance against it. It is precisely because of these perceptions that the efforts failed.

Efforts by Russia and Belarus to promote the highest levels of co-operation with Ukraine, namely its integration into the CIS, met with very limited success, notwithstanding the 1999 decision of the Ukrainian parliament to join the CIS Interparliamentary Assembly. The move by parliament to join a CIS institution was a stark and sudden reminder to pro-Western President Kuchma that there was a domestic constituency in Ukraine that did not necessarily share the geopolitical ambitions of the foreign policy elite in Kyiv. Nevertheless, as of March 2000, Ukraine remains beyond most key CIS institutions: it is not a signatory to the CIS Charter, or a member of the Economic Union.

Yet in the light of the sheer number of ties linking Ukraine with Russia and the post-Soviet region – trade flows, financial interests, ethnic ties – the ability of Kyiv to remain beyond the hegemonic pull of Russia is all the more surprising. To all intents and purposes Ukraine's involvement in the RSC along the North-eastern azimuth remains highly circumscribed in anything other than economic terms.

The Western azimuth

In the early days following independence, Ukraine pursued the creation of a subregional Central European collective security system. The fact that a collective security system was construed by potential participant states as well as by Russia as an effort to balance ('power balancing power', in the terminology of Lake *et al.*) against the latter put paid to these efforts.[1] However, partial regional success for Ukraine in participating in emerging collective security management was achieved with the attainment of stronger ties with NATO, primarily through PfP, something which reflected the changing nature of NATO as a security structure. After joining the PfP in 1994, Ukraine became a willing if only peripheral contributor to an emerging collective security system along the Western azimuth. Even the Kosovo crisis in 1999, which so badly disrupted the uneasy peace between Russia and NATO, leading to Moscow's temporary withdrawal from the PfP, did little to damage Ukraine's relations with NATO. Despite the fact that the Ukrainian parliament appeared to be virtually unanimously outraged by developments in Kosovo, the presidential administration continued to pledge its wholehearted support to continued co-operation with NATO within the framework of the PfP, a notable tribute to the strength of the ties which had developed between Kyiv and Brussels. This emerging security relationship served as an impetus for Kyiv to pursue economic and political integration along the Western azimuth.

The first stage towards the 'strategic objective' of integration with the EU, announced in 1996 by President Kuchma, was integration with subregional institutions along the Western azimuth. The desire to integrate with subregional institutions reflects Ukraine's recognition that key regional goals, i.e. EU membership and even closer ties with NATO, were effectively unattainable in the short term. Kyiv was convinced that not only would membership of subregional institutions prevent Ukraine from becoming isolated 'between East and West', but would also facilitate Ukraine's integration into regional structures. In the absence of viable alternatives, Ukraine was by 1994 intent on joining CEFTA, despite the growing obsolescence of the latter as many of its member states drew ever closer to the EU. Ukraine's continued failure to integrate with CEFTA, a stepping-stone along the way toward the key regional institution – the EU – must thus be seen as a major failure of Ukraine's regional policy. However, Kyiv's inability to form closer ties with the EU is an even greater failure. The signing of a partnership and co-operation agreement with the EU in 1994 remains the only real milestone in relations between the EU and Ukraine. The fact remains that Ukraine has overestimated its geopolitical importance in the region, and singularly failed to implement the economic and political reforms that are at the root of successful integration into the Western bloc and which are a prerequisite for Ukraine's entry into the EU. Indeed, rather than progress along the road of reform, Ukraine has actually made a number of retrograde steps in the last few years. As a result, Ukraine is even more distant from its strategic goal of integration with the EU in 2001 than it was in 1996.

However, another explanation for this failure is that Ukraine's objectives at the subregional level were hindered by neighbours along the Western azimuth, because of their own regional objectives. Indeed, regional level developments actively damaged subregional level developments because of the belief held by individual states that participation in subregional developments was likely to inhibit their own individual chances of membership of regional institutions. Thus fearful of being locked out of NATO integration and EU enlargement, CEES effectively cold-shouldered Ukraine along the Western azimuth, at least until 1994. There is certainly no evidence to suggest that Western institutions in any way encouraged the inclusion of Ukraine into subregional structures up until 1994, something which they could have easily be done with little added burden to themselves. After 1994, things changed somewhat, but then only with regard to NATO in that enlargement encouraged Poland to 'think regionally' and try and bring Ukraine in 'out of the cold' and avoid leaving it isolated. However, the opposite is true when it comes to the EU. As the CEES moved ever closer to EU membership, Ukraine became ever more marginalised on the EU's future eastern border.

The Southern azimuth

The regional order pursued by Ukraine along the Southern azimuth is inextricably linked to objectives along the North-eastern and Western azimuths. In particular, Southern azimuth objectives were pursued to the extent that they facilitated Ukraine's integration with the West, and hindered its integration, or prevented Ukraine from being too drawn into the hegemonic regional order of the North-east. For example, Kyiv hoped that ties with Turkey, the key BSEC state, would help integrate Ukraine into the BSEC more tightly. There are two key reasons that explain Ukraine's enthusiastic participation in the BSEC. First, the institution helped temper Russian influence in the region. This was because the co-operation between BSEC member states, led by an assertive Turkey and not an emasculated Russia, hinted at shared concerns for the soft security of the region, concerns which were not dominated by Russian priorities. Anything which tempered Moscow's ambitions was welcome in Kyiv. Second, Kyiv hoped that the BSEC might influence the route of the flows of Caspian oil westward, and hence reduce Ukraine's energy dependence on Russia. The diminished influence of Russia in conjunction with a new-found assertiveness on the part of Black Sea littoral states suggested the emergence of a collective security management approach, although the BSEC remains constrained by its limited financial clout.

If the BSEC merely *implies* confrontation between Ukraine and Russia, GUUAM is a different proposition; the objectives of GUUAM appear to be much more blatant. GUUAM can perceived as a limited and somewhat desperate attempt at power-restraining power, or balancing against Russia. 'Ganging up' against Russia for protection was one of the few means available for regional actors to pursue a common objective while limiting the interference of the regional hegemon.

However, the underlying regional objectives of GUUAM member states hint at an attempt at collective security management. The fact that member states were prepared to form a battalion, albeit under Ukrainian leadership, seeking ties with NATO, supports the contention that GUUAM has taken on collective security ambitions. It could also be seen as bandwagoning with NATO – after all, one of the goals of these ambitions was identical to that of the US, namely to determine the direction of Caspian energy flows in favour of the main member state's interests, which were antagonistic to those of Russia. The fact that GUUAM has also proposed a battalion to function under the aegis of NATO supports this contention.

GUUAM can thus be perceived as an anti-hegemonic, anti-Russian, anti-CIS phenomenon, and hence an anti-integrationist reaction to events along the North-eastern azimuth. Joining forces with other former Soviet republics was a means for Ukraine and other former Soviet republics to alleviate some of the pressures exerted on them by Moscow. The growth of trade ties and military co-operation between CIS non-Russian member states was evidence of the waning power of Russia to influence bilateral and subregional developments in its 'near abroad'. These subregional processes, especially the development of GUUAM, were not welcome by Russia. GUUAM was useful in impeding the attainment of CIS objectives, if only to pursue its own. The development of GUUAM within the CIS is from Moscow's perspective a pernicious development. *If* GUUAM states were to combine to produce a battalion, *if* Turkey was to become a member of GUUAM, as has been mooted, and *if* any of these events were to take place with the framework of the Partnership for Peace programme, the CIS as an integrative body would have sustained a meaningful blow, and GUUAM would have taken on the distinct shape of a collective security structure with links to a larger one, something which may even resemble bandwagoning. Whether or not these perspectives are exaggerated only time will tell. However, the decision in September 2000 for the member states to push for the institutionalisation of GUUAM, reiterating in the process their common interests and objectives, suggests that the options for GUUAM are far from exhausted.[2]

Nevertheless, the Southern azimuth remains one of little more than hope for Kyiv. By the end of 1999, there was little likelihood that Ukraine was going to become an indispensable part of the energy conduit taking energy resources westward, despite its prominence in GUUAM and willing participation in BSEC.

Theoretical implications

Systemic-level theories of regionalism

Realism and neorealism

As far as the North-eastern azimuth was concerned, Kyiv's prime preoccupation was with how a spurned Russia would respond to Ukraine's independence in 1991. Its second concern was with Russia's response to Ukraine's subsequent full-blown military and political, though not economic, de-integration from former Soviet structures. As the process of de-integration gained momentum, the world stood helplessly by while a political vacuum prevailed on the territory of the former Soviet Union. Ukraine's initial concerns were purely realist in their nature – a military response on the part of Moscow, while unlikely, was not ruled out by Kyiv.

As a result, in the first days of independence the policies adopted by Ukraine were those of a classic self-help state: a commitment to fully independent military forces. Ukraine's decision to nationalise the Soviet forces on its territory (other than strategic military forces) was thus a dramatic step congruent with that predicted by neorealist theory – although it was potentially highly destabilising, Kyiv's recourse to such action spoke volumes about the vulnerability Ukraine felt. In this instance, survival rather than power was the priority in Kyiv, as Waltz might have postulated.[3]

From a theoretical point of view there was, however, one key anomaly in Ukraine's post-independence behaviour. This related to Kyiv's willingness to adhere to its earlier commitment to denuclearise and start decommissioning its nuclear weapons. This was anomalous as the decision went against the grain of one of the main tenets of realist theory, namely the pursuit of self-help by states. However, the fact that the commitment to denuclearise was later reneged on as the international scene became more hostile to Ukraine only apparently supports the realist perspective. In practice, a bankrupt Ukraine wanted to retrospectively make money from the weapons after realising that it had committed itself to giving away a valuable commodity.

Although a Russian military threat failed to materialise, an economic and political offensive nevertheless ensued: by taking advantage of Ukrainian economic dependence on Russia, and on the CIS in general, Moscow strove to undermine Ukraine's independence and drive it ever more deeply into the CIS and into continued dependence on itself. Had Russia been successful, the Ukrainians themselves argue that that would have condemned Ukraine to 'vegetate in the backyard of history'.

It is argued by realists that the economic objectives underlying regional integration do not derive from the pursuit of welfare, but rather from the close relationship between political power and economic wealth.[4] From a Ukrainian perspective, Russia and the CIS were hardly associated with economic wealth, and by extension political power. Thus, regional integration along the North-eastern azimuth was not the preferred option – it was the wrong way to go. The fact that Ukraine's economic objectives lay in the West rather than the North-east strongly suggested that Ukraine sought the benefits that derive from economic wealth and political power. Ukraine's adaptation to the international environment, and its pursuit of security, required that it gain the economic and technological advantage conferred by subregional and regional integration with the West.

Ukraine's search for security in Western and Southern subregional alliances, some of which were suggested on Kyiv's initiative, bolsters the realist view that the formation of alliances is a natural form of self-help: balancing against perceived foes is one of the few options available for weak states in the presence of stronger foes. The ambition to create or participate in a subregional security structure, which included CEES and conspicuously excluded Russia, was an explicit demonstration of this point. Yet the effort to balance with CEES against Russia (especially the Baltic–Black Sea Security Zone) was an abject failure. Furthermore, the theory says little about the pursuit of membership of *non-security* subregional institution along the Western azimuth: membership of CEFTA was pursued with greater vigour than was membership of earlier security-based institutions (e.g. NATO-*bis* or Zone of Stability and Security).

Objectives along the Southern azimuth were an inherent part of Ukraine's strategy of integration with the Western azimuth: by attempting to become part of the energy transportation network, Ukraine hoped to become indispensable to Europe's energy needs. Supporting realist theory is the fact that relations along the Southern azimuth were also intended as a means of escaping the direct pressure coming from Russia: Black Sea alliances, co-operation in the creation of transportation corridors and participation in peacekeeping duties in the Caucasus all sent clear messages to Moscow that it could no longer simply dictate affairs to its former underlings. Specifically, the emergence of GUUAM hints at the readiness of former Soviet republics to balance, even if only tentatively, against Russia. In sum, the pursuit of both harmonious bilateral relations and membership of subregional institutions along the Western and Southern azimuths testifies to a willingness on the part of Kyiv to balance Russia.

Realists also argue that hegemons stimulate the formation of regions.[5] While Russia was clearly willing to contribute to the creation of a regional security grouping along the North-eastern azimuth, it nevertheless failed to successfully establish such a regime fully involving Ukraine – the latter was not willing to bandwagon with Russia. While Ukrainian perceptions were such that Kyiv saw Russia as a hegemon, it is also possible to conceptualise Russia as a declining hegemon, seeking actors with whom burdens could be shared, thanks to whom policies would be legitimised, and through whom actions would be internationalised in pursuit of self-interest. However, despite Moscow's willingness – as a declining hegemon – to take on the burden of regime formation, Kyiv was an extremely reluctant participant in the CIS, unwilling to trade the economic benefits for the political costs. Ukraine was simply unwilling to undertake the role of helping manage the decline of Russia: Kyiv was too suspicious of Moscow's motives to risk its sovereignty. Instead of successfully drawing Ukraine more deeply into the CIS, Moscow in fact elicited a counter-response on the part of Kyiv: the latter actively started to form or participate in subregional and regional groupings along its Western and Southern azimuths as a response to the perceived military and later economic threat emanating from Russia. Russia the hegemon elicited an inclination to alliance formation on the part of former Soviet republics. There is no evidence to suggest that Ukraine's albeit limited participation in the CIS was designed to restrict Russia, as is predicted by some versions of the theory. In contrast, Western and Southern hegemons, if they can be characterised as such (Germany/USA and Turkey, respectively) were not perceived as threats by Ukraine: instead, they were characterised as 'strategic' partners. Partnership was sought, and all the evidence suggests that progress towards closer ties with such hegemons was welcomed.

Some standard criticisms of the (neo)realist approach, however, have a particular resonance in CEE and the post-Soviet space. First, 'realism is particularly weak in accounting for change, especially where the sources of that change lie in the world political economy'.[6] The most telling example of such a criticism is the inability of the theory to have predicted the end of the Cold War and the implosion of the Soviet Union. The second criticism levelled at (neo)realism, namely that it neglects the role of domestic factors as determinants of foreign policy, is more easily dismissed. Waltz's work is particularly pertinent in this regard, especially as applied to Ukraine's post-independence behaviour. The realist contention that states, or more specifically policy-makers, assess threats and determine policy on the basis of perceived threat and aggressive intention, certainly contributes to an understanding of the twists and turns that the evolution of Ukrainian foreign and security policy underwent as Kyiv sought regional accommodation following independence.[7] Additional evidence of this is the Ukrainian parliament's vociferous denouncing of NATO attacks in Serbia and demands that Ukraine withdraw from the PfP. Only the constitutionally enshrined preponderance of presidential power over the parliament stopped these moves in their tracks. In other words, domestic factors are not wholly neglected in realist theory. Third, (neo)realism contends that states 'are extremely unwilling to assign importance to international institutions or to allow them to constrain their freedom of action'.[8] Certainly, in the light of Ukraine's 'strategic objective' of integration with the European Union, to say nothing of subregional institutions, the contention is discordant. Ukraine was seemingly only too willing to 'assign importance to international institutions' as evidenced by President Kuchma's unambiguous proclamation of the strategic goal of membership of the EU in 1996. The fact that Ukraine is far from attaining this goal in 2002 is attributable to Ukrainian bureaucratic inertia rather than the threat the EU presented to Ukraine's sovereignty. In this regard (neo)realism is at fault as it provides an 'inadequate analysis of economic integration and of the roles played by formal and informal international institutions'.[9] Wendt, while acknowledging a propensity toward anarchy in the international system, argues that the very intersubjectivity that characterises inter-state behaviour renders realism 'ill-suited as a comprehensive basis for systemic theory' in that it neglects the 'the nascent sociology of the international community'.[10] While in Ukraine's case it is true that Kyiv was 'extremely unwilling to assign importance to international institutions' along the North-eastern azimuth, the same just does not hold true for Ukraine's objectives along its Western azimuth: membership of the EU as a strategic objective has been doggedly adhered to. Indeed, Ukraine's 'strategic objective' of membership of the European Union hints at an importance ascribed to economic issues by Kyiv that even the neorealist version of the theory cannot accommodate. Significantly, non-security subregional organisations played a more prominent role in Ukrainian foreign and security policy than realist theory would have predicted. Indeed, economic ties with CEES which had joined NATO were seen as Ukraine's potential 'way in' to membership of subregional RSCs along the Western azimuth and eventually the EU; for Kyiv, prior to 2002, NATO membership had never really been on the cards. Thus, realist theory fails to explain why Ukraine's objective of membership of non-security subregional institutions was to serve the same legitimising role for Ukraine's western orientation that NATO served for CEES. As Balmaceda points out, along the Western azimuth 'bandwagoning does not seem to be fully capable of explaining Ukraine's international behaviour'.[11] Furthermore, the realist approach is ultimately somewhat barren in its explanatory power. It fails to account for Ukraine's initial de-integration from the Soviet Union: the sheer number and strength of ties linking the Ukrainian SSR and Russia were such that Ukrainian independence was an almost unthinkable phenomenon. The fact that it occurred despite these ties suggests that by neglecting to examine the precise nature of ties at the micro level the (neo)realist approach is overlooking potentially important independent/causal variables.

Structural interdependence

By allowing for the complexities of the type of interdependence, complex interdependence and regime change that characterised Ukraine's relationship with Russia in the years following independence, the theory of structural interdependence addresses a key flaw of realist theory, namely the inability of realist theory to explain the changed nature of the security threat Ukraine faced from Russia from around 1994 onwards, namely the politico-economic rather than military challenges emanating from Moscow.[12] The theory helps explain how Ukraine came to be threatened by the vulnerabilities that are a natural corollary of interdependence between states, and why the probability of a successful and voluntary reintegration of Ukraine into the post-Soviet space was so unlikely.

The very real, albeit asymmetrical, interdependence (the first theme of the theory of structural interdependence, as opposed to mere interconnectedness) that existed between Ukraine and Russia was demonstrated by Ukraine's extreme sensitivity and vulnerability to costs imposed by Russia in terms of energy. Kyiv was also badly hit by (i.e. sensitive to) the price increases the Russian side imposed as prices were brought up to world level – Kyiv could do little to cushion the shocks of such increases (i.e. it was highly vulnerable). Not that Russia was totally invulnerable – Kyiv's moves to undermine the reliability of Russian supplies to the West were a painful reminder to Moscow of the 'strategic' role this once loyal ally played. Interdependence was indeed a two-way process.

However, somewhat awkwardly for the theory of structural interdependence, the albeit asymmetric interdependence between Ukraine and Russia along the North-eastern azimuth failed to adequately stimulate or promote harmonious ties between them either on a bilateral level, or within subregional or regional structures. In fact the opposite was true: Ukraine, rather than remain dependent on Russia as the sole source of energy supplies and hence vulnerable and sensitive to any disruption in those supplies, desperately sought alternative supplies, something which motivated its ambitions along the subregional dimension on the Southern azimuth and was tied to objectives along the Western azimuth. Russia's corresponding vulnerability, its reliance on Ukraine as the key transit route for gas and oil supplies to the West, was acted on by Moscow from very early on – the building of alternative pipelines around Ukraine, had it been completed rapidly, would have significantly reduced Ukraine's bargaining position vis-à-vis Russia, and their interdependence would have been reduced, with Ukraine coming off very much worse. In fact, Ukraine's vulnerabilities, in the absence of successes along the

Southern azimuth would have endured, while Russia's would have dissipated. Interdependence was hardly conducive to integration in this particular instance.

Ukraine's reluctance to build on its interdependence with Russia can in part be explained by the second theme of structural independence theory, namely complex interdependence and the role of its three key components – multiple channels of contact, hierarchy of issues, and salience of use of force, most particularly the latter two. First, as far as the hierarchy of issues was concerned, competing military security concerns for both states dominated the agenda between them in the early years following Ukrainian independence. Although tensions over the Crimea, Sevastopol, the BSF, air defence and nuclear weapons reached their peak under the presidency of Kravchuk, they certainly did not immediately disappear on the election of his successor, Leonid Kuchma. Second, these tensions were further exacerbated by the fact that at least on the part of Ukrainians there was the perception that for Russia the use of force was highly salient. The war in Chechnya, the attack on the Russian parliament, Russian 'peacekeeping' duties throughout the former Soviet Union, ongoing events in Moldova, all fostered the suspicion that post-Soviet Russia was not merely threatening the use of force, but was actually using it. It is probable that the very thing that prevented the total breakdown in relations were the multiple channels of contact that existed between the two states on an inter-state, intergovernmental and transnational level. Indeed, there are suggestions that despite the formal independence from each other of the two states, there remains a vein of intimacy between them that strongly suggests that Ukraine's independence is a myth and that the two are *de facto* integrated.[13]

The third theme of the theory, that of regime change, exposes the salience of wider issues in Ukraine's efforts to remain aloof from regional developments along its North-eastern azimuth. There are four features to regime change: the role of economic processes, the overall power structure in the world, the power structure within issue areas and the role of international organisations.

As far as economic processes are concerned, the growing obsolescence of the technological base of the former Soviet Union was evident to policy-makers in Kyiv – integration with the CIS suggested a further ossification of Ukraine's fast-dating but occasionally still impressive technology. This was in direct contrast with what Kyiv believed integration with the West would offer. A second economic factor explaining Ukraine's desire to leave the network that made up the former Soviet Union, and its refusal to get drawn more deeply into the CIS was a demand at the popular level for an improvement in standards of living. Nothing more emphatically supports this view than the overwhelming and uniform popular support for independence across Ukraine, driven as it was by the hoped for economic benefits of independence – a process not held up by amorphous concepts linked to national identity or suchlike.

To say that with the collapse of the Soviet Union the overall power structure in the world had changed, is merely to reiterate an often-stated truism. However, to suggest that Ukraine sought solutions along the Western and Southern azimuths at the expense of the North-eastern azimuth, and that objectives along the former two of those azimuths were intertwined and linked to objectives along the North-eastern azimuth is to make a less obvious claim. With a decline in Russian power, the regime change was so great owing to the overhaul of the overall power structure in the world, that Ukraine was able to adopt a hitherto unthinkable policy stance.

This new policy stance was most evident in the change that took place in the power structure within the issue areas affecting the former Soviet Union, the second feature of regime change. As should by now be evident, Kyiv adopted a pro-active role in bringing about this change in the power structure within certain key issue areas. Indeed, the collapsing power of Russia meant not only that regime change was inevitable, but also that Ukraine was likely to adopt a prominent role in the push for regime change. There is strong empirical support for the contention that Ukraine was the catalyst that brought about the change in the 'implicit and explicit principles, norms, rules and decision-making procedures around which actors' expectations converge'.[14] For example, Ukraine was highly pro-active in preventing the emergence of a post-Soviet successor regime. Furthermore, Kyiv pursued with vigour the creation of a sub-CIS regime along the Southern azimuth, which challenged the CIS.

Moscow exerted great efforts to manage its political, military and economic decline by linking issue areas, for example by making the continued supply of cheap energy to the republics conditional on their membership of the CIS. However, despite Ukraine's dependence on Russian energy, Moscow could not prevent Ukraine's military and political deintegration from the Soviet Union; neither was it able to compel Ukraine to integrate fully with the CIS. Indeed, arguably, the CIS itself provided a forum within which regime change could be arranged and managed. Furthermore, the very weakness of the CIS emboldened some of its members to support regime change whether Ukraine led or not, much to the consternation of the strongest member of the institution.

The role of the key international institution along the North-eastern azimuth, the CIS, was in Kyiv's eyes to be limited to that of ensuring a 'civilised divorce'. However, while the break with the former Soviet Union has not been total, Ukraine remains estranged from Russia. The role of the CIS in managing this change has been circumscribed, to say the least, by Kyiv efforts to impede ambitions for the institution, as well as the inadequate institutional framework of the body itself. As for the CIS itself, it could be argued that, at best, it has not drastically impeded the type of regime change favoured by Ukraine; at worst it has hindered the evolution of normal inter-state ties on the territory of the former Soviet Union.

If the structural interdependence theory successfully helps explain the process via which Ukraine managed the change from its status as a former constituent republic of the USSR to an independent state, the attempt to use the theory to fully account for Ukraine's western orientation meets with mixed results. Ukraine was interdependent with states to its west to the smallest possible degree – shuttle trade with Poland was amongst the most tangible measures of those relations. While arguably the West was vulnerable to a disruption of energy supplies coming via Ukraine, this vulnerability was something of a phantom – Ukraine needed the income from the transportation of supplies. In other words, there was interconnectedness rather than interdependence, something which tends not to be conducive to integration.

As far as complex interdependence along the Western azimuth was concerned, the multiple channels of contact certainly enhanced relations with states along that azimuth, as did the lack of threat to the military security of those states presented by an independent Ukraine (certainly once nuclear weapons had been eliminated), as did also the lack of salience of the use of military force (reinforced by the decision to denuclearise). That this was not enough to make Ukraine an alluring candidate for integration is hardly a moot point.

In terms of regime change, the economic success of the West was such that integration with it was seen as a solution to many of Ukraine's long-term problems, if only Ukraine could contribute to a change of regime that was willing to include it. However, the fact that Ukraine was not a key actor in the management of this change (i.e. Ukraine could bring about a deintegration from the Soviet Union and avoid full integration with the CIS, but not bring about its integration with the West), merely reflected not only the overall power structure in the world, but highlighted where that power lay. Ukraine's efforts to link issue areas by, for example, trying to participate in the transportation of Caspian oil as a means of facilitating its integration with the West merely highlighted its inability to influence developments. Thus despite all of its efforts, Ukraine's relations with key international institutions along the Western azimuth remained highly circumscribed, much more so in the case of the EU than with NATO. In sum, all the ingredients necessary to explain Ukraine's lack of success along the Western azimuth are present.

Overall, by making an allowance for the compelling prerogatives of realism, the all-pervasive impact of technology, and the challenges presented by economic competitiveness, on the one hand, and economic interdependence, on the other, the theory of structural interdependence provides a plausible explanatory framework for understanding Ukraine's regional behaviour along the various azimuths. Yet this very comprehensiveness equates to a lack of parsimony; with so many potentially causal variables capable of explaining Ukraine's objective of avoiding full integration along the North-eastern azimuth, it is difficult to pinpoint the impact of any one variable at any given time. Additionally, the theory of structural interdependence does not commit itself to placing causal variables in any sort of hierarchy or primacy of effect. Indeed, as the political constellation changed, so did the priorities of the actors. So, for example, up until 1994 Ukraine was concerned with the military threat presented by Russia, and hence military de-integration was an absolute priority for Kyiv. Yet by 1994, as Russia's relative military impotence grew ever more evident, the threat had become primarily economic. Underlying this economic threat was a concern as to the damage economic integration within the CIS could do to Ukraine's independence and sovereignty. Thus the theory tells us very little about how the nature of the issue-areas which formed the focus of policy-makers at any given time changed – how one lost salience at the expense of the others. The theory also fails to allow for factors from beyond a given region: as the West became more interested in Ukraine from 1994 onwards, there was a corresponding impact on Ukraine's prospects along the Western azimuth, which nonetheless subsequently failed to materialise primarily due to Kyiv's inability to implement meaningful structural economic reform. Finally, it is plausible to argue that Ukraine's objectives along the North-eastern azimuth, that is of remaining a minimal participant in subregional and regional processes, were achieved despite the complexity of the interdependence between Ukraine and its former Soviet brethren.

As expected, and despite its ubiquitousness, Globalisation Theory struggles to contribute to an understanding of Ukraine's regional behaviour. The theory fails to explain the salience of security issues that affected Ukraine's regional planning, especially in the early years of independence. It also fails to account for the extent to which Ukraine was prepared to endure the profound economic downturn that a disruption of ties with Russia brought, in pursuit of pastures new in the West.

In sum, the first two of the systemic theories examined provide some insight into the peculiarities of Ukraine's situation and its efforts to adjust throughout the 1990s to the repercussions of having been part of a collapsed empire. Of the three theories, however, realist theory most convincingly encapsulates the context of threat and uncertainty that Ukraine found itself in, in the few years following independence, and hence has most to contribute during this early period. The fact that Kyiv's preoccupation with military and security issues only subsided once the context had become less threatening and Ukraine's international status had become institutionalised, meaning that it could turn its attention to economic affairs, suggests that realist theory needs to be supplemented by other explanations. The theory of structural interdependence complements realism by virtue of the fact that it successfully explains this transition from a preoccupation with solely hard security issues to soft security issues, for example, Ukraine's dire economic status.

Regional-level theories of regionalism

Neofunctionalism

As was stated in the introductory chapter, the relevance of neofunctionalism to regionalism outside the European Union is questionable. However, neofunctionalism does partially explain Ukraine's willingness to subsume its independence to that of the EU – Kyiv believed membership would enhance its security and increase its prosperity. Furthermore, it is arguable that Kyiv was reliant on and hopeful of the functional, political and cultivated spill-over that comes with closer ties with the Union as long as such spill-over is again compensated for by enhanced security and increased prosperity. These hopes in part explain the disappointment of the Ukrainians at not even being offered the prospect of membership of the EU at Helsinki in 1999.

Neoliberal institutionalism

The main tenet of neoliberal institutionalism is that institutions are the solution to problems thrown up by the collective action demands of increasingly interdependent states. Nevertheless, in contrast to functionalism, neoliberal institutionalism is firmly state-centric. This is a major plus of the theory, as along the North-eastern azimuth the CIS had different functions, according to whose perspective was adopted. From Moscow's point of view, the CIS was to serve as a replacement for the Soviet Union. In contrast, as Ukraine struggled to come terms with the dilemmas of independence, the CIS was perceived as a means of achieving a 'civilised divorce'. Furthermore, for the Ukrainians the role of the CIS was to be strictly restricted to economic issues. They only allowed themselves to be drawn reluctantly into other areas, as in the case of the air-defence agreement. While clearly the CIS could have functioned as a forum for multilateral communication, maintaining transparency and the plethora of other benefits institutions are deemed to offer, in practice its utility was highly circumscribed by the fact that it was dominated by Russia. The fact is that, in contrast to Russia, on anything other than economic issues, Ukraine saw the CIS as a means to an end – de-integration – rather than an end in itself.

For Ukraine, history and experience seemed to suggest that institutions along the Western azimuth functioned as liberal institutionalists suggested they should: they were fora that were security-enhancing by virtue of the fact that they reduced the uncertainty connected with collective action and interdependence. Furthermore, the sheer density of institutions along the Western azimuth (in contrast to the dearth of such institutions along the North-eastern azimuth) meant that the benefits of such fora (information provision, communication, facilitating transparency, etc.) were mutually reinforcing. While the North-eastern azimuth offered the all-or-nothing CIS, the Western azimuth offered a plethora of alternatives which indicated an ever more complex yet integrated whole, something demanded by increasing co-operation. The fact that those options were not available to Ukraine suggested that it was not yet interdependent with states along its Western azimuth.

Once again, the Southern azimuth can also be seen as a continuation of the Western azimuth – the creation of GUUAM reflected Ukraine's inability to cope with Russia on an individual basis, and the need for collective action if objectives were to be achieved along this azimuth. Thus while the co-operation behind the creation of GUUAM was driven by alliance formation in pursuit of the objective of transporting Caspian oil, it also resulted in an ever denser network of political, economic and even military co-operation between those particular former Soviet republics.

Constructivism

The post-imperial setting in which Ukraine and Russia found themselves means that the extensive cultural, social, ethnic and familial ties that linked them were inadequate to sustain the sense of community that once existed between them. While there is lingering nostalgia in Eastern and Southern Ukraine caused by the shared sense of history, mutual sympathy and loyalty, and compatibility of economic and political values with Russia, such emotions have not yet been mobilised sufficiently to drive integration. While there is, admittedly, support for closer ties with the CIS, it was inadequate to ensure the election of the Communist candidate for the presidency, Petro Symonenko, who stood on a platform of deeper integration with the CIS in the 1999 presidential elections.

Constructivism does, however, show that despite the highly circumscribed and dated shared structural context, the limited opportunities for the expression of the power of systemic processes and strategic practices linking Ukraine with states along the Western azimuth, Kyiv was intent from the earliest days of independence on forging ties with them in pursuit of community formation. Kyiv emphasised Ukraine's Central European social and collective identity, even if that meant that a gloss had to be put on the data and myths that supposedly portrayed Ukraine's European credentials. This was done especially in terms of the role of systemic processes (such as highlighting instances of historical interdependence and transnational convergence) and strategic practice (such as repeated instances of co-operation in the past, while underplaying divisive historical events. The single most outstanding example of Ukraine's willingness to consign divisive events to history was the signing of a Declaration on Agreement and Unity with Poland in 1997). Furthermore, it can be argued that the CEES, with Ukraine in tow, are striving for membership of key regional institutions because they share, or in Kyiv's case, strive to share, community values, norms and values. While this is perhaps bending the tenets of the theory somewhat, the spirit of the theory is maintained. Nevertheless, the simple fact remains that Ukraine remains beyond the integration process to its west, on the grounds that Ukraine currently just does not share the norms and values of its western neighbours, has failed to fully democratise itself, and has not created the infrastructure for the development of a market economy. This is what really lies behind Ukraine's lack of success in the integration process along the Western azimuth.

New Wave regionalism

As expected, New Wave regionalism fills a gap in Hurrell's framework by elaborating on the important link between economics and politics, something which was at best implicit in other theories. Despite being more of an approach than a theory, New Wave regionalism does indeed shed light on Ukraine's regional behaviour and the extent to which political factors guided Ukraine's efforts to participate in regional institutions, or more accurately, PTAs.

Along the North-eastern azimuth, it was precisely the suspicion that PTAs were being used by Russia as political instruments to engineer the renewed subordination of other CIS member states that prevented Ukraine from fuller participation in the CIS. This suspicion was fuelled by Russia's crude exploitation of CIS institutional mechanisms to explicitly link the economic policies adopted by the institution with the political status of member states. It was precisely because regionalism within the CIS was 'a *political* process characterised by economic policy co-operation and coordination' [italics in original] that Ukraine steered clear to the extent that it did.[15] Although secondary to the preservation of independence, welfare considerations were important to Kyiv, which is why it sought to encourage yet at the same time limit the functioning of the CIS to economic issues.

Along the Western azimuth, New Wave regionalism helps explain both why Ukraine strove for and failed to gain membership of key subregional institutions or make much process in establishing closer ties with the EU. While the benefits of greater aggregate power conferred on members in pursuit of EU membership was not lost on Kyiv, the political aspect of regionalism was both over- and underestimated. For example, in the international arena, Kyiv prioritised the political over the economic – membership of CEFTA and the EU was pursued as a political objective, to the detriment of economic reform, despite the warnings from both Central and East European capitals and Brussels. Thus, by highlighting the economic dimension of regionalism as a political process, New Wave regionalism exposes the flaw of Ukraine's over-focus on the international political dimension of membership of CEFTA and the EU at the expense of the economic.

Conversely, Kyiv underestimated the importance of domestic political factors for participation in PTAs. This was evidenced by the apparent impunity with which the incumbent abused his power in the 1999 presidential elections, as well as his dismissal of the international condemnation of his response to the publicisation of his implication in the murder of a journalist critical of his regime. The unambiguous message sent by the EU to Kyiv as to the need to temper its authoritarian tendencies, (re)introduce freedom of the press, and permit free and fair elections as a *sine qua non* for closer ties demonstrates that PTAs can be used 'to help prompt and consolidate economic and political reforms in prospective members'.[16] By allowing for the prerogatives of domestic political factors in the formation of or participation in PTAs, New Wave regionalists highlight an important variable which affected Ukraine's subregional and regional prospects and one which has been underestimated by other theories.

In sum, New Wave regionalism both helps explain the rationale behind Ukraine's stance towards the CIS and lays bare the flaws in Ukraine's strategy in pursuit of membership of subregional and regional institutions along the Western azimuth.

'Subregional' regionalism

As discussed in Chapter 1, 'subregional' regionalists have sought to fill the niche left by other theories of regionalism by focusing on the generally grey transitional area that exists between the state and the regional institution.

Along the Western azimuth, subregional opportunities were enthusiastically grasped by Ukraine following independence. This was because subregional institutions in Central and Eastern Europe offered one of the few means of 'rejoining Europe' available to Kyiv, along with the other theoretical advantages that 'subregional' regionalists claimed would accrue from membership. In practice, along the Western azimuth Ukraine struggled to overcome the flaws inherent to the process: for the CEES, membership of subregional institutions was an inadequate substitute for membership of the regional institution to which they all aspired, the EU. The former could never replace the latter, and would be abandoned at the first opportunity, despite the efforts of 'subregional' regionalists to encourage the EU to support the former. Yet, problematically for Kyiv, although Visegrad/CEFTA, as effectively transitory phenomena, were in a sense doomed before they had started, Ukraine could do little other than strive for membership of them – its options were so tightly circumscribed.

Problems were exacerbated by the nature of relations between regional and subregional institutions. By not encouraging the CEES to think collectively, and indeed by evaluating their membership prospects on an individual basis, the EU engendered a competitiveness that undermined the process of subregionalism and which left Ukraine looking vulnerable and isolated on the eastern borders of the CEES. Furthermore, in the shorter term, barriers to, for example, CEFTA membership appeared insurmountable; yet in the longer term CEFTA was in danger of becoming irrelevant as key member states abandoned the institution for membership of the EU.[17] Despite the best intentions of 'subregional' regionalists, along the Western azimuth, the benefits of subregionalism have not materialised and as such the phenomenon is in danger of becoming obsolete.[18]

There is little doubt that, along the Southern azimuth, both GUUAM and indeed the BSEC would have evolved more successfully had they successfully garnered the support of key Western regional institutions. Both of the subregional institutions failed to attract either the support of the EU or NATO, closer ties with which most GUUAM and many BSEC member states aspired to. Moscow did not look upon GUUAM favourably, to say the least; the BSEC was merely tolerated. The lack of support of the wealthy regional bodies and its effects are plain to see.

Of the two subregional institutions, theoretically, GUUAM is the more interesting. Even if GUUAM as a grouping of heterogeneous states has not exactly prospered, then at least it has continued to survive and, against the odds, institutionalise in the face of adversity and impecuniosity.[19] Furthermore, it has evolved despite the fact that the collectivism of GUUAM has provided member states with little in the sense of proportionally greater influence as predicted by the proponents of subregionalism. Neither is it a staging post *en route* to membership of regional institutions, nor is it a forum for equal status negotiations with other institutions – it is treated far too cautiously by Western regional states for those advantages to obtain. For these reasons, ultimately, 'subregional' regionalism disappoints – it struggles to readily explain the enigma of GUUAM's continued existence, something which realists, for example, can as a matter of course.

In sum, empirical findings both negate and support the arguments of 'subregional' regionalism. Along the Western azimuth, the validity of treating subregional developments as a distinct phenomenon from regional developments is questionable: the existence of CEFTA, for example, is so closely tied to prospects for EU membership that it resembles an ante-chamber. The built-in obsolescence of subregional institutions, in the sense that they tend to exist to promote the attainment of regional goals of member states, merely reinforces this view. If along the Western azimuth, the existence of subregional institutions as a distinct entity is questionable, arguably along the Southern azimuth the opposite is true. GUUAM as a distinctly subregional institution, bereft of regional support, is a particularly interesting theoretical phenomenon; it is a body which is burdened by the major disadvantages of subregionalism, is blessed with few of the advantages, yet continues to endure.

Domestic-level theories of regionalism

Regionalism and state coherence

On independence, and indeed nearly a decade on, Ukraine lacks convincing territorial and ethnic integrity, continues to be emaciated by limited economic viability and remains barely politically coherent. In other words, according to the theory, Ukraine in all of these key respects barely satisfies the prerequisites for partaking in regionalism. This did not stop Ukraine from trying to participate in the subregional and regional developments along the Western azimuth and subregional developments along the Southern azimuth. However, in theoretical terms, Ukraine's lack of success along the key azimuth, the Western one, could be partially attributed to its fractured internal state and its proto-sovereign status. There can be little doubt that a Ukraine in its current fractured and barely viable state would present NATO and the EU with an indigestible problem. In this regard, the theory of state coherence is supported.

From a theoretical point of view, in the longer term, Ukraine's regional prospects along the Western azimuth appear dim. Although in the early years of independence separatism was an unthinkable prospect, there are increasing signs that as Ukraine continues to stagnate, Galician separatism is being viewed as a preferable alternative (by Galicians at least) to continued decline within a unitary Ukraine.[20] Whether or not policy-makers in Brussels, Berlin, Warsaw or even Moscow would agree is debatable.

Regime type and democratisation

The democratisation of Ukraine was far more fundamental to its participation in subregional and regional developments along the Western azimuth than policy-makers in Kyiv had envisaged in the years following independence. Even as late as 1999 the Ukrainian political elite was guided by the belief that Ukraine's geopolitical position mattered more to the EU and NATO than did the minutiae of domestic events. This misapprehension was exposed by two events in 1999 and 2000 respectively.

The opprobrium of the international community heaped on Kuchma following his re-election in the 1999 presidential elections reflected the scale of corruption in bringing about his victory. It was the EU's exasperation with the lack of democracy in Ukraine which lay behind Brussels' decision not to offer Kyiv even the prospect of EU membership at some unspecified time in the future in Helsinki in 1999. This alone reveals the close link between democracy and regionalism.

However, Ukraine as a democracy plumbed new depths with the death of a Ukrainian journalist, allegedly on the orders of the president, late in September 2000. It was because of Ukraine's failure as a democracy that the link between regionalism and democracy was made explicit by the West. Whether or not Kuchma was involved in ordering the murder of the journalist, as apparently demonstrated by a recording of him doing so, is a moot point. The inadequacy of his subsequent response to the event is not. In pursuit of 'the truth', Ukraine as a democracy, with Kuchma as its president, failed to satisfy even the most basic criteria of the term: transparency, openness and accountability. Ukraine's response was not lost on the EU. Ukraine was subsequently marginalised along the Western azimuth, with the Council of Europe calling for the suspension of Ukraine's membership of the body (on the grounds of lack of press freedom). At the end of 2000, Ukraine's regional prospects along the Western azimuth looked dim indeed.

Kuchma had totally failed to grasp the point that what mattered within Ukraine would impact on its external relations, especially along the Western azimuth. From a theoretical point of view, Ukraine was failing regionally because 'the culture, perceptions and practices that permit compromise and the peaceful resolution of conflicts without the threat of violence within countries come to apply across national boundaries toward other democratic countries'.[21] The use of violence within Ukraine implied that it could not be trusted to participate in the regional institution to which it aspired according to the norms and principles of that institution.

* * *

The power of systemic-level theories shines through in the above analysis. They still show themselves capable of explaining macro-level behaviours, and even in some instances micro-level behaviour. Indeed, systemic theories provide a view of the broad picture, and thereby provide a context without which any examination of Ukraine's regional behaviour comes across as somewhat two-dimensional. It is the systemic approach that provides an opportunity to examine 'the arch' of which the keystone is an integral part and critical component. Amongst these theories, the robustness of the realist approach continues to present a formidable challenge to newer pretenders. However, with its allowance for the economic aspects of international relations, complex interdependence takes up where realism leaves off.

Regional-level theories complement systemic-level theories. Ukraine's pursuit of institutional membership along the Western azimuth strongly suggests that international institutions play a more prominent role in international relations than realist theory in particular can account for. However, while the neofunctionalist approach provides some limited insight into Ukraine's regional behaviour, as does the neoliberal institutionalist approach, both struggle to provide a coherent and consistent explanation along all three azimuths.

Domestic-level theories perhaps currently lack the academic rigour to compete with the aforementioned two levels. This is not to denigrate the contribution of domestic-level theories: without a sufficient appreciation of the subtleties and intricacies of the keystone, it might be difficult to appreciate how it fits into the whole. It is evident that international relations still lacks a theory that is capable of accounting for the variety of variables and the intricate interplay between them that are international relations.

Notes

Introduction

1 D. A. Lake and P. M. Morgan, 'The New Regionalism in Security Affairs', in D.A. Lake and P. M. Morgan, (eds), *Regional Orders – Building Security in a New World* (Pennsylvania: Pennsylvania State University Press 1997) p. 6.
2 CEES will be deemed to include Poland, Hungary, Slovakia (and formerly Czechoslovakia), and along the South-western azimuth, Romania, Moldova and Bulgaria.
3 Quoted in O. L. Valevsky and M. M. Honchar, *Struktura Heopolitichnych Interesiv Ukrainy*, Vypusk 45 (Kyiv: Natsionalny Institut Stratehichnych Doslidzen 1995) p. 42.
4 For more detail on this issue see R. Wolczuk, 'Relations between Ukraine and Romania in the Context of NATO Enlargement', *Ukrainian Review*, 44(4), Winter 1997, pp. 34–41.
5 For a more detailed analysis of these issues see R. Wolczuk, 'Ukraine and Europe: Relations Since Independence', *Ukrainian Review*, 44(1), Spring 1997, pp. 38–53 and also 'Ukraine in the Context of NATO Enlargement', *Ukrainian Review*, 44(3), Autumn 1997, pp. 3–23.
6 J. Sherr, *Ukraine's New Time of Troubles*, G67 (Conflict Studies Research Centre: Camberley 1998) pp. 18–19.
7 For a more detailed examination of Ukraine's foreign and security policy regarding these objectives see R. Wolczuk, 'The Evolution of Ukraine's Foreign and Security Policy 1991–1994', *Slavic Military Studies*, 12(3) (September 1999) pp. 18–37.

1 A theoretical context

1 The term 'pivot' was used by the British foreign secretary, Malcolm Rifkind. Quoted in J. E. Mroz and O. Pavliuk, 'Ukraine: Europe's Linchpin', *Foreign Affairs*, 75(3), May/June 1996, p. 59. See also S. W. Garnett, *Keystone in the Arch: Ukraine in the Emerging Security Environment of Central and Eastern Europe* (Washington: Carnegie Endowment for International Peace 1997).
2 J. Hillen and M. P. Noonan, 'The Geopolitics of NATO Enlargement', *Parameters*, Autumn 1998, p. 21.
3 *Financial Times*, 5 May 1998.
4 See H. J. Mackinder, *Democratic Ideals and Reality* (New York: Norton 1962) for a collection of Mackinder's classic papers including the seminal 'The Geographical Pivot of History' (1904); for a more modern application of Mackinder's work read C.S. Gray *The Geopolitics of Superpower* (Kentucky: University of Kentucky Press 1988). More dated examinations of Ukraine's geopolitical context include R. Kjellen, *Die Politische Probleme des Weltkriegs* (Leipzig) 1918, and also F. Naumann, *Werke* (Köln and Opladen 1966).

5 Gray, *The Geopolitics of Super Power*, pp. 1–2.

6 On the establishment of norms in international relations see P. Keal, *Unspoken Rules And Superpower Dominance* (London: Macmillan Press 1983).

7 Hillen and Noonan, 'The Geopolitics of NATO Enlargement', p. 25.

8 Lake and Morgan 'The New Regionalism in Security Affairs' in Lake and Morgan, pp. 3–20.

9 R. Rosecrance, 'Regionalism and the Post-Cold War Era', *International Journal*, XLVI, Summer 1991, p. 373.

10 The notion of regional security complex is used in preference to the term 'region', the definition of which is plagued with difficulties. Efforts to establish outer geographical or 'scientific' limits to a 'region', while useful in explaining the term 'region', also cloud understanding. One effort in the field of geography for classifying regional systems differentiated between at least two types of region. A homogenous or uniform region is an 'area within which the variations and co-variations of one or more selected characteristics fall within some specified range of variability around a norm, in contrast with areas that fall outside the range. Such a region . . . is a result of the process of regionalisation.' In other words, a region is formed when a degree of cohesiveness is conferred on an area on the basis of specified and shared attributes. In contrast, a region of 'coherent organisation' or 'functional region is defined as one in which one or more selected phenomena of movement connect localities within it into a functional whole', that is where the behaviour of localities is organised so that the behaviour of the localities functions as a whole. See B. J. L. Berry and T. D. Hankins, *A Bibliographic Guide to the Economic Regions of the United States* (Chicago: University of Chicago Press 1963) Department of Chicago Research Paper, No. 87, p. 134. Taken from D. Grigg, 'The Logic of Regional Systems', *Annals of the Association of American Geographers*, No. 55, 1965, p. 473. Most definitions of regionalism in International Relations take advantage of both to come to an unsatisfactory amalgam. For example, Russet suggests that, on the one hand, cultural and social homogeneity, external behaviour and, on the other hand, economic interdependence and geographic proximity are necessary in the formation of a 'region'. B. M Russett, 'International Regimes and the Study of Regions', *International Studies Quarterly*, 13(4), December 1969, pp. 123–33. Cantori and Spiegel, while arguing for geographic proximity and regular international interaction, also propose common historical, linguistic, cultural, ethnic and social bonds (as opposed to homogeneity) and a sense of identity the distinctiveness of which is underlined by actors from beyond the region. L. J. Cantori and S. L. Spiegel (eds), *The International Politics of Regions: A Comparative Approach* (Englewood Cliffs, NJ: Prentice-Hall 1970). See also, L. J. Cantori and S. L. Spiegel, 'The Analysis of Regional International Politics: The Integration Versus the Empirical Systems Approach', *International Organization*, 27(4), 1973, pp. 465–94. Katzenstein's efforts to escape from the ambiguities of 'geographical proximity', 'homogeneity' and 'regular international interaction', by defining 'a region as a set of countries markedly interdependent over a wide range of different dimensions' fail to avoid the 'unavoidable empirical ambiguities and differences in analytical perspectives' he himself highlights. P.J. Katzenstein, 'Regionalism in Comparative Perspective', *Co-operation and Conflict*, 31(2), 1996, p. 130.

11 B. Buzan, *People, States and Fear: An Agenda for International Security Studies in the Post-Cold War Era*, 2nd ed. (Boulder, Colo.: Lynne Rienner 1991) p. 190.

12 Externalities help address this problem. D. A. Lake, 'Regional Security Complexes: A Systems Approach' in Lake and Morgan, pp. 45–67.

13 In addition to the Western, Russian, Central European and the CIS azimuths, Sherr conceptualises two other 'quasi-azimuths': 'the development of . . . relations with resource rich regions of the Russian Federation itself' and 'the azimuth of Black Sea co-operation'. See J. Sherr, 'Ukraine's New Time of Troubles', G27 (Sandhurst, UK: Conflict Studies Research Centre October 1998) p. 19.

14 Although Lake rejects institutional definitions on the grounds that not all RSCs are institutionalised. Lake 'Regional Security Complexes' in Lake and Morgan, pp. 46–7.
15 R. Cooper, 'The Meaning of 1989', *Prospect*, December 1999, p. 29.
16 In the case of the OSCE the criteria are recognised statehood and agreement with certain basic norms and adherence to the Helsinki Principles of 1975 and 1992, and the Budapest Document of 1994; the Council of Europe require adherence to legal norms and respect for human rights.
17 P. M. Morgan, 'Regional Security Complexes and Regional Orders' in Lake and Morgan, pp. 21–44.
18 Ibid., p. 34.
19 *ITAR-TASS*, 1 March 1993. See P.M. Morgan, 'Regional Security Complexes and Regional Orders' in Lake and Morgan, p. 34.
20 C. A. Snyder, 'Regional Security Structures' in C. A. Snyder (ed.), *Contemporary Security and Strategy* (London: Macmillan Press, 1999) pp. 102–19.
21 Ibid., p. 107.
22 S. Kay, *NATO and the Future of European Security* (Oxford: Rowan & Littlefield, 1998) pp. 1–2.
23 K. Deutsch, *Political Community and the North Atlantic Area: International Organisation in the Light of Historical Experience* (Princeton: Princeton University Press 1957), p. 5. Also, see P. M. Morgan, 'Regional Security Complexes and Regional Orders' in Lake and Morgan, p. 37.
24 Ibid., p. 38. As ever, the perennial problem for the study of integration remains bogged down in definitions. As Haas pointed out, 'the task of selecting and justifying variables and explaining their hypothesised interdependence cannot be accomplished without an agreement as to possible conditions to which the process is expected to lead. In short, we need a dependent variable'. See E. Haas, 'The Study of Regional Integration: Reflections on the Joy and Anguish of Pretheorising' in L. N. Lindberg and S. A. Scheingold (eds), *European Integration: Theory and Research* (Cambridge, MA: Harvard University Press 1971) p. 18 and B. Rosamond, *Theories of European Integration* (London: Macmillan Press 2000) pp. 11–12.
25 According to Lake and Morgan 'integrating regional politics into nascent models of multilevel games will produce theories of staggering complexity' a problem compounded by the fact that methodological tools are lacking. See Lake and Morgan, 'The New Regionalism in Security Affairs', in Lake and Morgan, p. 14.
26 B. Buzan, *People, States and Fear*, p. 19.
27 Ibid., p. 19.
28 For an in depth analysis of post-independence constitutional developments in Ukraine, see the unpublished PhD thesis by K. Wolczuk, *Politics of Statebuilding – The Constitutional Process in Ukraine 1990–1996*, University of Birmingham, 2000.
29 B. Buzan, *People, States and Fear*, pp. 19–20.
30 Ibid., p. 20.
31 Ibid., p. 19.
32 Ibid., p. 19.
33 Ibid., p. 117.
34 For an early comparative perspective on regionalisation see, for example, E. Haas, 'International Integration: the European and the Universal Process', *International Political Communities: An Anthology* (Garden City, NY: Doubleday, Anchor Books) pp. 93–129. For a post Cold War perspective, see P.J. Katzenstein, 'Regionalism in Comparative Perspective', pp. 123–59; M. Alagappa, 'Regionalism and Conflict Management: A Framework for Analysis', *Review of International Studies*, 21, 1995, pp. 359–87; J.H. Mittelman, 'Rethinking the "New Regionalism" in the Context of Globalisation', *Global Governance*, 2, 1996, pp. 189–213.
35 A. Hurrell, 'Regionalism in Theoretical Perspective', in L. Fawcett and A. Hurrell, *Regionalism in World Politics* (Oxford: Oxford University Press 1998) p. 37.

36 K. Waltz, *Theory of International Politics* (Reading, Mass.: Addison-Wesley, 1979) p. 72.
37 P. Cloke, C. Pilo and D. Sadler, *Approaching Human Geography* (New York: Paul Chapman Publishing 1991) p. 10.
38 Ibid., p. 49.
39 The sheer diversity of (neo)realist theories, suggests that it is meaningful to talk about a (neo)realist approach, as such theories tend to share a common core of assumptions and beliefs.
40 Waltz, *Theory of International Politics*, p. 91.
41 Ibid., p. 58.
42 Hurrell, 'Regionalism in Theoretical Perspective', p. 48.
43 S. M. Walt, *The Origins of Alliance* (Ithaca, NY: Cornell University Press 1987). Walt defines an alliance as 'a formal or informal arrangement for security co-operation between two or more sovereign states' in contrast to Snyder's definition of an alliance as a 'formal association of states for the use (or non-use) of military force, intended for either the security or the aggrandisement of their members, against specific other states'. See G. H. Snyder, 'Alliance Theory: A Neorealist First Cut', *Journal of International Affairs*, 44, 1990, p. 104.
44 Hurrell, 'Regionalism in Theoretical Perspective', in Fawcett and Hurrell, p. 50.
45 R. O. Keohane and J. S. Nye, *Power and Interdependence*, 2nd edition (Boston: Scott Foresman and Company 1989) p. 9.
46 Ibid., p. 13.
47 Ibid., p. 43.
48 W. Wallace, *The Transformation of Western Europe* (London: Pinter 1990) p. 54.
49 Hurrell, 'Regionalism in Theoretical Perspective', in Fawcett and Hurrell, p. 55.
50 Early neo-functionalists identified four process mechanisms, which contributed to the formation of regional organisation: the functional linkages of tasks; increasing flows or transactions; linkages and coalitions and, finally, the formation of pressure groups. Later research adds three more: regional group formation; ideological-identitive appeal and the involvement of external actors in the process. The integrative potential of a given region is determined by four structural features: the economic equality of units, elite value complementarity, pluralism and the capacity of member states to adapt and respond. In addition to structural features, perceptual conditions are deemed important. These included the perceived equity of distribution of benefits, perceptions of cogency and low visible costs. See J. S. Nye, 'Comparing Common Markets: A Revised Neo-Functionalist Model', in F. Kratochwil and E. D. Mansfield (eds), *International Organization: A Reader* (New York: HarperCollins College Publishers) pp. 286–300.
51 E. B. Haas, *The Uniting of Europe: Political, Social and Economic Forces 1950–1957* (Stanford, Calif.: Stanford University Press 1968) pp. xxxv–xxxvi.
52 Hurrell, 'Regionalism in Theoretical Perspective', in Fawcett and Hurrell, pp. 56–7.
53 Ibid.
54 C. E. Wallander, *Mortal Friends, Best Enemies – German-Russian Co-operation After the Cold War* (Ithaca: Cornell University Press 1999) pp. 38–9.
55 Wallander points out that institutions differ from co-operation in that the former – that is, 'explicit, persistent and connected sets of rules that prescribe behavioural roles and constrain activity' – facilitate the latter. Wallander, *Mortal Friends*, p.16. For an outstanding analysis of institutions see D. C. North, *Institutions, Institutional Change and Economic Performance* (Cambridge: Cambridge University Press 1990); and R. O. Keohane, 'International Institutions: Two Approaches' in Kratochwil and Mansfield, *International Organization*, pp. 44–61.
56 K. Deutsch, S. Burrell and R. Kann, *Political Community in the North Atlantic Area* (Princeton: Princeton University Press, 1958).
57 A. Wendt, 'Collective Identity Formation and the International State', *The American Political Science Review*, 88(2) June, 1994, p. 385.

58 Ibid., p. 389.
59 E. Mansfield and H. Milner, 'The New Wave of Regionalism', *International Organization*, 53(3), Summer 1999, pp. 589–627.
60 Ibid., p. 591.
61 Ibid., p. 608.
62 However, the welfare benefits of regionalism remain unclear and inconsistent as 'economic analyses indicate that regionalism's welfare implications have varied starkly over time and across PTAs', ibid., p. 595.
63 Ibid., p. 601.
64 A. J. Bayles, 'Sub-regional Organizations: The Cinderellas of European Security', *NATO Review*, 2(45), March 1997, pp. 27–31.
65 Ibid., pp. 27–8.
66 A. Cottey 'Introduction' in A. Cottey (ed.), *Subregional Co-operation in The New Europe – Building Security, Prosperity and Solidarity from the Barents to the Black Sea* (London: Macmillan Press 1999), p. 3.
67 Bayles, 'Subregional Organizations', p. 28.
68 Cooper, 'The Meaning of 1989'.
69 A. Bjurner, 'Reflections on Subregionalism and Wider European Security' in R. Dwan (ed.), *Building Security in Europe's New Borderlands – Subregional Co-operation in the Wider Europe* (London M.E. Sharpe: 1999), pp. 11–12
70 Bayles, 'Subregional Organizations', p. 28.
71 Ibid. p. 27.
72 See R. Wolczuk 'The Evolution of Ukraine's Foreign and Security Policy'.
73 'Greater Ukraine' is a colloquialism for Central, Eastern and Southern Ukraine collectively.
74 Arel suggests that 3/4 of Ukrainians living west of the Dnipro are Ukrainophone, while 3/4 of the population to the east is Russophone. For a comprehensive discussion of the much misunderstood issue of language use see D. Arel and V. Khmelko, 'The Russian Factor and Polarization in Ukraine', *The Harriman Review*, 9(1), 1996, pp. 81–91.
75 D. Arel and V. Khmelko, 'The Russian Factor and Polarization in Ukraine', p. 84.
76 Hurrell, 'Regionalism in Theoretical Perspective', in Fawcett and Hurrell, p. 67.
77 M. W. Doyle, 'Kant, Liberal Legacies and Foreign Affairs', *Part I, Philosophy and Public Affairs*, 12(3), Summer 1983, pp. 205–35. See also, M.W. Doyle, 'Liberalism and World Politics', *American Political Science Review*, 80(4), December 1986, pp. 1151–69; B. Russett, *Grasping the Democratic Peace: Principles for a Post-Cold War World* (Princeton: Princeton University Press 1993); B. Russett, 'Can a Democratic Peace Be Built', *International Interactions*, 18(3), Spring 1993, pp. 277–82. The key article on the subject is M. Small and J. D. Singer, 'The War-proneness of Democratic Regimes, 1816–1865', *Jerusalem Journal of International Relations*, 1(4), Summer 1976, pp. 50–69.
78 B. Russett, *Grasping the Democratic Peace: Principles for a Post-Cold War World* (Princeton: Princeton University Press 1993) p. 31 (italics in original).
79 The democratic peace theory has been subject to swingeing criticism, most notably by Mearsheimer, who is so dismissive of it that he questions the very basis on which it purports to be a theory. See J. J. Mearsheimer, 'Back to the Future: Instability in Europe After the Cold War', *International Security*, 15(1), Summer 1990, pp. 5–56; see also C. Layne, 'Kant or Cant: The Myth of the Democratic Peace', *International Security*, 19(2), Fall 1994, pp. 5–49.
80 N. Woods, 'The Uses of Theory in the Study of International Relations' in N. Woods (ed.), *Explaining International Relations Since 1945*, (Oxford: Oxford University Press 1996) p. 11.
81 R. E Stake, *The Art of Case Study Research*, (London: Sage Publications 1995) p. 12.

2 Ukraine's relations with Slavic states

1 Garnett, *Keystone in the Arch*, p. 41.
2 Ibid., p. 57.
3 'Russian Official Advocates Border Revision', SOVSET, 24 June 1992 in N. V. Lamont, *Territorial Dimensions of Ethnic Conflict: The Moldovan Case* (Kansas: Foreign Military Studies Office 1996). A former version of the article appeared as 'Ethnic Conflict in the Transdniester' in *Military Review*, December – February 1995.
4 'Treaty on the Principles of Relations Between the RSFSR and the Ukrainian SSR', Article 6. See *Radyanska Ukraina*, 21 Nov. 1990, p. 1.
5 On 5 February 1954, a resolution of the Presidium of the RSFSR Supreme Soviet launched an initiative to transfer Crimea to the jurisdiction of the Ukrainian SSR. This initiative was then followed on 19 February 1954 by a decree of the Presidium of the USSR Supreme Soviet transferring the territory. The decision was enshrined in the 'Law on the Transfer of the Crimean Oblast from the RSFSR to the Ukrainian SSR' on 26 April 1954 by Supreme Soviet of the USSR. A thorough discussion of the legalities of the transfer of Crimea to Ukraine is discussed in *Narodna Armiya*, 23 November 1996. A detailed elaboration on the laws of the transfer is provided by the Ukrainian minster of justice, Serhiy Holovatyi, in *Narodna Armiya*, 26 December 1996.
6 It was in part to deal with the 'Russian' problem in Crimea that the OSCE was invited in by Kyiv to act as a dispassionate observer. Author's conversation with Michael Wygant, head of the OSCE Mission to Ukraine, Kyiv July 1997.
7 *Komsomolskaya Pravda*, 22 January 1992, in R. Solchanyk, 'Russia, Ukraine and the Imperial Legacy', *Post-Soviet Affairs*, 9(4), 1993, pp. 359–60.
8 *Zerkalo Nedeli*, 23 August, 1996.
9 *Pravda Ukrainy*, 14 January 1992.
10 For example, on 5 April 1992 the Ukrainian President Kravchuk in his decree 'On Urgent Measures Necessary for the Creation of Military Forces of Ukraine' ordered the formation of a Ukrainian Navy on the basis of units of the BSF located on Ukraine's territory. In turn, on 7 April 1992, President Yeltsin responded with the decree 'On the Transfer of the Black Sea Fleet to the Russian Federation'. On 8 April, Directive no. 8, 'On the Formation of Ukraine's Navy', was issued by the Ukrainian minister of defence. On 9 April, over the phone, both presidents agreed to halt the claims and counter-claims; in N. Savchenko, *Anatomia Neobyalvlenoy Voyny* (Kyiv: Ukrainska Perspektiva 1997) pp. 44–61.
11 'Ukrainian–Russian Summit at Dragomys', *RFE/RL Research Report*, 1(30), 24 July 1992, p. 38. James Sherr suggests that in January 1992 a 50:50 split was agreed between the two parties; see J. Sherr, 'Russia–Ukraine *Rapprochement*?: The Black Sea Fleet Accords', *Survival*, 39(3), Autumn 1997, p. 36.
12 Savchenko, *Anatomia Neobyalvlenoy Voyny*, pp. 135–6.
13 M. A. Smith, *Russian Hegemony in the Near Abroad* (Sandhurst: Conflict Studies Research Centre July 1994) p. 9. gopher://marvin.nc3a.nato.int:70/00/secdef/csrc/f40mas.txt.
14 Ibid., p. 9.
15 S. Kudriachov, S. Odarych, Y. Orobets and M. Tomenko, *Carta Sevastopolya: Triumph Presidentiv, Trahedia Ukrainy* (Kyiv: Ukrainska Perspektiva 1997) p. 14.
16 Ibid., p. 12.
17 *Narodna Armiya*, 27 February 1997.
18 *Summary of World Broadcasts*, SU/2470, 2471 and 2473.
19 Savchenko, *Anatomia Neobyalvlenoy Voyny*, pp. 261–9.
20 *Narodna Armiya*, 27 February 1997.
21 For a thorough discussion of the legalities surrounding the division of the Black Sea Fleet by the Ukrainian minister of justice, Serhiy Holovatyi, see *Narodna Armiya*, 29 October 1996. Article 2 of the new constitution affirms the sovereignty of Ukraine over

all its territory; Article 133 codifies the status of Sevastopol as Ukrainian territory. See *Narodna Armiya*, 26 December 1996.

22 *Narodna Armiya*, 27 February 1997.

23 Ibid.

24 *Narodna Armiya*, 8 May 1997.

25 Sherr, *Ukraine's New Time of Troubles*, p. 28.

26 Ibid.

27 Sherr, 'Russia–Ukraine *Rapprochement*?' p. 38.

28 Conversation with author, Kyiv, July 1997. This view is confirmed by an official from the Ukrainian Ministry of Foreign Affairs who added that a finalised version of the treaty had been ready some two years earlier but remained unsigned on the insistence of Moscow (conversation with author, Kyiv, July 1997). Puzzlingly, the eventual version signed was, from Moscow's point of view, slightly inferior to the original version. Sherr supports this interpretation arguing that the eventual agreements were 'more favourable to Ukraine than those which Russia had, to all intents and purposes, torpedoed in October 1996'. See Sherr, *Ukraine's New Time of Troubles*, p. 28. See also J. Sherr, *A New Storm Over the Black Sea Fleet* (Sandhurst: Conflict Studies Research Centre, 1996).

29 Kudriachov, Odarych, and Orobets, *Carta Sevastopolya*, pp. 2–3.

30 *Den*, 13 May 1997.

31 In December 1995 a protocol of intent on the demarcation of borders between Ukraine and Russia was signed. *SWB* SU/2491. By September 1996, an agreement was reached on the necessity of starting the legal delimitation of borders. *SWB* SU/2712. So little progress was made that in February 1997 the Ukrainian foreign minister hinted that Ukraine might unilaterally delimit its border. SWB SU/2843, 2844. Russia's intransigence was perceived as being caused by the BSF issue and the status of Sevastopol/ Crimea.

32 *Zerkalo Nedeli*, 23 August, 1996; see also *Den*, 13 February 1997.

33 While Kudriachov *et al.*, argue that the Russians refused point blank to discuss the delimitation of marine borders (Kudriachov, Odarych and Orobets, *Carta Sevastopolya*, pp. 2–3), Sherr suggests that a sub-commission on the issue, 'on 22 October 1996 took up in detail the demarcation of the Sea of Azov and the Kerch Strait' (Sherr, 'Russia–Ukraine *Rapprochement*, p. 36). By 1998, little progress had been made on the sea's status; see *Narodna Armiya*, 18 September 1998.

34 *Kyiv Post*, 01 April 1999.

35 'Monitoring Foreign and Security Policy of Ukraine: On The Ratification of Black Sea Fleet Agreements by Ukraine', *The Ukraine List* (UKL) 39, p. 4.

36 Ibid., p. 5.

37 *Ukraine – Country Report*, Economist Intelligence Unit, 1999, 1st Quarter, p. 13.

38 *Kyiv Post*, 1 April 1999.

39 Sherr, 'Russia–Ukraine *Rapprochement*', p. 40.

40 The short-lived and non-militarised Ukrainska Narodna Republica (1917–1920) failed to mobilise any military forces, something which ultimately led to its downfall.

41 Stephen J. Zaloga. 'Armed Forces in Ukraine', *Jane's Intelligence Review*, March 1992, pp. 131–4. According to data in *Krymskaya Pravda*, 5–9 January 1992, the fleet was made up of 45 major warships, 28 submarines, 300 medium and small vessels, 151 airplanes and 85 helicopters. The discrepancy is probably attributable to the vested interests of underestimating the extent of the fleet by local actors.

42 Garnett, *Keystone in the Arch*, p. 113.

43 For a more elaborated exploration of the role of nuclear weapons in Ukraine's foreign policy formation between 1991 and 1994 see R. Wolczuk, 'The Evolution of Ukraine Foreign and Security Policy 1991–1994', *Slavic Military Studies*, 12(3), September 1999 pp. 18–37.

44 See Sherr, 'Russia–Ukraine *Rapprochement*'. For a more detailed breakdown on the make up of the fleet see Kuzio, *Ukrainian Security Policy, passim*. For an exposé see Savchenko, *Anatomia Neobyavlenoy Voyny*.

45 Savchenko, *Anatomia Neobyavlenoy Voyny*, p. 137.
46 The decision to 'hand over' the entire fleet contributed to Minister of Defence Morozov's eventual resignation in October 1993.
47 In Article 4 of the Accords, Ukraine was allocated 18.3 per cent of the fleet with the remaining 81.7 going to Russia (this division was on the basis of a 50:50 split, with Ukraine forfeiting the bulk of its portion in lieu of its debt to Russia). As the BSF was estimated to make up 10 per cent of the total Soviet fleet, a 50:50 division technically meant that Ukraine was in theory getting just 5 per cent of the total fleet. This meant Ukraine was to end up with one third of the 16 per cent it was entitled to according to the formula, which allocated the wealth of the Soviet Union to the various republics in proportion to population size of the republic. As the Ukrainian population made up 16 per cent of the population of the Soviet Union, it was entitled to 16 per cent of its wealth. However, the further reduction of this 50 per cent to 18.7 per cent meant that Ukraine was getting less than 2 per cent of total Soviet fleet forces. See Savchenko, *Anatomia Neobyavlenoy Voyny*, pp. 269–70
48 Sherr, 'Russia–Ukraine *Rapprochement*', p. 36.
49 Ibid., p. 40.
50 Ibid., p. 42.
51 The terms were for Russia to lease out facilities for $97 million per annum. Ukrainian analysts have calculated that Ukraine leased out 18232.62 hectares of Crimea for the sum of $0.53 per square metre per annum *including* the cost of the leasing out 4,591 buildings. No provision was made for recompensing Ukraine for stationing the Russian portion of the fleet for the 6 years during which the treaty and agreements were negotiated. As far as the division of the fleet was concerned, in line with the already agreed 50:50 split, and an earlier concession by the Ukrainians, the final split was 81.3 per cent of the fleet going to Russia, and the remaining 18.7 per cent going to Ukraine; Ukraine was compensated by a reduction in its energy debt by $521 million (for the 31.7 per cent ceded to Russia), a significant reduction on the $2,992.78 million Ukraine was demanding in August 1995. This suggests a total valuation of the fleet at some $1.6 billion, a significant reduction on the $80 billion Kyiv originally claimed the fleet was worth. Kudriachov, Odarych and Orobets, *Carta Sevastopolya*, pp. 7–8
52 Sherr, *Ukraine's New Time of Troubles*, p. 29.
53 M. M. Balmaceda, 'Gas, Oil and the Linkages between Domestic and Foreign Policies: The Case of Ukraine', *Europe-Asia Studies*, 50(2), 1998, pp. 257–86.
54 I. Burakovsky and V. Biletsky, *Ukraine's Way to the European Union – A View from Ukraine*, Analytical Report No.12 (Kyiv: Centre for Peace, Conversion and Foreign Policy of Ukraine, 1999) p. 7.
55 *Ukraine – Country Report*, Economist Intelligence Unit, 1997, 2nd Quarter, p. 38.
56 *Zerkalo Nedeli*, 21 March 1998.
57 Balmaceda, 'Gas, Oil and the Linkages between Domestic and Foreign Policies', p. 258.
58 *Ukraine – Country Report*, Economist Intelligence Unit, Quarterly issues between 1997 and 1999.
59 Ibid.
60 Balmaceda, 'Gas, Oil and the Linkages between Domestic and Foreign Policies', p. 258.
61 *Ukraine – Country Report*, Economist Intelligence Unit, 2nd Quarter 1999, p. 23.
62 *Holos Ukrainy*, 5 August 1998. The article discusses the vagaries of gas and oil pricing and transportation, taking them into account when drawing its conclusions. According to the Economist Intelligence Unit, Ukraine failed to benefit from the dramatic price decrease obtained by Germany when gas prices fell from $100 to $40 per cubic metre. These figures suggest that Ukraine was overpaying by $2 billion per annum. See *Ukraine – Country Report*, Economist Intelligence Unit, 2nd Quarter, 1999, pp. 22–3.
63 O. M. Smolenksy, 'Ukraine's Quest for Independence: The Fuel Factor', *Europe-Asia Studies*, 47(1), 1995, p. 69.
64 *Kyiv Post*, 25 Feb. 1999.

65 Balmaceda, 'Gas, Oil and the Linkages between Domestic and Foreign Policies', p. 259. See also *Holos Ukrainy*, 12 June 1998, for details of amounts transported and growth prospects.
66 *The European*, 7 March 1993.
67 Balmaceda, 'Gas, Oil and the Linkages between Domestic and Foreign Policies', p. 268
68 *Ukraine – Country Report*, Economist Intelligence Unit, 1st Quarter 1999, p. 23.
69 *Financial Times*, 19 October 2000.
70 Balmaceda, 'Gas, Oil and the Linkages between Domestic and Foreign Policies', p. 269
71 Ibid., pp. 263–4. For more details on Ukraine's gas infrastructure see *Holos Ukrainy*, 3 February 1998, 16 October 1998 and also 17 November 1998.
72 *Ukraine – Country Report*, Economic Intelligence Unit, 2nd Quarter 1998, p. 23. As a prelude to ownership, Shell and UkrGazProm agreed to jointly evaluate both the physical and financial aspects of the gas pipeline and storage systems. From a geopolitical point of view, of interest is the fact that Ukraine's relations with Shell had been developing for some time. According to one report, Western interest (and Shell's in particular) in the Ukrainian gas infrastructure was promoted in a letter from President Clinton to President Kuchma in April 1997. See *Zerkalo Nedeli*, 20 December 1997, *Uriadovy Kurier*, 9 October 1997 and *Zerkalo Nedeli*, 11 October 1997, on the development of Shell's interest in Ukraine, including its role in the transportation of Caspian oil, and extraction of gas in the Black Sea region.
73 At the end of October, the prime minister, Victor Yushchenko, visited Western capitals to discuss the possibility of granting concessions to private companies to operate Ukraine's gas pipeline network. *Financial Times*, 23 October 2000.
74 *International Herald Tribune*, 21 October 2000. However, Gaz de France suggested that the signed document was only regarding a feasibility study. See Tammy Lynch, 'Ukraine – A New Territorial Pact', *The NIS Observed: An Analytical Review*, Vol. V, No, 15, October 2000.
75 Smolenksy, 'Ukraine's Quest for Independence', p. 85
76 *Ukraine- Aircraft and Parts*, Bain & Company for the Commercial Service of the US, Kyiv, August 1995.
77 *Narodna Armiya*, 11 February 1997.
78 The Russian RSC-Energia was a 25 per cent partner in the consortium Ukraine's Yuzhmash and Yuzhnoye Design Bureau joint 15 per cent partners; Boeing had 40 percent and Kvaerner Maritime of Norway, 20 percent. *Kyiv Post*, 01 April 1999.
79 The Russian companies involved are Rosobschemach and Ascond; in addition to the ubiquitous Yuzhmash and the Yuznoye Design Bureau on the Ukrainian side, Khartron, a company based in Kharkiv, was also involved. *Kyiv Post*, 25 March 1999. Khartron was in fact a top-secret producer of space technology in the Soviet Union. Amongst other things, it produced the control system for the *Mir* space station. The company is particularly keen on tighter ties with Russia: 'we are keen that our Russian customers become participants in the company: we will give them shares; they will give us orders'. *Zerkalo Nedeli*, 14 March 1998.
80 *Ukraine – Aircraft and Parts*.
81 *Narodna Armiya*, 13 Jan. 1998; also 13 Feb. 1998.
82 *Zerkalo Nedeli*, 15 February 1997
83 *Zerkalo Nedeli*, 9 September 1997.
84 *Narodna Armiya*, 13 March 1998.
85 *Zerkalo Nedeli*, 9 September 1997.
86 *Narodna Armiya*, 13 August 1998.
87 Although the treaty required both parties to harmonise economic legislations, Sherr points out that no-one asked 'how Ukraine could harmonise economic legislation with Russia and the European Union at the same time'. See Sherr, *Ukraine's New Time of Troubles*, p. 30.

88 M. Honchar, O Moskalets and S Nalivka, 'Vidhomin Serpnevoho Strusu', *Polityka I Chas*, 2, 1999, p. 45. Artificial efforts to inject some life into Ukrainian–Russian economic relations, as in the case of the economic co-operation treaty, tend to be flawed. First, the agreement lacks a mechanism for implementing its well-meaning objectives, namely a significant growth in trade between the two. Second, the agreement as an inter-state document pays little heed to the essentially inter-manufacturer co-operation needed for the achievement of its objectives, notwithstanding the wide-ranging ownership of such enterprises by the state. As such, the agreement is little more than a set of recommendations. Furthermore, no provision within the agreement is made for the harmonisation of its requirements with those of the norms and standards demanded by the EU, WTO or other significant international financial bodies. See *Zerkalo Nedeli*, 21 March 1998.
89 Honchar, Moskalets and Nalivka, 'Vidhomin Serpnevoho Strusu', p. 38.
90 I. Burakovsky and V. Biletsky, *Ukraine's Way to the European Union*, p. 15.
91 *Den*, 17 December 1996.
92 *Den*, 17 December 1996.
93 Garnett, *Keystone in the Arch*, p. 49.
94 *Den*, 27 February 1997.
95 K. J. Mihalisko, 'Belarus: Retreat to Authoritarianism' in K. Dawisha and B. Parrott (eds), *Democratic Changes and Authoritarian Reactions in Russia, Ukraine, Belarus and Moldova* (Cambridge: Cambridge University Press 1997) p. 248.
96 V. Paznyak, 'Belarus: in Search of a Security Identity', in R. Allison and C. Bluth (eds), *Security Dilemmas in Russia and Eurasia* (London: RIIA 1998) p. 159.
97 O. Y Manachinski, *Suchasni Voyenno-Politychny Vidnosyny Ukrainy iz Sumizno-Prylehlymy Derzavami*, Vypusk 2 (Kyiv: Natsionaly Institut Stratehichnych Doslidzen 1996) p. 9.
98 K. J. Mihalisko, 'Belarus: Retreat to Authoritarianism', p. 274.
99 Ibid., p. 273.
100 V. Paznyak, 'Belarus: in Search of a Security Identity', p. 165.
101 *Agence France-Presse*, 25 February 1998.
102 *Reuters*, 26 February 1999.
103 *RFE/RL*, 10 April 1999. For an overview of military agreements signed between Russia and Belarus on a bilateral and multilateral basis see, M.B. Olcott, A. Åslund and S.W. Garnett, *Getting it Wrong – Regional Co-operation and the Commonwealth of Independent States* (Washington DC: Carnegie Endowment for International Peace 1999) pp. 77–108.
104 G. Sanford, 'Belarus on the Road to Nationhood', *Survival*, 38(1), Spring 1996, p. 138.
105 M. M. Balmaceda, '*Belarus and Russia after Yeltsin*', paper presented at the Special Seminar on Belarus, University of Bath, 10–11 February 2000.
106 *Agence France-Presse*, 25 February 1999.
107 *Associated Press*, 28 April 1999.
108 M. M. Balmaceda, '*Belarus and Russia after Yeltsin*'.
109 *Den*, 14 May 1997.
110 *Den*, 27 February 1997.
111 *Narodna Armiya*, 11 September 1996.
112 *Nezavisimost*, 16 September 1997.
113 *Voice of America*, 7 March 1998.

3 The North-eastern azimuth: subregional and regional integration

1 R. Solchanyk, 'Russia, Ukraine and the Imperial Legacy', *Post-Soviet Affairs*, 9(4), 1993, pp. 356–7.
2 G. Sanford, 'Belarus on the Road to Nationhood', p. 148.
3 *Narodna Armiya*, 10 June 1997.

4 I. Pritzel, *National Identity and Foreign Policy: Nationalism and Leadership in Poland, Russia and Ukraine* (Cambridge: Cambridge University Press 1998) p. 280.
5 *Holos Ukrainy*, 11 June 1996.
6 *Nezavisimost*, 16 September 1997.
7 O. Hrynkevych, 'Things Return to Their "Natural" State: Russia, Belarus and the "New Commonwealth"', *Politics and the Times*, February 1996, pp. 85–91.
8 *Reuters*, 15 March 1999.
9 *Argumenty I Fakty*, 3 August 1999.
10 *Den*, 14 May 1997.
11 According to reports, 'Yeltsin, acting as Gorbachev's spokesman, informed Kravchuk that the Soviet President was prepared to let Ukraine make any amendments to the text of the Union treaty that it desired, but only under one condition: that it sign the document . . . Kravchuk responded that if Ukraine were to propose its version the result would not be a confederative state but a commonwealth of states.' See R. Solchanyk, 'Russia, Ukraine and the Imperial Legacy', p. 354.
12 Garnett, *Keystone in the Arch*, p. 61.
13 Olcott, Åslund and Garnett, *Getting it Wrong*, passim.
14 Author's discussion with an official from the Ukrainian Ministry of Foreign Affairs, Kyiv, July 1997.
15 *Argumenty I Fakty*, No. 50, 1991, p. 1.
16 Garnett, *Keystone in the Arch*, p. 62.
17 Ibid., pp. 62–3.
18 It is worth pointing out that while the CIS was explicitly integrative (as codified in the Minsk Agreement and CIS Charter), the institutional structures designed to implement these agreements were either consultative or not empowered to impose on member states legally binding decisions. Olcott, Åslund and Garnett, *Getting it Wrong*, p. 10.
19 Indeed, so fearful of the renewal of empire were the Ukrainians, that they even insisted that the word 'commonwealth' be written with a lower case 'c' to avoid conferring on the institution any state-like attributes that might be inferred if an upper case 'C' was used. *Holos Ukrainy*, 11 June 1996.
20 *RFE/RL*, 17 January 1992.
21 *RFE/RL*, 24 April 1992.
22 See Bohdan Horyn, the noted Ukrainian parliamentarian and activist's article 'Ukraina I SND' in *Narodna Armiya*, 6 August 1996, for a more detailed breakdown of the incongruence between the Ukrainian constitution and the CIS Charter.
23 *RFE/RL*, 16 Nov. 1992
24 As of 1 September 1997, the CIS was made up of 74 committees, 54 of which Ukraine participated in: 27 as a full member, and the other 27 as an observer. V. Tkachenko, *Spivdruznist Nezaleznych Derzav ta Natsionalni Interesy Ukrainy* (Kyiv: Institut Hromadskoho Suspilstva 1998) p. 20. Although the charter was ready in January 1993, Ukraine (along with Moldova and Turkmenistan) has, as of 2002, still not signed, nor has the Supreme Rada ratified it.
25 *RFE/RL*, 30 November 1992.
26 *RFE/RL*, 1 December 1992.
27 *RFE/RL*, 30 March 1992.
28 A. Rudnyk, *Politychna Karta SND* (Kyiv: Ukrainska Perspektyva 1996) p. 7.
29 Tkachenko, *Spivdruznist Nezaleznych Derzav ta Natsionalni Interesy Ukrainy*, p. 41.
30 Ibid., p. 41.
31 *RFE/RL*, 15 Sep. 1993.
32 Primakov quoted in Tkachenko, *Spivdruznist Nezaleznych Derzav ta Natsionalni Interesy Ukrainy*, p. 42.
33 Ukrainian researchers point to the proposed voting system in the CIS Interparliamentary Assembly as a good example of this. Voting in this institution was to be on the basis of one vote per delegation with proposals requiring 'a consensus' (i.e. unanimity) in order to be carried. However, hidden amongst the clauses was the suggestion that 'the one

vote per delegation will apply as long as no other decisions have been taken which supersede the aforementioned point'. A good example of the possible emergence of such a 'superseding decision' was the suggestion made in the Russian Duma in April 1995 for voting to take place 'on a quota basis', i.e. with votes weighed according to percentage of the population, with Russia getting something like 40 per cent of the vote (in line with the fact that it has 40 per cent of the total CIS population) and Ukraine 17 per cent. If decisions in the CIS body were subsequently to be made on the basis of a qualified majority (which has been mooted, incidentally), something easily achieved by the Russians thanks to the trusted support of the Belarussians and some of the Muslim republics, the Ukrainians could be easily outvoted on all major issues, demeaning their role in the body to that of observers. A. Filipenko, 'The CIS Economic Union: Pros and Cons', *Politics and the Times*, October–December, 1995, pp. 58–65.

34 *Uriadovy Kurier*, 8 June 1996.

35 Events in both Russia and Ukraine highlight the need to distinguish between positions taken up by the respective governments and legislatures of the two states. I am indebted to Professor Neil Malcolm for reminding me of this point.

36 *Ukraine – Country Report*, Economist Intelligence Unit, 2nd Quarter, 1999, p. 13.

37 *RFE/RL*, 3 March 1999. The importance of the CIS IPA has been dismissed by Nationalists in the Ukrainian parliament on the grounds that it can hold consultations and make recommendations, but not enforce anything.

38 For a more detailed analysis of the evolution of Ukraine's foreign and security policy, see R. Wolczuk, 'The Evolution of Ukraine Foreign and Security Policy 1991–1994', *Slavic Military Studies*, 12(3), September 1999, pp. 18–37.

39 *RFE/RL*, 5 February 1992.

40 *RFE/RL*, 8 April 1992.

41 *RFE/RL*, 18 May 1992. Georgia joined the CIS in October 1993 under what it saw as duress. Apparently Shevardnadze was told, 'if you want gas, oil, raw materials then join the CIS'; see *RFE/RL*, 11 October 1993. The Azeri parliament refused to ratify former President Mutabilov's decision in December 1991 committing Azerbaijan to CIS membership; subsequently, following the election of President Aliev, the parliament reversed its decision in September 1993; see *RFE/RL*, 21 Sep. 1993, and 20 March 1996.

42 *RFE/RL*, 9 Oct. 1992.

43 *Narodna Armiya*, 6 August 1996. Olcott *et al.* argue that this interest was triggered by hopes for an injection of funds into Ukraine's military infrastructure. Olcott, Åslund and Garnett, *Getting it Wrong*, p. 91.

44 Tkachenko, *Spivdruznist Nezaleznych Derzav ta Natsionalni Interesy Ukrainy*, p. 67.

45 *Den*, 1 March 1997. V. Zerebestky, a member of the Ukrainian parliament and a member of the Parliamentary Committee of Foreign Affairs stated that the agreement needed to be subjected to ratification by the parliament. However, the right-wing-dominated committee refused to process the agreement as the left-wing-dominated parliament would have been certain to ratify it. In the view of Zerebetsky, such a ratification would legitimise Russia's presence on Ukraine's territory beyond the parametres of the treaty signed between the two states in 1997, something that was unacceptable to the committee (conversation with author, Kyiv, July 1997).

46 *RFE/RL*, 24 April 1992.

47 Smith, *Russian Hegemony in the Near Abroad*, p. 3.

48 *RFE/RL*, 13 January 1992.

49 *RFE/RL*, 7 October 1992.

50 *Uriadovy Kurier*, 18 January 1997.

51 Author's conversation with an official from the Ministry of Foreign Affairs, Kyiv, November 1999.

52 *Holos Ukrainy*, 11 June 1996.

53 *RFE/RL*, 1 December 1998.

54 Filipenko, 'The CIS Economic Union: Pros and Cons'.

55 Ibid.
56 *RFE/RL*, 29 Nov 1994.
57 *RFE/RL*, 26 Jan. 1995 and 25 April 1995.
58 Solchnanyk, 'Russia, Ukraine and the Imperial Legacy'.
59 *Narodna Armiya*, 3 June 1997.
60 *RFE/RL*, 19 Sep. 1997.
61 *RFE/RL*, 23 July 1998 (authors italics).
62 N. V. Lamont, *Territorial Dimensions of Ethnic Conflict: The Moldovan Case*, Foreign Military Studies Office, Fort Leavenworth, K.S., p. 2; a version of the article appeared as 'Ethnic Conflict in the Transdniester' in *Military Review*, December–February 1995.
63 *RFE/RL*, 22 Nov. 1992.
64 *Nezavisimaya Gazeta*, 5 February 1997.
65 Garnett, *Keystone in the Arch*, p. 69.
66 *Zerkalo Nedeli*, 10–16 January, 1998
67 *Zerkalo Nedeli*, 25–31 October 1997.
68 *Uriadovy Kurier*, 18 January 1997.
69 *RFE/RL*, 27 June 2000.
70 Honchar, Moskalets and Nalivka, 'Vidhomin Serpnevoho Strusu', p. 39.
71 *Uriadovy Kurier*, 29 March 1997.
72 Olcott, Åslund and Garnett, *Getting it Wrong*.
73 *Uriadovy Kurier*, 5 May 1996.
74 Sherr, *Ukraine's New Time of Troubles*, p. 32.
75 Mansfield and Milner, 'The New Wave of Regionalism', p. 611.
76 Ibid., p. 611.
77 I. Bremmer, S. Clement, A. Cottey and T. Dokos, 'Emerging Subregional Co-operation Processes: South-Eastern Europe, The Newly Independent States and the Mediterranean', in Cottey, '*Subregional Co-operation in the New Europe*', p. 227.

4 Ukraine's relations with Central and East European neighbours

1 T. Bukkvol, *Ukraine and European Security* (London: Royal Institute of International Affairs 1997) p. 75.
2 For an overview of relations see P. J. Potichnyj (ed.), *Poland and Ukraine – Past and Present* (Toronto: CIUS 1980).
3 Manachinski, *Suchasni Voyenno-Politychny Vidnosyny Ukrainy*, p. 68.
4 Quoted in O. L. Valevsky and M. M. Honchar, *Struktura Heopolitichnych Interesiv Ukrainy*, Vypusk 45 (Kyiv: Natsionalny Institut Stratehichnych Doslidzen 1995) p. 42.
5 Ilya Prizel, 'The Influence of Ethnicity on Foreign Policy – The Case of Ukraine' in Roman Szporluk (ed.), *National Identity and Ethnicity in Russia and the New States of Eurasia* (London: M.E. Sharpe 1994) p. 112.
6 *Nashe Slovo*, 31 Jan. 1993.
7 Ian Brzezinski, 'Polish–Ukrainian Relations: Europe's Neglected Strategic Axis', *Survival*, 35(3), Autumn 1993, p. 26.
8 Indeed, this phrase was used by the Polish dissident Jacek Kuron in 1980. Adrian Karatnycky, 'A Polish Voice', *New Leader*, 15 June 1981.
9 Bukkvol, *Ukraine and European Security*, p. 76.
10 M. M. Balmaceda, 'Ukraine, Russia, and European Security: Thinking Beyond NATO Expansion', *Problems of Post-Communism*, 45(1), January/February 1998, pp. 21–9.
11 *SWB*, 26 May 1993.
12 The only bilateral document known by the researcher to have been signed by the Ukrainian SSR was with Poland. The agreement between the Ukrainian SSR and the Polish Committee of National Liberation concerning the evacuation of the Ukrainian population from Polish territory and the Polish population from the territory of the

Ukrainian SSR was signed on 9 Sep. 1944 in Lublin. The protocol of 6 May 1947 marked the completion of the operation. R.M. Slusser and J.F. Triska, *A Calendar of Soviet Treaties, 1917–1957* (Stanford: Stanford University Press 1959), p. 216.

13 *Ukraina na Mizhnarodny Areni. Zbirnik Dokumentiv I Materialiv 1991–1995. Knyha 1*, Ministerstvo Zakordonnych Sprav Ukrainy (Kyiv: Yurinkom Inter 1998) p. 250.

14 Ibid., p. 385.

15 Garnett, *Keystone in the Arch*, pp. 86–91.

16 It needs to be recalled that for a long time much of Western Ukraine had been part of Poland. Conversely much of the population of south-eastern Poland is ethnically Ukrainian.

17 For example, Leonid Kuchma in his speech to the Polish Sejm on 26 June 1996. Additionally, *Przeglad Srodkowoeuropejski, Bezpieczenstwo Europy, Obronnosc, Integracja, No 14*, Padziernik 1995, p. 30. See also Janusz Dobrosz in *Gazeta Wyborcza*, 22 May 1997.

18 *Nashe Slovo*, 22 Sep. 1991.

19 I. Brzezinski, 'The Geopolitical Dimension', *The National Interest*, Spring 1992, p. 51.

20 *Nashe Slovo*, 1 February 1992.

21 *Nashe Slovo*, 23 May 1993.

22 According to a UN Human Development Report, Ukrainian standards of living were estimated to have declined by 80 per cent between 1991 and 1995. *Ukraine. Human Development Report* (Kyiv: United Nations Development Programme 1995).

23 Garnett, 'Poland: Bulwark or Bridge?', *Foreign Policy*, 2, 1996, Spring, p. 71.

24 Bukkvol, *Ukraine and European Security*, p. 75

25 *Nashe Slovo*, 31 Jan. 1993.

26 *Uriadovy Kurier*, 8 June 1996.

27 Y. Berdesha, M. Honchar, and O. Moskalets, *Mistse Polshchi v Polititsi Bezpeky Ukrainy* (forthcoming).

28 *Narodna Armiya*, 8 Oct. 1996.

29 *Nashe Slovo*, 14 Dec. 1997.

30 I. Kobrinskaja, *Dlugi Koniec Zimnej Wojny* (Warsaw: Centrum Stosunkow Miedzynarodowych 1998) p. 146.

31 *Uriadovy Kurier*, 24 May 1997.

32 Berdesha, Honchar and Moskalets, *Mistse Polshchi v Polititsi Bezpeky Ukrainy*.

33 For example, a route from Tengiz, via Atyrau, Tikhoretsk, Novorossiysk, the Bosphorus, Wilhelmshaven to Leuna was estimated to be 9,310 kilometres in comparison to the 4,700 kilometres if the route was to go from Tengiz via Baku, Supsa, the Yuzhniy pipeline to Brody, Plock, Shwedt and Leuna. 'Caspian Oil to European Markets through Ukraine', Project Presentation for the Business Forum of the European Bank for Reconstruction and Development by the State Committee for Oil, Gas and Oil Refining Industry of Ukraine, May 1998.

34 *Zerkalo Nedeli*, 27 June–4 July 1997.

35 *Uriadovy Kurier*, 24 May 1997.

36 By linking the new Yuzniy pipeline with Druzhba, oil could also be transported to Slovakia, the Czech Republic, Hungary, Austria and Germany.

37 *Nashe Slovo*, 11 October 1996.

38 In light of the financial hardship that drove such cross-border transactions, it is somewhat ironic that these flows of people were categorised as 'tourist' for purposes of official statistics.

39 Mieczyslaw Kowerski, 'Wplyw handlu z Ukraina na rozwoj wojewodztw przygranicznych', *Gospodarka Narodowa*, 3, 1998.

40 Berdesha, Honchar and Moskalets, *Mistse Polshchi v Polititsi Bezpeky Ukrainy*. As an aside, it is worth highlighting how much of the trade between two such industrialised parties is made up of raw materials. For example, in 1996, 37.8 per cent of total Ukraine exports to Poland were made up of ore and metals, whilst 38 per cent of Ukrainian imports from Poland were made up of energy resources.

41 *Narodna Armiya*, 5 Jan. 1998. This border crossing, between Krakovec and Korchova, was the fifth such crossing between Poland and Ukraine. Many more exist between Poland and Germany.
42 Kowerski, 'Wplyw handlu z Ukraina'.
43 *Uriadovy Kurier*, 20 March 1997.
44 *Gazeta Wyborcza*, 22 May 1997.
45 *Gazeta Wyborcza*, 21 May 1997.
46 *Uriadovy Kurier*, 24 May 1997.
47 *Zerkalo Nedeli*, 27 December 1997.
48 *Zerkalo Nedeli*, 7 May 1998.
49 *Financial Times (Special Supplement – Hungary)*, 22 November 2000.
50 *Narodna Armiya*, 13 February 1997 and 14 October 1998.
51 O. Mirus, 'Ne Metodom vyrishenya a shlyachom dosyahnenya', *Polityka I Chas*, May 1996, pp. 43–9.
52 A. Zolnayi, 'Uhorski Partnery Chekayut na Propozytsiyi', *Polityka I Chas*, May 1995, pp. 56–9.
53 Hungarian-CEFTA Trade, Central and Eastern Europe Business Information Centre, http://iepnt1.itaiep.doc.gov/ eebic/cables/1997/jan/bud42.htm.
54 *Zerkalo Nedeli*, 7 May 1998.
55 In fact Tarasiuk was told that 'the EU makes no exceptions for anyone, and the demands of the Schengen Agreement are rigourously applied to all sides', *Zerkalo Nedeli*, 7 May 1998.
56 The pipeline has a capacity of about 20 million tons, though since 1993 only about 12 million tons (including 6–7 millions for the Czech Republic) has traversed the pipeline. See 'Slovakia: Economic Relations with the Russian Federation', *RFE/RL*, http://iepnt1.itaiep.doc.gov/eebic/CEFTA/CABLES/BRA1035.HTM
57 'Slovakia: Natural Gas Agreement with Russia Criticised', *RFE/RL*, http://www.rferl.org/nca/features/1997/05/ F.RU.970522145848.html
58 See 'Slovakia: Economic Relations with the Russian Federation', *RFE/RL*, http://iepnt1.itaiep.doc.gov/eebic/CEFTA/CABLES/BRA1035.HTM
59 For a wider ranging discussion of this period see N. Dima, *Bessarabia and Bukovina: The Soviet-Romanian Territorial Dispute* (New York: Columbia University Press 1982).
60 It has been suggested that in 1950 the Romanians agreed to 'give' the island to the USSR at the latter's request. N. Dima, *Bessarabia and Bukovina, passim*.
61 'The Treaty on the Regime of the Soviet-Romanian Border, Co-operation and Mutual Assistance in Border Issues', concluded between the two states in February 1961 was in fact based on the 1947 Paris Treaty, the 1948 Protocol and the 1949 Treaty.
62 Press Release of the Ukrainian Government: '*On The Situation Concerning The State Border Between Ukraine and Romania*', 27 Jan. 1997.
63 *Demokratychna Ukraina*, 5 Dec. 1991.
64 *OMRI Daily Digest*, 7 Dec. 1995.
65 *UNIAN News Agency*, 10 Feb. 1995.
66 Antonescu was the Romanian premier from 1940, and generalissimo and commander of Romanian armies after joining in Germany's war against the Soviet Union in 1941. See *Holos Ukrainy*, 26 June 1996, for the Romanian response.
67 Press release of the Ukrainian government: '*Finalization of the Draft Treaty between Ukraine and Romania on Good-Neighbourly Relations and Co-operation*', 27 Jan. 1997.
68 *Narodna Armiya*, 26 Dec. 1996.
69 *Ukraina I Svit*, 8 Feb. 1997.
70 According to a member of the Ukrainian parliament, Volodymyr Zerebetski, a member of the Committee on Foreign Affairs and the CIS 'The problem lies in the fact that while the land border between the USSR and Romania was agreed, they did not agree on the marine border – oil was plentiful and nobody paid that much attention to the issue' (conversation with the author, Kyiv 1997).

71 *Holos Ukrainy*, 22 Jan. 1997.
72 Ukrainian legislation (designed so as to eliminate the dangers associated with giving the Russian minority resident in Ukraine joint citizenship as demanded by Moscow) permits the possession of only one citizenship, while Romanian legislation allows for dual citizenship.
73 *Holos Ukrainy*, 22 Jan. 1997.
74 Although the declaration was enshrined in the law 'On National Minorities' (adopted in June 1992), the latter failed to fulfil the objectives of the declaration – because of the increasing threats to the territorial integrity of Ukraine, the law failed to mention the issue of territorial autonomy, despite securing extensive rights for national minorities. As a result, in its place, a new law is being proposed by the member of parliament for Chernivtsi Oblast in Northern Bukovina, Ivan Popescu, 'On indigenous people, national minorities and ethnic groups in Ukraine', which would provide for this territorial autonomy.
75 According to the Ukrainians the issue appears to hinge on the inhabitability of the island. They believe that if classified as 'habitable', international law provides for a 12-mile exclusion zone, something that does not apply in the case of uninhabitability (author's conversation with Volodymyr Zerebetski).
76 Article 2 refers to a separate agreement regarding all of these matters, activated through an exchange of letters by the two foreign ministers, at the same time as the main treaty.
77 Author's translation.
78 T. R. W. Waters, 'Problems, Progress and Propsects in a Post-Soviet Borderland: The Republic of Moldova', gopher://marvin.nc3a.nato.int:70/00/secdef/csrc/s29.txt, p. 5 (originally published in *Boundary and Security Bulletin*, 5(1), Spring 1997).
79 *UN Report – Moldova*, http://www.un.md/NEW/PUBS/NHDR/chap1.html, p. 4.
80 M. Orr, '14 Army and the Crisis in Moldova', April 1992, gopher://marvin.nc3a.nato.int:70/00/secdef/csrc/k11, p. 1.
81 Waters, 'Problems, Progress and Propsects', p. 2.
82 In *Bezopasnonst. Informatsionnyi Sbornik Fonda Natsionalnoi I Mezhdunarodnoi Bezopasnosti*, nos. 1 and 2 (January and February), taken from *Transition*, 20 October 1995, p. 6.
83 Waters, 'Problems, Progress and Prospects', p. 2.
84 Ibid.
85 I. F. Selivanova, *Trans-Dniestria*, http://www.rand.org/publications/CF/CF129/CF-129.chapter4.html, p. 3.
86 At the same time, the Republic of Gagauzia was established in southern Moldova by the minority of Gagauzes who were driven by similar of fears of Romanisation. The Gagauz make up 3.5 per cent of the population of Moldova, and are located mainly in the south of the country.
87 N. V. Lamont, *Territorial Dimension of Ethnic Conflict: The Moldovan Case* (Kansas: Foreign Military Studies Office, 1996) p. 3; (a version of this article entitled, 'Ethnic Conflict in Transdniester', appeared in *Military Review*, December–February 1995).
88 Ibid.
89 Waters, 'Problems, Progress and Propsects'.
90 Lamont, *Territorial Dimension of Ethnic Conflict*, p. 5.
91 Ibid., p. 6.
92 Ibid., p. 7.
93 P. Baev, 'Peacekeeping and Conflict Management in Eurasia', in R. Allison and C. Bluth (eds), *Security Dilemmas in Russia and Eurasia* (London: Royal Institute of International Affairs 1998) pp. 211–12.
94 For details of numbers of troops involved and ordinance possessed by these forces see G. B. Solomon (Special Rapporteur), *Peacekeeping in the Transdniester Region: A Test Case for the CSCE* (Draft Special Report), November 1994, http://www.intnet.net/pub/COUNTRIES/Moldova/Moldova.conflict.data.

95 Solomon, *Peacekeeping in the Transdniester Region: A Test Case for the CSCE*, p. 9.
96 According to Baev, Lebed 'worked a miracle' preventing either the disintegration of the 14th Army or anarchy with units getting involved in combat operations. Baev, 'Peacekeeping and Conflict Management in Eurasia', p. 211. For comments on the role of the Russian Ministry of Defence, see T. Kuzio, *Ukrainian Security Policy*, p. 78.
97 Radio Kyiv Report 7 and 8, March 1993, as translated in 'Moldovan–Ukrainian Rapprochement', SOVSET, 11 March 1993; taken from Lamont, *Territorial Dimension of Ethnic Conflict*, p. 18.
98 *RFE/RL*, 18 February 1994.
99 *RFE/RL*, 12 January 1994.
100 *RFE/RL*, 1 December 1992.
101 Lamont, *Territorial Dimension of Ethnic Conflict*, pp. 12–13.
102 *RFE/RL*, 14 March 1994.
103 *RFE/RL*, 11 April 1994.
104 *RFE/RL*, 22 February 1994.
105 *RFE/RL*, 9 June 1994.
106 *RFE/RL*, 12 August 1994.
107 *Transition*, 20 October 1995, p.10.
108 *Holos Ukrainy*, 8 May 1997.
109 *Uriadovy Kurier*, 9 May 1997; also S. Garnett and R. Lebenson, 'Chy Nastane Myr u Prydnistrovyi?', *Polityka I Chas*, January 1999, p. 58 (author's translation of article).
110 G. B. Solomon (Special Rapporteur), *Peacekeeping in the Transdniester Region: A Test Case for the CSCE* (Draft Special Report), November 1994, p. 12.
111 *Narodna Armiya*, 18 October 1997.
112 *Holos Ukrainy*, 5 November 1997.
113 Garnett and Lebenson, 'Chy Nastane Myr', p. 59.
114 Ibid., p. 60.
115 Ibid., p. 61.
116 *Uriadovy Kurier*, 13 March 1997; see also *Den*, 20 June 1997.
117 *Den*, 20 June 1997.
118 *The Ukrainian Weekly*, 25 July 1999, No. 30, Vol. LXVII.
119 RFE/RL, 3 August 2000.
120 Garnett and Lebenson, 'Chy Nastane Myr', p. 60.
121 Ibid., p. 61.

5 The Western azimuth: subregional and regional integration

1 Kobrinskaja, *Dlugi Koniec Zimnej Wojny*, p. 40.
2 Ibid., pp. 40–2.
3 S.R. Burant, 'Foreign Policy and National Identity: A Comparison of Ukraine and Belarus', *Europe-Asia Studies*, 47(7), 1995, pp. 1125–44.
4 Conversation with an official from the Polish Ministry of Foreign Affairs, Warsaw, August 2000.
5 L. Pastusiak (Rapporteur), *Subregional Co-operation Among Central European Countries And Their Struggle Toward Membership of Transatlantic Structures* (Draft Special Report), Sub-Committee on Transatlantic And European Relations, AN104, PC/TER (96) 4.
6 H. Shmanko and E. Kish, 'Vishegradski Chotyrykutnyk', *Polityka I Chas*, January 1994, p. 50.
7 For example, at a meeting of Ukrainian and Polish parliamentary deputies, and foreign and defence ministry officials, the Poles were explicitly urged by the Ukrainians to assist Ukraine in its efforts at membership of the Visegrad triangle. Konferencja Polsko-Ukrainska nt. 'Droga Ukrainy do Europy', *Sprawy Miedzynarodowe*, 1992, Vol. 4–6, pp. 149–70.

8 However, Ukraine is unlikely to gain entry until it has signed bilateral treaties on free trade with all the CEFTA states; become a member of the WTO; signed an association agreement with the EU (the partnership and co-operation agreement signed between Ukraine and EU allows for the creation of a free trade area between the two starting from 1998; a free trade area is a prerequisite to an association agreement).
9 Kobrinskaja, *Dlugi Koniec Zimnej Wojny*, p. 67.
10 The CEI was formed in 1989 by Italy, Austria, Hungary, Yugoslavia and subsequently Czechoslovakia. Poland joined in 1991 despite the objections of Prague which was concerned at the damage Polish membership may do to its own ambitions. The organisation was designed to establish a platform for co-operation on political and economic issues in the region. It was also designed to facilitate the process of preparation undertaken by member states for eventual entry into the European Union. See R. Wolczuk, 'Ukraine and Europe', p. 42.
11 Speech to the Polish Sejm on 26 June 1996.
12 *Uriadovy Kurier*, 20 March 1997.
13 O. Pavliuk, 'Ukrainian–Polish Relations: A Pillar of Regional Stability', in M. Wohlfeld (ed.), *The Effects of Enlargement on Bilateral Relations in Central and Eastern Europe* (Paris: Institute for Security Studies, Western European Union 1997) p. 46.
14 *Zerkalo Nedeli*, 21 March 1998.
15 *Holos Ukrainy*, 5 June 1998.
16 V. Horbulin, 'Ukraine's Place in Today's Europe', *Politics and the Times*, October–December 1995, pp. 10–15.
17 See, for example, President Kuchma's speech to the Western European Union. *Uriadovy Kurier*, 8 June 1996, nos 104–5.
18 *Polityka Bezpieczenstwa I Strategia Obronna RP*, 2 November 1992.
19 Garnett, 'Poland: Bulwark or Bridge?', p. 77.
20 Kobrinskaja, *Dlugi Koniec Zimnej Wojny*, p. 67.
21 The speech of I. Raciu to the NATO Consultative Committee on 30 May 1994 was published in the Romanian press under the title 'Partnership for Peace will save Romania'. See Kobrinskaja, *Dlugi Koniec Zimnej Wojny*, p. 69.
22 Ibid., p. 68.
23 Ibid., p. 65.
24 Ibid., p. 67.
25 Although at the same time as PfP was announced, the alliance proclaimed that 'we expect and would welcome NATO expansion that would reach to democratic states to our East', no timescale was mentioned. P. Kolodziejczyk, 'Poland – A Future NATO Ally', *NATO Review*, No. 5, 1994, p. 7. The issue of the integration of Central and East European States into the European Union was finally discussed at the summit of leaders of the EU in December 1994. Similarly, one of the first explicit and unambiguous references to Poland's membership of NATO was made in September 1994 at a meeting of NATO defence ministers.
26 Pastusiak, *Subregional Co-operation Among Central European Countries*.
27 Zbigniew Brzezinski quoted in *Nashe Slovo*, 21 April 1996. On Nicholas Burns, see Kobrinskaja, *Dlugi Koniec Zimnej Wojny*, p. 89.
28 On a visit of the speaker of the speaker of the Polish Sejm to Kyiv in October 1995, the then Prime Minister Marchuk urged the Poles to be cautious about joining NATO, in response to which the speaker Zych replied they would 'not retreat'. *SWB*, 9 October 1995.
29 *Nashe Slovo*, 21 April 1996.
30 For more details on this see the report 'Poland–NATO' which was the result of discussions at the Euro-Atlantic Association and the Stefan Batory Foundation. See also W. Cimoszewicz, 'Building Poland's Security: Membership of NATO a Key Objective', *NATO Review*, No. 3, 1996, pp. 3–5; also Kolodziejczyk, 'Poland – A Future NATO Ally', pp. 7–10.

31 This was made clear by Polish Defence Minister Zbigniew Okonski, *PAP News Wire*, 27 Sep. 1995.
32 For example, in his speech to the OSCE in Lisbon in December 1996, President Kuchma argued that 'Ukraine, more than any other country, has the full right to touch on the issue of non-stationing of nuclear weapons on the territories of the states of Central and Eastern Europe, and to be able to depend on understanding and support for its position', *Uriadovy Kurier*, 5 December 1996.
33 Garnett, 'Poland: Bulwark or Bridge?' pp. 66–82.
34 Ibid., p. 81.
35 There is some confusion on who initiated the idea of the charter. Kuzio argues that 'on a visit to NATO in June 1995 by the Ukrainian foreign minister, Ukraine was offered a special relationship with the alliance along the lines of the one promised to Russia'. T. Kuzio, *Ukraine Under Kuchma* (New York: St Martin's Press 1997) p. 194. However, according to Roman Luchinski, the late director of the NATO Information Centre in Kyiv, it was the Ukrainians who proposed the idea, one which apparently NATO originally scoffed (conversation with author, Kyiv 1997) Roman Zwarych, a Rukh member of parliament, suggested that Ukraine's position toward NATO only became crystallised following the Copenhagen Agreement in the summer of 1996 (conversation with author, February 2000).
36 *Den*, 5 Feb. 1997.
37 R. Wolczuk, 'Ukraine and Europe: Relations Since Independence', *Ukrainian Review*, 44(1), Spring 1997, pp. 38–53.
38 Pavliuk, 'Ukrainian–Polish Relations', p. 46.
39 *Uriadovy Kurier*, 22 May 1997.
40 The full charter is in *Narodna Armiya*, 11 July 1997.
41 Conversation with official from the Ministry of Foreign Affairs, Kyiv, July 1997.
42 Inevitably, the signing of the document exacerbated internal domestic tensions. Marchenko, a member of parliament and a member of the Progressive Socialist Party, regarded the document as illegal as it was not subjected to ratification. He was almost definitely right in arguing that it was not subjected to ratification as it was unlikely to have been ratified by the left-wing dominated parliament (conversation with author, Kyiv 1997).
43 Sherr, *Ukraine's New Time of Troubles*, p. 21.
44 Ibid., p. 21.
45 Author's conversation with Roman Lishchynski, head of NATO Information Centre in Kyiv, 1997.
46 *STRATFOR Global Intelligence Update*, 26 March 1999.
47 *Kyiv Post*, 1 April 1999.
48 *Reuters*, 1 April 1999.
49 *Kyiv Post*, 8 April 1999.
50 Ibid. See also *Kyiv Post*, 22 April 1999.
51 Burakovsky and Biletsky, *Ukraine's Way to the European Union*, p. 31.
52 Information gleaned from various editions of *Ukraine – Country Report*, Economist Intelligence Unit.
53 O. Pavliuk, *The European Union and Ukraine: The Need for a New Vision, Policy Paper Based on the Study on the Current State and Prospects of Relations Between the European Union and Ukraine*, 1999, p. 12.
54 Sherr, *Ukraine's New Time of Troubles*, p. 12.
55 Ibid., p. 11.
56 Only Spain, the United Kingdom, Denmark, Ireland and Luxembourg had ratified the agreement by that stage. See *Uriadovy Kurier*, 8 June 1996, nos 104–5, for the text of the speech delivered to the WEU.
57 Pavliuk, *The European Union and Ukraine*, p. 12.

58 Sherr argues that the West was not blameless in the problems encountered by Kyiv in the implementation of reform. First, he suggests that the West misdiagnosed the problem, and as a result 'the dominant Western models of reform – macroeconomic rather than institutional in focus, financial and economic rather than political–economic in emphasis – were derived from 'medicine' successfully applied to poorly functioning or dilapidated market economies instead of the command economy which Ukraine inherited'. Second, the national–economic cause of the collapse of the Soviet Union was misperceived as a politico-ideological issue. The third mistake, ironically, was to neglect political and institutional issues at the expense of economic and technical solutions. See Sherr, Ukraine's *New Time of Troubles*, pp. 9–10.
59 Ibid., p. 10.
60 Kowerski, *Wplyw Handly z Ukraina*.
61 Burakovsky and Biletsky, *Ukraine's Way to the European Union, passim.*
62 Honchar, Moskalets and Nalivka, 'Vidhomin Serpnevoho Stusu', *passim.*
63 *Kyivski Vidomosti*, 17 Jan. 1997.
64 *Nashe Slovo*, 5 April 1997.
65 Author's conversation with Eva Figel, the second secretary at the Polish Embassy in Kyiv in June 1997.
66 Conversation with official from the Ministry of Foreign Affairs, in Kyiv, October 1999.
67 Conversation with Boris Hudyma, the ambassador of the Permanent Mission of Ukraine to the EU, February 2000, Wilton Park, Steyning.
68 *Wall Street Journal Europe*, 15 September 2000.
69 *RFE/RL*, 2(39), 24 October 2000.
70 Discussion with a senior advisor to Volodymyr Horbulin, the secretary of the National Security and Defence Council, in Kyiv, October 1999.
71 Jan B. De Weydenthal, 'Poland's Eastern Policy', *RFE/RL Research Report*, 3(7), 18 Feb. 1994, p. 13.
72 Kobrinskaja, *Dlugi Koniec Zimnej Wojny*, p. 38.
73 According to the United States Energy Information Administration, while the anticipated growth in energy consumption in Western Europe is expected to continue more or less unabated, the bulk of the increase will be made up by gas, much of it provided by Russia, with some 33 per cent of known reserves, the largest in the world. Http://www.eia.doe.gov/oiaf/ieo98/gas.html#wptrc
74 Http://www.eia.doe.gov/emeu/cabs/ukraine.html
75 Bukkvol, *Ukraine and European Security*, p. 76.
76 Http://www.eia.doe.gov/oiaf/ieo98/gas.html#wptrc
77 'Russian Oil and Gas Exports Fact Sheet', June 1998, United States Energy Information Administration.
78 *Uriadovy Kurier*, 12 Oct. 1996.
79 *RFE/RL*, 2(39), 24 October 2000.
80 Ibid.
81 Kobrinskaja, *Dlugi Koniec Zimnej Wojny*, p. 117.
82 Kobrinskaja, *Dlugi Koniec Zimnej Wojny*, p. 43.
83 Kuzio, *Ukrainian Security Policy*, pp. 79–80.
84 *Rossiyskaya Gazeta*, 28 Oct. 1996.
85 *Obshchaya Gazieta*, 21–27 September 1996. Author's translation taken from Kobrinskaja, *Dlugi Koniec Zimnej Wojny*, p. 107.
86 A. Bayles, 'Sub-regional Organizations: The Cinderellas of European Security', *NATO Review*, 2(45), March 1997, p. 27.
87 Indeed, in Kyiv in July 1997, in conversation with the EU Political Officer the author was told, that 'if Poland doesn't want to spoil its chances of membership, it had better not get too close to Ukraine'.
88 Conversation with analyst at the Ukrainian Institute of Strategic Studies, in Kyiv in 1997, who confirmed the widespread nature of the belief.

89 Sherr, *Ukraine's New Time of Troubles*, p. 22.
90 Ibid., p. 24.
91 Ibid., p. 20.
92 I would like to thank Professor Neil Malcolm for his insight into this contentious area.
93 See for example A. Cottey 'The Visegrad Group and Beyond: Security Co-operation in Central Europe', pp. 69–89, in Cottey, *Subregional Co-operation in the New Europe*.
94 Ibid., p. 82.
95 Mansfield and Milner, 'The New Wave of Regionalism', p. 614.
96 A. Kupich, 'The Central European Free Trade Agreement: Problems, Experiences, Prospects', in Cottey, *Subregional Co-operation in the New Europe*, pp. 90–112.
97 For arguments on the relationship between co-operation and integration see A. Bjurner, 'Reflections on Subregionalism', p. 15.
98 Ibid., pp. 93–94.
99 Mansfield and Milner, 'The New Wave of Regionalism', p. 603.
100 A. Bayles, 'The Role of Subregional Co-operation in Post-Cold War Europe: Integration, Security, Democracy', in Cottey, *Subregional Co-operation in the New Europe*, pp. 176–177. The two way nature of the relationship between regionalism and democratisation was made highlighted by Cottey who argued that 'when the strategic situation changed – with the break-up of the Soviet Union – and Slovakia appeared to be turning away from the goals of democratisation and Western integration shared by the other three states, the Visegrad group became moribund'. See Cottey 'The Visegrad Group' p. 88.
101 Mansfield and Milner, 'The New Wave of Regionalism', p. 606.
102 Ibid., p. 606.

Part IV The Southern azimuth

1 Monitoring Foreign and Security Policy of Ukraine, June 1998 Expert Poll, http://www.public.ua.net/~potekhin/ ucpccrs/MONITOR/EXPOLL/poll98-2.htm

6 Relations with Black Sea littoral neighbours

1 Once the delimitation and demarcation of the Black Sea boundary between Ukraine and Russia got underway, problems soon emerged in terms of the boundaries in the Azov Sea (linked to the Black Sea by the Kerch Straits). While both sides agreed to treat the Azov Sea as a lake or 'internal waters', the Ukrainians insisted on full delimitation and demarcation of boundaries, something that the Russians were opposed to. *Holos Ukrainy*, 30 May 1998. Moscow was concerned that if Kyiv's proposal was implemented 'the Sea of Azov would *de facto* and *de jure* cease to be an internal sea, thus meaning that foreign warships and fishing fleets could enter'. *Narodna Armiya*, 18 September 1998.
2 Ukraine's maritime trade is estimated at between 30–40 million tons. *Narodna Armiya*, 5 May 1998.
3 These are the Ukrainian names for the Danube, Dniester and Dnepr respectively.
4 There are an estimated 70 billion cubic metres of gas on the shelf around the Crimean peninsula. *Holos Ukrainy*, 27 March 1997. An 11000 square kilometre area around Crimean peninsula has also been estimated to contain about 1.3 billion barrels of oil-equivalent hydrocarbons. Http://www.business-europa.co.uk/ukraine/cr07.html
5 R. B. Peele, 'The Importance of Maritime Chokepoints', *Parameters*, Summer 1997, p. 64.
6 Much discussion has taken place over the size of the Caspian hydrocarbon deposits. The size of the deposits are in turn, likely to impact on the route taken to bring them to market. Such is the cost of some of the proposed pipelines, that they are only likely to be viable in the event of very substantial resources. It has been estimated that the current favourite pipeline, Baku–Ceyhan, costed at between \$2.5–3 billion, needs 6 billion barrels of

proven reserves to make it viable. *New York Times News Service*, 20 November 2000. BP Amoco has estimated Azerbaijan oil reserves alone at 7 billion barrels, or 0.7 per cent of world reserves. The Azeri state oil company has put reserves at 17.5 billion barrels. (Gas reserves are put at 850 billion cubic metres, or 0.6 per cent by BP Amoco.) *Financial Times (Special Supplement – Azerbaijan)*, 22 November 2000. Jaffe and Manning have long urged caution in making estimates owing to the distorting effect they have had on US policy formation for the region. A. M. Jaffe and R. A. Manning, 'The Myth of the Caspian 'Great Game': The Real Geopolitics of Energy', *Survival*, 1 January 1998, http://www.aliyev.com/archive/19980101Survival.htm

7 Balmaceda, 'Gas, Oil and the Linkages', p. 276.
8 J. A. Corwing and J. Maksymiuk, 'Sparring Over Sevastopol', *RFE/RL Weekday Digest*, 11 February 1999.
9 For an overview of the nature of these facilities see Sherr, 'Russia–Ukraine Rapprochement?', pp. 33–50.
10 In 1997 Russia exported 3.5 million barrels per day (bbl/d), of which 0.9 million bbl/d were transported through the Druzhba pipeline, a 70 per cent utilization rate. 'Russian Oil and Gas Exports Fact Sheet', United States Energy Information Administration, June 1998.
11 Balmaceda, 'Gas, Oil and the Linkages', p. 261.
12 *Ukrainian Statehood in the Twentieth Century* (Kyiv: Political Thought 1996) p. 215.
13 *Holos Ukrainy*, 6 May 1992
14 *Finansova Ukraina*, 28 January 1997.
15 'Ukraine in Turkish Foreign Policy', in *Ukrainian Statehood in the Twentieth Century*, p. 217.
16 *Uriadovy Kurier*, 16 May 1998.
17 Sherr, *Ukraine's New Time of Troubles*, p. 5.
18 R. Wolczuk, 'Relations between Ukraine and Romania in the Context of NATO Enlargement', *The Ukrainian Review*, 44(4), Winter 1997, pp. 34–41.
19 *OMRI Daily Digest*, 7 Dec. 1995.
20 The treaty acquired formal legal status only in November 1997, *Uriadovy Kurier*, 13 November 1997.
21 Article 2 refers to a separate agreement regarding all of these matters, activated through an exchange of letters by the two foreign ministers, at the same time as the main treaty.
22 *Holos Ukrainy*, 15 January 1998.
23 G. Velea, 'Having joined the struggle for Caspian oil, Ukraine does not rule out co-operation with Romania'.
24 *Holos Ukrainy*, 20 March 1998.
25 *Zerkalo Nedeli*, 8 Feb. 1997.
26 *Uriadovy Kurier*, 12 November 1996.
27 *Uriadovy Kurier*, 4 Jan. 1997; *Zerkalo Nedeli*, 8 Feb. 1997.
28 This was an offer Kyiv rejected at the time, though it agreed to provide observers.
29 *Den*, 26 Feb. 1997.
30 *Zerkalo Nedeli*, 27 June–4 July 1997.
31 *Narodna Armiya*, 15 September 1998.
32 Route 3 is planned to run along the Berlin–Wroclaw–Lviv–Kyiv axis while route 5 runs via Trieste–Liubliana–Budapest–Chop–Lviv. The most important from Ukraine's point of view is route 9 which goes through Helsinki–Kyiv-Odesa–Dmytrovgrad and from there on up to the Euro-Asian transport corridor thereby linking Northern Europe and the Baltic region with the Transcaucasus. Route 7, the Danube waterway option, goes through Ukraine only tangentially via the ports of Izmail and Reni. *Holos Ukrainy*, 5 May 1998. Although it was originally planned that a firm decision as to the routes would be made at the third Pan European conference in Helsinki in June 1997, no decision was forthcoming. A decree (number 346) 'On the Confirmation of the Programme for the Building and Functioning of the National Network of the International Transport

Corridors in Ukraine' (sic) was issued by the Ukrainian Cabinet of Ministers on 20 March 1998.

33 'Caspian Sea Region', United States Energy Information Administration, October 1997.

34 Ukraine has six oil refineries, with a total refinement capacity of 63 million tons of oil. Since 1991, when 38 million tons of oil were refined, the amounts refined fell into a precipitous decline, with only 16 million (a figure which also included 3.5 million tons of oil extracted in Ukraine) refined in 1995. *Holos Ukrainy*, 22 April 1997. However, the superior quality of Caspian oil (as compared to that of the Russian oil that the refineries were designed to process) meant that a substantial investment was necessary if processing was to take place in Ukraine. *Holos Ukrainy*, 23 June 1998.

35 *Kyiv Post*, 11 September 1998.

36 *Kyiv Post*, 6 November 1998; *Kyiv Post*, 11 September 1998. Indeed, in 1998, Ukraine imported 28 million tons (or some 70 per cent) of oil from Russia, up from the 17.8 million tons in 1994, though down from the 55.1 million tons of 1989, a figure which included oil for re-export from Ukraine.

37 O. M. Smolenksy, 'Ukraine's Quest for Independence: The Fuel Factor', *Europe-Asia Studies*, 47(1), 1995, pp. 67–90. At the beginning of the 1990s, there were also efforts to gain access to Iraqi oil, which flowed from Kirkuk to Ceyhan, from where a pipeline was to be built to Samsun. These plans were put paid to by the ongoing Iraqi crisis. *Holos Ukrainy*, 23 June 1998.

38 *Finansova Ukraina*, 12 November 1996.

39 *Finansova Ukraina*, 18 Feb. 1997.

40 Discussion with official from the Ministry of Foreign Affairs, Kyiv, July 1997.

41 There were a plethora of other proposals. One option involved transporting the oil by tanker from the port of Novorossiysk to a new terminal which would be built in Burgas (Bulgaria), on the Black Sea, and then onto Alexandroupolis (in Greece), on the Aegean Sea, and from there possibly to Genoa by tanker. However, this route required a 320-kilometre pipeline between the two terminals. A further disadvantage was that all the ports involved in the route were limited to a 120,000 tanker capacity. Another alternative was from Burgas to Constanta (in Romania). From there the oil would go either by pipeline on into Europe, and/or by river tankers (with the associated danger of ecological catastrophes) by the Danube into Hungary. (In a similar vein, at the beginning of 1998, a pre-feasibility study was initiated between the Romanians and Italians for a $1.2 billion pipeline between Constanta and Trieste with a capacity of 34 million tons. Adina Borta, 'Romania to participate in ENI-coordinated SEEL project'.) Yet another alternative was from a terminal planned at Burgas to a terminal planned at Flora on Albania's Black Sea coast; the two terminals would then be linked by a new pipeline. While the route benefits from being able to use the very largest tankers from Albania onwards out of the Mediterranean Sea, the option was unappealing because of the political instability in the region and the expense of so much extra building of new terminals. Nevertheless, the revival of the marine links in the region was taking place with some urgency as evidence by the opening of sea ferry links between Poti in Georgia and both Burgas (in Bulgaria) and Constanta (in Romania). *Zerkalo Nedeli*, 27 June–4 July 1997. Yet another route involves crossing the Black Sea (from any one of a number of ports), and avoiding the Bosphorus via a pipeline leading from just before the Bosphorus to a terminal on the Sea of Marmora. Turkey was not keen on this option, much preferring the Ceyhan route because of the transit fees the route would generate.

42 A. Cohen, 'The New Great Game: Oil Politics in the Caucasus and Central Asia', *The Heritage Foundation*, Backgrounder No. 1065, 1996.

43 The consortium behind the pipeline was the Caspian Pipeline Consortium, the ownership of which was split as follows: Russia was allocated 24 per cent of shares, Kazakhstan 19, and Oman 7; the remaining 50 per cent was split between a number of oil concerns including Chevron, Lukoil, Shell, Mobil, British Gas and others.

44 However, by early 1998, little progress had been made in obtaining the necessary right of way, and the various federal permits necessary for the laying of the pipeline. As a result, in February 1998 the Western partners in the pipeline froze the $2 billion fund for the building of the pipeline, and started demanding a shake-up in the management of the Consortium, which was led at the time by the Russians *Wall Street Journal*, 2 Feb. 1998. However, in May 1998, an investment feasibility study was secured by the CPC, which would then need approval.

45 'Russian Oil and Gas Exports Fact Sheet', United States Energy Information Administration, June 1998.

46 Signed in 1936, the Montreaux Treaty guaranteed the free and unhindered passage of vessels though the Bosphorus Straits, while guaranteeing the sovereignty of Turkey. In that pre-nuclear and pre-supertanker era, an average of 17, usually grain carrying, ships per day, weighing on average 13 tons, traversed the straits. By 1994, these figures had risen to 110 ships, sometimes reaching 200,000 tons, carrying nuclear waste and other hazardous materials passing through the straits daily. Nearly 25 per cent of the shipping going through the straits was Russian. *The Reuter European Business Report*, 31 January 1995.

47 For example, vessels longer than 200 metres were only to be allowed through during daytime and then only during favourable weather, while ship height was set at 60 metres. The new measures were endorsed (and therefore legitimised) by the International Maritime Organization. *APS Review Oil Market Trends*, 17(43), 31 October 1994.

48 *The Christian Science Monitor*, 9 June 1994.

49 *Holos Ukrainy*, 28 July 1998.

50 Socar, the Azeri state oil company, originally planned to bring oil from Baku to Supsa by an existing 900-kilometre long, 500-millimetre diametre pipeline, which was in need refurbishment at a cost of $315 million. However, in April 1998 it was discovered that an all new pipeline was required, as a result of which a proposal for a 1,050-millimetre diametre pipeline capable of transporting 600,000 barrels a day was made; the projected cost was $590 million. *Wall Street Journal*, 13 April 1998.

51 The pipeline was to be built by the Azerbaijan International Oil Consortium (AIOC), a consortium headed by BP and Statoil (a Norwegian company) and a number of US companies. In September 1994, the Consortium signed a $8 billion contract to develop three Caspian oil fields over 30 years. In 1998, contracts were signed to invest $13 billion over 15 years. *New York Times*, 21 July 1998.

52 *Den*, 10 June 1997.

53 Indeed, in June 1997, Iranian Foreign Minister Ali Akbara Velayati paid a visit to Ukraine, during which it was agreed that Iran would provide Ukraine with 1 million tons of oil in exchange for 50 turbines to be used in power stations. Soon after, US pressure put paid to these plans. *Den*, 10 June 1997.

54 *Zerkalo Nedeli*, 27 June–4 July 1997

55According to one estimate, it was between $8.50 and $10 per ton cheaper to transport the oil via the Ukrainian route than by the cheapest of the other routes. *Kyiv Post*, 6 November 1998. Other earlier estimates suggested that the route through Ukraine would reduce the costs of transportation by $20–30 per ton. *Uriadovy Kurier*, 24 May 1997.

56 EBRD Project Summary Document, February 1998. The author, in conversation with Melanie Yuniacke of the EBRD in February 1999 discovered that the loan had been suspended. The terminal has been plagued by financial problems from the outset. Owing to the lack of progress, a joint stock company was floated in the hope that more funds would be released by Western institutions. *Den*, 29 Jan. 1997. UkrNaftoTerm – Ukrainian Oil Terminal – was a special purpose state-owned joint-stock company, created at the beginning of 1997, and which would own the eventual terminal. Significantly, a 50 per cent stake in UkrNaftoterm was held by the owners of the Druzhba pipeline, the network to which the terminal would eventually be linked up (and which had provided the majority of the funding up until that point).

57 In an associated vein, UkrTransNafta is also the co-founder (along with Georgia and Azerbaijan) of the company that will be responsible for the projected Euro-Asian transport corridor which would run from Odesa to the Caucasus; an agreement on its creation was signed between Ukraine, Georgia and Azerbaijan on the 'Co-operation, construction and functioning of the AETC' at the end of 1996. *Uriadovy Kurier*, 4 January 1997.
58 Prior to the creation of UkrTransNafta, Ukrainian prospects for participation in the pipeline were starting to look grim. However, once it was established, 'investors started to queue up', *Den*, 24 May 1997.
59 An additional 51-kilometre link was to be created with the Kremenchuk–Odesa oil pipeline, which would then supply the Odesa and Kherson Oil Processing plants with oil. By January 1997, 28 kilometres of pipeline had been laid. *Den*, 29 Jan. 1997.
60 *Narodna Armiya*, 15 September 1998.
61 Baku's Black Gold: June Oil Highlights. http://usiahq.usis.usemb.se/abtusia/posts/XA1/wwwtjn97.txt
62 Apparently an agreement regarding the project was ready for signing by 1995 and suddenly halted when a presidential decree wound up the joint stock company specially created for the project, 'Ukrzahranneftehaztroy'. *Zerkalo Nedeli*, 2–8 Aug. 1997. See *Uriadovy Kurier*, 24 June 1997 for details on the signing of the pipeline. The reasons for the long delay in the signing of the agreement are unclear, although Ukrainian observers attribute this to the 'interfering hand' of Russia, although they do not specify the precise mechanism of this interference. *Holos Ukrainy*, 21 February 1997. In preparation for the building of the pipeline (and evidence of the serious intent of Kyiv), the Ukrainians set up a state-owned corporation (as opposed to joint-stock company) called 'Ukrzahranneftehaztroy' (the Ukrainian Foreign Oil and Gas Transportation Company) on 4 March 1997. *Zerkalo Nedeli*, 2–8 Aug. 1997.
63 *Holos Ukrainy*, 23 June 1998; *Kyiv Post*, 11 September 1998.
64 *Porty Ukrainy*, (4) 1998, p. 53.
65 It has been suggested that officials were 'satisfied with hundreds of dollars made from Russian energy transporters instead of looking further afield and receive thousands of dollars from non-Russian energy sources'. *Zerkalo Nedeli*, 8 Feb. 1997.
66 A solution to this apparent under-utilisation worked in favour of the Novorossiysk route proposed by the Caspian Pipeline Consortium. However, this was regarded as a short-term solution as, if Kazakhstan's both offshore *and onshore* potential was to be realised, the capacity of the 'Russian' Novorossiysk option would be exceeded.
67 *Financial Times*, 4 December 1998. See also *The Economist*, 5–11 December 1998.
68 *The Economist*, 28 November–4 December 1998.
69 Letter to *The Economist*, 2–8 January 1999, from Jan Kalicki, Counsellor to the Department of Commerce, Washington DC. However, as has been pointed out 'Baku–Ceyhan is also self-defeating – its success depends on conditions that undermine its ends. The . . . commercial viability of the project depends on high oil prices sustained over a prolonged period . . . But high oil prices provide the Kremlin with the resources to be mischievous in Chechnya, exporting its power and ignoring international pressures', i.e. the opposite of that which the US administration wishes. *Christian Science Monitor*, 24 January 2000.
70 For an update on events see *Financial Times (Special Supplement – Azerbaijan)*, 22 November 2000.
71 *Christian Science Monitor*, 24 January 2000.

7 The Southern aimuth: subregional and regional integration

1 Author's conversation with Mikhailo Honchar from the National Institute of Strategic Studies, Kyiv 1999.
2 Perhaps giving a clue as to the source of the project is the fact that the idea was proposed in 1990 by the former Turkish ambassador to the United States, Sükrü Elekdag.

3 Ö. F. Gençkaya 'The Black Sea Economic Co-operation Project: A Regional Challenge to European Integration'. A paper presented at the 'Europe '92: International Conference on the European Community' at East Carolina University, Greenville, USA, 19–21 March 1992.
4 Ibid.
5 D. A. Connelly, 'Black Sea Economic Co-operation', *REF/RL Research Report*, 3(26), 1 July 1994, pp. 31–8.
6 *Narodna Armiya*, 24 July 1997.
7 Black Sea Economic Co-operation. Http://www.turkey.org/bsec2.htm
8 On the establishment of the BSEC in 1992, signatories to the Summit Declaration included Albania, Armenia, Azerbaijan, Bulgaria, Georgia, Greece, Moldova, Romania, Russia, Turkey and Ukraine. By 1997 Poland, Tunisia, Egypt, Israel and Slovakia, had joined as observers.
9 Gençkaya, 'The Black Sea Economic Co-operation Project'.
10 Ibid.
11 *Holos Ukrainy*, 22 October 1998.
12 *Holos Ukrainy*, 27 October 1998.
13 *Holos Ukrainy*, 27 October 1998.
14 According to one journalist '90 per cent of the Black Sea can now be declared dead, a victim of hydrogen sulphide gas that is continuing to rise from the depths of the sea and contaminate its upper layers . . . the Black Sea will be totally destroyed by the year 2040 if the present trend continues'. It has been estimated that $15 billion is needed to decontaminate the Black Sea. TED Case Studies: Black Sea Pollution and Tourism.
15 *Holos Ukrainy*, 23 March 1993.
16 Moldova joined the original trio when, as a result of the Flank Limitations Agreement (a modification to the 1990 Treaty on Conventional Forces in Europe), Russia was offered significant concessions regarding the deployment of increased numbers of weapons in the Transcaucasus, Ukraine and Moldova. This was a sufficient stimulus for Kishinev to seek the relative security of GUA, despite or perhaps because of the ominous presence of the 14th Army in Transdniester. It is misleading to put a date on the actually precise inception of GUAM, as its non-institutionalised nature renders this a difficult task. Nevertheless, by late 1996 it was clear that this group of states was formally co-ordinating policies on significant issues. On the realignment of Uzbekistan with GUAM in 1999, the group came to be formally known as GUUAM.
17 *Financial Times*, 5 September 1997.
18 *Uriadovy Kurier*, 4 Jan. 1997.
19 *Zerkalo Nedeli*, 8 Feb. 1997.
20 *Zerkalo Nedeli*, 10 March 1997.
21 Ibid.
22 If nothing else, then Ukrainian pipe manufacturers were going to benefit from the building of the pipelines. For example, at a follow-up meeting in Baku between 21 and 22 April, Ukrainian firms were contracted to build pipes and compressors to go along the Baku–Supsa route. *Uriadovy Kurier*, 24 April 1997.
23 *Den*, 26 Feb. 1997.
24 Ibid.
25 Ibid.
26 The Azeris were irritated by the fact that Russia had supplied the Armenians with free weapons. The Ukrainians agreed to peacekeeping activity subject to it being sanctioned by a United Nations mandate. *Den*, 26 March 1997. The principle of the territorial integrity of Azerbaijan, which was supported by Ukraine, was established at the Lisbon conference. *Uriadovy Kurier*, 27 March 1997.
27 *Holos Ukrainy*, 5 November 1997.
28 *Narodna Armiya*, 15 September 1998.
29 *Uriadovy Kurier*, 27 March 1997.

30 *Den*, 26 Feb. 1997
31 In addition to the fact that the Ukrainians did not want to be seen as legitimising Russian activities in the Caspian region with their co-operation, there was also a cost consideration to be taken into account. As CIS peacekeepers, the Ukrainians would not benefit from the generous expenses they would be paid if they were there under the aegis of the OSCE or UN, their preferred option. Nevertheless, this was a financial burden they were willing to shoulder. *Narodna Armiya*, 17 September 1998.
32 *Uriadovy Kurier*, 30 October 1997.
33 *Holos Ukrainy*, 11 June 1998.
34 *Narodna Armiya*, 17 September 1998.
35 *Den*, 26 March 1997.
36 *Holos Ukrainy*, 10 September 1998.
37 *Wall Street Journal Europe*, 15 September 2000.
38 Olcott, Åslund and Garnett, *Getting it Wrong*, p. 168.
39 *Zerkalo Nedeli*, 28 February 1998.
40 R. Wolczuk, 'Ukraine and Europe: Relations Since Independence', *The Ukrainian Review*, 44(1), Spring 1997, pp. 38–53.
41 *Den*, 26 March 1997.
42 *Zerkalo Nedeli*, 10 March 1997.
43 Ibid.
44 Ibid.
45 *Holos Ukrainy*, 11 Dec. 1998.
46 *Zerkalo Nedeli*, 8 Feb. 1997.
47 Ibid.
48 Ibid.
49 *Holos Ukrainy*, 11 June 1998.
50 *New York Times*, 6 November 1998. Although, confusingly, the USA $750,000 grant for a feasibility project into the viability of Odesa–Brody line seems to contradict this somewhat.
51 *Kyiv Post*, 10 November 1998.
52 *Zerkalo Nedeli*, 7–14 November 1997.
53 Iran was a country with which Ukraine had on more than one occasion tried to establish strong ties – e.g. for energy source purposes, trade such as turbines etc. See Balmaceda, 'Gas, Oil and the Linkages'.
54 Sherr, *Ukraine's New Time of Troubles*, p. 5.
55 *Kyiv Post*, 6 November 1998.
56 *The Economist*, 28 November to 4 December 1998.
57 One way in which the Americans hoped to get involved financially was via subsidies through the Overseas Investment Corporation and the Export-Import Bank. The United States was also behind Turkish efforts to provide subsidies for the Baku–Ceyhan pipeline. *New York Times*, 8 November 1998.
58 *Kyiv Post*, 11 September 1998. Though, as has been mentioned, in a conversation with a representative of the EBRD in London in February 1999, the author was told the whole package was in suspension.
59 *Holos Ukrainy*, 28 July 1998. Signatories to the charter include Azerbaijan, Turkey, Georgia, Russia Turkmenistan, Kazakhstan, Romania, Bulgaria and Poland.
60 Until the BSTDB determined an alternative, the EBRD was to be the depository of capital payments.
61 Foreign Policy Briefing No. 63, http://www.cato.org/pubs/fpbriefs/fpb-063es.html
62 *International Herald Tribune*, 21 October 2000
63 I. Bremmer, 'Southern Tier Subregionalism', *Perspectives on Central Asia*, Vol. II, No. 4, July 1997, p. 2, (http://www.cpss.org/casianw/perca0797.txt).
64 Cottey, *Subregional Co-operation in the New Europe*, p. 5.
65 O. Pavliuk, 'The Black Sea Economic Co-operation: Will Hopes Become Reality?' in Cottey, *Subregional Co-operation in the New Europe*, p. 137.

66 Cottey, *Subregional Co-operation in the New Europe, passim.*
67 O. Pavliuk, 'The Black Sea Economic Co-operation', p. 140.
68 A. Bjurner, 'Reflections on Subregionalism', p. 12.
69 Ibid., pp. 145–7.
70 Ibid., p. 131.
71 Ibid., p. 135.
72 I. Bremmer, S. Clement, A. Cottey and T. Dokos, 'Emerging Subregional Co-operation Processes: South-Eastern Europe, The Newly Independent States and the Mediterranean', in Cottey, *Subregional Co-operation in the New Europe*, p. 230.

8 Conclusion

1 Lake and Morgan, *Regional Orders, passim.*
2 *Wall Street Journal Europe*, 15 September 2000.
3 K. Waltz, *Theory of International Politics.*
4 Hurrell, 'Regionalism in Theoretical Perspective', in Fawcett and Hurrell, p. 48.
5 Ibid., p. 50.
6 R. O. Keohane, 'Theory of World Politics: Structural Realism and Beyond', in R.O. Keohane (ed.), *Neorealism and its Critics* (New York: Columbia University Press 1986) p. 159.
7 R. Wolczuk, 'The Evolution of Ukraine Foreign and Security Policy 1991–1994', *Journal of Slavic Military Studies*, 12(3), September 1999, pp. 18–37 .
8 J. M. Grieco, 'Realist International Theory and the Study of World Politics', in M. W. Doyle and G. J. Ikenberry (eds), *New Thinking in International Relations Theory* (New York: Westview Press 1997) p. 184
9 Keohane and Nye, *Power and Interdependence*, p. v.
10 Wendt, 'Collective Identity Formation and the International State', p. 394.
11 M. M. Balmaceda, 'Institution, Alliance and Stability: Thinking Theoretically About International Relations in Central-East Europe', *European Security*, 6(3), Autumn 1997, p. 98.
12 Keohane and Nye, *Power and Interdependence, passim.*
13 'How Ukraine's Fake Independence Promotes "Collective Security"', *Soviet Analyst*, 23(8), 1996, pp. 1–6.
14 S. Krasner, *International Regimes* (Ithaca, NY: Cornell University Press 1983).
15 Mansfield and Milner, 'The New Wave of Regionalism', p. 591.
16 Ibid., p. 601.
17 See O. Pavliuk 'Subregional Relations and Cooperative Initiatives in East-Central Europe', in R. Dwan, *Building Security in Europe's New Borderlands*, p. 50 and p. 63.
18 According to Pavliuk, 'as the NATO Madrid summit of 1997 approached, western states increasingly perceived subregional co-operation as a useful tool for "cushioning" possible new dividing lines between "ins" and "outs"', ibid., p. 48. For the proposed benefits of subregionalism also see also A. Cottee, 'Europe's Security Architecture and the New "Boundary Zones"', in R. Dwan, *Building Security in Europe's New Borderland*, p. 175.
19 Pavliuk in fact refers to GUUAM 'as an example of a rather successful newly emergent subregional initiative'; see Pavliuk, ibid., p. 60.
20 Galicia (*Halychyna*) is a region of Western Ukraine, on the border with Poland that was the cradle of Ukrainian nationalism and has remained its hotbed.
21 B. Russett, *Grasping the Democratic Peace: Principles for a Post-Cold War World* (Princeton: Princeton University Press 1993) p. 31.

Bibliography

General texts on International Relations (English language)

Alagappa, M. 'Regionalism and Conflict Management: A Framework for Analysis', *Review of International Studies*, 1995, Vol. 21, pp. 359–87.

D'Anieri, P. 'Dilemmas of Interdependence: Autonomy, Prosperity and Sovereignty in Ukraine's Russia Policy', *Problems of Post-Communism*, 7(1), Jan./Feb. 1997.

Berry, B. J. L. and T. D. Hankins *A Bibliographic Guide to the Economic Regions of the United States*, Department of Chicago Research Paper, No. 87, (Chicago: University of Chicago Press 1963).

Brecher, M. B. Steinberg, and J. Stein 'A Framework for Research on Foreign Policy Behaviour', *Journal of Conflict Resolution*, 13(1), March 1969, p. 80.

Bueno de Mesquita, B. 'The Benefits of a Social-Scientific Approach to Studying International Affairs', in N. Woods, *Explaining International Relations Since 1945* (Oxford: Oxford University Press 1996).

Buzan, B. *People, States and Fear: An Agenda for International Security Studies in the Post-Cold War Era*, 2nd edn (Boulder, Colo.: Lynne Rienner 1991).

Cantori, L. J. and S. L. Spiegel (eds), *The International Politics of Regions: A Comparative Approach* (Englewood Cliffs, NJ: Prentice-Hall 1970).

Cantori, L. J. and S. L. Spiegel 'The Analysis of Regional International Politics: The Integration Versus the Empirical Systems Approach', *International Organisation*, 27(4), 1973.

Cloke, P., C. Pilo and D. Sadler *Approaching Human Geography* (New York: Paul Chapman Publishing 1991).

Cooper, R. 'The Meaning of 1989', *Prospect*, December 1999.

Deutsch, K., S. Burrell and R. Kann *Political Community in the North Atlantic Area* (Princeton: Princeton University Press, 1958).

Doyle, M. W. 'Kant, Liberal Legacies and Foreign Affairs', Part I, *Philosophy and Public Affairs*, 12(3), Summer 1983, pp. 205–35.

Doyle, M. W. 'Liberalism and World Politics', *American Political Science Review*, 80(4), December 1986, pp. 1151–69.

Doyle, M. W. and G. J. Ikenberry (eds) *New Thinking in International Relations Theory* (New York: Westview Press 1997).

Gray, C. S. *The Geopolitics of Superpower* (Kentucky: University of Kentucky Press 1988).

Grigg, D. 'The Logic of Regional Systems', *Annals of the Association of American Geographers*, No. 55, 1965, p. 473.

Haas, E. 'International Integration: The European and the Universal Process', *International Political Communities: An Anthology* (Garden City, NY: Doubleday, Anchor Books).

Haas, E. B. *The Uniting of Europe: Political, Social and Economic Forces 1950–1957* (Stanford, California: Stanford University Press 1968).

Haas, E. 'The Study of Regional Integration: Reflections on the Joy and Anguish of Pretheorising', in L. N. Lindberg and S. A. Scheingold (eds), *European Integration: Theory and Research* (Cambridge, MA: Harvard University Press 1971).

Hillen, J. and M. P. Noonan 'The Geopolitics of NATO Enlargement', *Parametres*, Autumn 1998.

Hurrell, A. 'Regionalism in Theoretical Perspective', in L. Fawcett and A. Hurrell, *Regionalism in World Politics* (Oxford: Oxford University Press 1998).

Katzenstein, P. J. 'Regionalism in Comparative Perspective', *Co-operation and Conflict*, 31(2), 1996, p. 130.

Kay, S. *NATO and the Future of European Security* (Oxford: Rowman & Littlefield, 1998).

Keal, P. *Unspoken Rules and Superpower Dominance* (London: Macmillan Press 1983).

Keohane, R. O. (ed.) *Neorealism and its Critics* (New York: Columbia University Press 1986).

Keohane, R. O. and J. S. Nye *Power and Interdependence*, 2nd edn (Boston Scott Foresman and Company: 1989).

Kjellen, R. *Die Politische Probleme des Weltkrieges* (Leipzig 1918).

Krasner, S. *International Regimes* (Ithaca, NY: Cornell University Press 1983).

Kratochwil, F. and E. D. Mansfield (eds) *International Organisation: A Reader* (New York: HarperCollins College Publishers).

Lake, D. A. and P. M. Morgan (eds) *Regional Orders – Building Security in a New World* (Pennsylvania: Pennsylvania State University Press 1997).

Layne, C. 'Kant or Cant: The Myth of the Democratic Peace', *International Security*, 19(2), Fall 1994, pp. 5–49.

Mackinder, H. J. *Democratic Ideals and Reality* (New York: Norton 1962).

Manfield, E. D. and H. V. Milner, 'The New Wave of Regionalism', *International Organization*, 53(3), Summer 1999, pp. 589–627.

Mearsheimer, J. J. 'Back to the Future: Instability in Europe After the Cold War', *International Security*, 15(1), Summer 1990, pp. 5–56.

Mittelman, J. H. 'Rethinking the "New Regionalism" in the Context of Globalisation', *Global Governance*, 2, 1996, pp. 189–213.

Naumann, F. *Werke* (Köln and Opladen 1966).

North, D. C. *Institutions, Institutional Change and Economic Performance* (Cambridge: Cambridge University Press 1990).

Rosamond, B. *Theories of European Integration* (London: Macmillan Press 2000).

Rosecrance, R. 'Regionalism and the Post-Cold War Era', *International Journal*, XLVI, Summer 1991, p. 373.

Russett, B. M. 'International Regimes and the Study of Regions', *International Studies Quarterly*, 13(4), December 1969, pp. 123–33.

Russett, B. *Grasping the Democratic Peace: Principles for a Post-Cold War World* (Princeton: Princeton University Press 1993).

Russett, B. 'Can a Democratic Peace Be Built', *International Interactions*, 18(3), Spring 1993, pp. 277–82.

Small, M. and J. D. Singer 'The War-proneness of Democratic Regimes, 1816–1865', *Jerusalem Journal of International Relations*, 1(4), Summer 1976, pp. 50–69.

Snyder, G. H. 'Alliance Theory: A Neorealist First Cut', *Journal of International Affairs*, 44, 1990, p. 104.

Snyder, C. A. (ed.) *Contemporary Security and Strategy* (London: Macmillan Press, 1999).

Stake, R. E. *The Art of Case Study Research* (London: Sage Publications 1995).
Wallace, W. *The Transformation of Western Europe* (London: Pinter 1990).
Wallander, C. E. *Mortal Friends, Best Enemies – German–Russian Co-operation After the Cold War* (Ithaca, NY: Cornell University Press 1999).
Walt, S. M. *The Origins of Alliance* (Ithaca, NY: Cornell University Press 1987).
Waltz, K. *Theory of International Politics* (Reading, Mass.: Addison-Wesley, 1979).
Wendt, A. 'Collective Identity Formation and the International State', *The American Political Science Review*, 88(2), June, 1994, p. 385.
Woods, N. 'The Uses of Theory in the Study of International Relations', in N. Woods (ed.), *Explaining International Relations Since 1945* (Oxford: Oxford University Press 1996) p. 11.

Specialised texts on Ukraine's International Relations – English language sources

Allison, R. and C. Bluth (eds) *Security Dilemmas in Russia and Eurasia* (London: Royal Institute of International Affairs 1998).
Arel, D. and V. Khmelko 'The Russian Factor and Polarization in Ukraine', *The Harriman Review*, 9(1), 1996, pp. 81–91.
Balmaceda, M. M. 'Institution, Alliance and Stability: Thinking Theoretically About International Relations in Central-East Europe', *European Security*, 6(3), Autumn 1997, p. 98.
Balmaceda, M. M. 'Ukraine, Russia, and European Security; Thinking Beyond NATO Expansion', *Problems of Post-Communism*, 45(1), January/February 1998, pp. 21–9.
Balmaceda, M. M. 'Gas, Oil and the Linkages between Domestic and Foreign Policies: The Case of Ukraine', *Europe-Asia Studies*, 50(2), 1998, pp. 257–86.
Balmaceda, M. M. 'Belarus and Russia after Yeltsin', paper presented at the Special Seminar on Belarus, University of Bath, 10–11 February 2000.
Bayles, A. 'Sub-regional Organisations: The Cinderellas of European Security', *NATO Review*, 2(45), March 1997, p. 27.
Burant, S. R. 'Foreign Policy and National Identity: A Comparison of Ukraine and Belarus', *Europe-Asia Studies*, 47(7), 1995, pp. 1125–44.
Brzezinski, I. 'The Geopolitical Dimension', *The National Interest*, Spring 1992, p. 51.
Brzezinski, I. 'Polish–Ukrainian Relations: Europe's Neglected Strategic Axis', *Survival*, 35(3), Autumn, 1993, p. 26.
Bukkvol, T. *Ukraine and European Security* (London: Royal Institute of International Affairs 1997) p. 75.
Burakovsky, I. and V. Biletsky *Ukraine's Way to the European Union – A View from Ukraine*, Analytical Report No.12 (Kyiv: Centre for Peace, Conversion and Foreign Policy of Ukraine, 1999) p. 7.
'Caspian Oil to European Markets through Ukraine', Project Presentation for the Business Forum of the European Bank for Reconstruction and Development by the State Committee for Oil, Gas and Oil Refining Industry of Ukraine, May 1998.
'Caspian Sea Region', United States Energy Information Administration, October 1997.
Cimoszewicz, W. 'Building Poland's Security: Membership of NATO a Key Objective', *NATO Review*, No. 3, 1996, pp. 3–5.
Cohen, A. 'The New Great Game: Oil Politics in the Caucasus and Central Asia', *The Heritage Foundation*, Backgrounder No. 1065, 1996.

Cottee, A. (ed.) *Subregional Co-operation In The New Europe – Building Security, Prosperity and Solidarity from the Barents To The Black Sea* (London: Macmillan Press 1999).

Dawisha, K. and B. Parrott *Democratic Changes and Authoritarian Reactions in Russia, Ukraine, Belarus and Moldova* (Cambridge: Cambridge University Press 1997) pp. 330–40.

Decree (Number 346) 'On the Confirmation of the Programme for the Building and Functioning of the National Network of the International Transport Corridors in Ukraine' (sic), issued by the Ukrainian Cabinet of Ministers on 20 March 1998.

Dima, N. *Bessarabia and Bukovina: The Soviet-Romanian Territorial Dispute* (New York: Columbia University Press 1982).

Dwan, R. (ed.), *Building Security in Europe's New Borderlands: Subregional Co-operation in the Wider Europe* (London: M.E. Sharpe 1999).

Filipenko, A. 'The CIS Economic Union: Pros and Cons', *Politics and the Times*, October–December, 1995, pp. 58–65.

Garnett, S. W. *Ukraine: Europe's New Frontier* (Sandhurst: Conflict Studies Research Centre July 1996) pp. 3–4.

Garnett, S. W. *Keystone in the Arch: Ukraine in the Emerging Security Environment of Central and Eastern Europe* (Washington DC: Carnegie Endowment for International Peace 1997).

Garnett, S. W. *Getting it Wrong – Regional Co-operation and the Commonwealth of Independent States* (Washington DC: Carnegie Endowment for International Peace 1999) pp. 77–108.

Gençkaya, Ö. F. 'The Black Sea Economic Co-operation Project: A Regional Challenge to European Integration', paper presented at the 'Europe '92: International Conference on the European Community' at East Carolina University, Greenville, USA, 19–21 March 1992.

Horbulin, V. 'Ukraine's Place in Today's Europe', *Politics and the Times*, October – December 1995, pp. 10–15.

Hrynkevych, O. 'Things Return to Their "Natural" State: Russia, Belarus and the "New Commonwealth"', *Politics and the Times*, February 1996, pp. 85–91.

Jaffe, A. M. and R. A. Manning, 'The Myth of the Caspian "Great Game": The Real Geopolitics of Energy', *Survival*, 1 January 1998, http://www.aliyev.com/archive/19980101Survival.htm

Kolodziejczyk, P. 'Poland – A Future NATO Ally', *NATO Review*, No. 5, 1994, p. 7.

Kuzio, T. *Ukraine Under Kuchma* (New York: St Martin's Press 1997) p. 194.

Kuzio, T. *Ukrainian Security Policy* (Washington DC: Praeger 1995).

Lamont, N. V. *Territorial Dimensions of Ethnic Conflict: The Moldovan Case* (Kansas: Foreign Military Studies Office 1996).

Lieven, A. 'Russian Opposition to NATO Expansion', *The World Today*, October 1995, pp. 196–9.

Lynch, T. 'Ukraine – A New Territorial Pact', *The NIS Observed: An Analytical Review*, Vol V, No. 15, October 2000.

Mansfield, E. and H. Milner, 'The New Wave of Regionalism', *International Organization*, 53(3), Summer 1999, pp. 589–627.

Mihalisko, K. J. 'Belarus: Retreat to Authoritarianism', in K. Dawisha and B. Parrott, (eds), *Democratic Changes and Authoritarian Reactions in Russia, Ukraine, Belarus and Moldova* (Cambridge: Cambridge University Press 1997) p. 248

Monitory Foreign and Security Policy of Ukraine, June 1998 Expert Poll, http://www.public.ua.net/~potekhin/ ucpccrs/MONITOR/EXPOLL/poll98-2.htm.

Mroz, J. E. and O. Pavliuk 'Ukraine: Europe's Linchpin', *Foreign Affairs*, 75(3), May/June 1996, p. 59.

Nordberg, M. 'Domestic Factors Influencing Ukrainian Foreign Policy', *European Security*, Vol. 7, No. 3, (Autumn 1998), p. 77.

Pastusiak, L. (Rapporteur) *Subregional Co-operation Among Central European Countries And Their Struggle Toward Membership of Transatlantic Structures* (Draft Special Report), Sub-Committee on Transatlantic And European Relations, AN104, PC/TER (96) 4.

Pavliuk, O. 'Ukrainian–Polish Relations: a Pillar of Regional Stability', in M. Wohlfeld (ed.), *The Effects of Enlargement on Bilateral Relations in Central and Eastern Europe* (Paris: Institute for Security Studies, Western European Union 1997) p. 46.

Pavliuk, O. *The European Union and Ukraine: The Need for a New Vision, Policy Paper Based on the Study on the Current State and Prospects of Relations Between the European Union and Ukraine*, 1999, p. 12.

Paznyak, V. 'Belarus: in Search of a Security Identity', in R. Allison and C. Bluth, (eds), *Security Dilemmas in Russia and Eurasia* (London: RIIA 1998) p. 159.

Peele, R. B. 'The Importance of Maritime Chokepoints', *Parametres*, Summer 1997, p. 64.

Potichnyj, P. J. (ed.) *Poland and Ukraine – Past and Present* (Toronto: CIUS 1980).

Pritzel, I. *National Identity and Foreign Policy: Nationalism and Leadership in Poland, Russia and Ukraine* (Cambridge: Cambridge University Press 1998) p. 280.

Pritzel, I. 'The Influence of Ethnicity on Foreign Policy – The Case of Ukraine', in Roman Szporluk (ed.), *National Identity and Ethnicity in Russia and the New States of Eurasia* (London: M.E. Sharpe 1994) p. 112.

'Russian Oil and Gas Exports Fact Sheet', United States Energy Information Administration, June 1998.

Sanford, G. 'Belarus on the Road to Nationhood', *Survival*, 38(1), Spring 1996, p. 138.

Selivanova, I. F. *Trans-Dniestria*, http://www.rand.org/publications/CF/CF129/CF-129.chapter4.html, p. 3.

Sherr, J. *A New Storm Over the Black Sea Fleet* (Sandhurst: Conflict Studies Research Centre 1996).

Sherr, J. 'Ukraine's New Time of Troubles', G27 (Sandhurst: Conflict Studies Research Centre October 1998) p. 19.

Sherr, J. 'Russia–Ukraine *Rapprochement*?: The Black See Fleet Accords', *Survival*, 39(3), Autumn 1997, p. 36.

Slusser, R. M. and J. F. Triska, *A Calendar of Soviet Treaties, 1917–1957* (Stanford: Stanford University Press 1959), p. 216.

Smith, M. A. *Russian Hegemony in the Near Abroad* (Sandhurst: Conflict Studies Research Centre July 1994) p. 9. gopher://marvin.nc3a.nato.int:70/00/secdef/csrc/f40mas.txt.

Smolenksy, O. N. 'Ukraine's Quest for Independence: The Fuel Factor', *Europe-Asia Studies*, 47(1), 1995, pp. 67–90.

Solchanyk, R. 'Russia, Ukraine and the Imperial Legacy', *Post-Soviet Affairs*, 9(4), 1993, pp. 359–60.

Solomon, G. B. (Special Rapporteur), *Peacekeeping in the Transdniester Region: A Test Case for the CSCE* (Draft Special Report), November 1994, http://www.intnet.net/pub/COUNTRIES/Moldova/Moldova.conflict.data.

'How Ukraine's Fake Independence Promotes "Collective Security"', *Soviet Analyst*, 23(8), pp. 1–6.

TED Case Studies: Black Sea Pollution and Tourism.

Udovenko, H. 'An Open, Predictable and Pragmatic Foreign Policy', *Politics and the Times*, October–December 1995, pp. 16–23.

Ukraine – Aircraft and Parts, Bain & Company.

Ukraine – Country Report, Economic Intelligence Unit (quarterly issues between 1996–1999).

Ukrainian Economic Trends, quarterly update, June 1997 (Kyiv: Ukrainian-European Policy and Legal Advice Centre 1997).

Ukraine. Human Development Report (Kyiv: United Nations Development Programme 1995).

Ukrainian Statehood in the Twentieth Century (Kyiv: Political Thought 1996) p. 215.

Weydenthal, Jan B. De 'Poland's Eastern Policy', *RFE/RL Research Report*, 3(7), 18 Feb. 1994, p. 13.

Wilson, A. *Ukrainian Nationalism in the 1990s* (Cambridge: Cambridge University Press 1997).

Wolczuk, K. *Politics of Statebuilding – The Constitutional Process in Ukraine 1990–1996*, University of Birmingham, 2000.

Wolczuk, R. 'Ukraine and Europe: Relations Since Independence', *Ukrainian Review*, 44(1), Spring 1997, pp. 38–53

Wolczuk, R. 'Ukraine in the Context of NATO Enlargement', *Ukrainian Review*, 44(3), Autumn 1997, pp. 3–23.

Wolczuk, R. 'Relations between Ukraine and Romania in the Context of NATO Enlargement', *Ukrainian Review*, 44(4), Winter 1997, pp. 34–41.

Wolczuk, R. 'The Evolution of Ukraine's Foreign and Security Policy 1991–1994', *Slavic Military Studies*, 12(3), September 1999, pp. 18–37 .

Zaloga, Stephen J. 'Armed Forces in Ukraine', *Jane's Intelligence Review*, March 1992, pp. 131–4.

Specialised texts on Ukraine's International Relations – non-English language sources

Berdesha, Y., M. Honchar, and O. Moskalets, *Mistse Polshchi v Polititsi Bezpeky Ukrainy* (forthcoming).

Garnett, S. and R. Lebenson, 'Chy Nastane Myr u Prydnistrovyi?', *Polityka I Chas*, January 1999, p. 58.

Honchar, M., O. Moskalets and S. Nalivka, 'Vidhomin Serpnevoho Strusu', *Polityka I Chas*, 2, February 1999, p. 40.

Kobrinskaja, I. *Dlugi Koniec Zimnej Wojny* (Warsaw: Centrum Stosunkow Miedzynarodowych 1998).

'Konferencja Polsko–Ukrainska nt. "Droga Ukrainy do Europy"', *Sprawy Miedzynarodowe*, 4–6, 1992, pp. 149–170.

Kowerski, M. 'Wplyw Handlu z Ukraina na Rozwoj Wojewodztw Przygranicznych', *Gospodarka Narodowa*, 3, 1998.

Kudriachov, S., S. Odarych, Y. Orobets and M. Tomenko, *Carta Sevastopolya: Triumph Presidentiv, Trahedia Ukrainy* (Kyiv: Ukrainska Perspektiva 1997).

Manachinski, O. Y. *Suchasni Voyenno-Politychny Vidnosyny Ukrainy iz Sumizno-Prylehlymy Derzavami*, Vypusk 2 (Kyiv: Natsionaly Institut Stratehichnych Doslidzen 1996).

Mirus, O. 'Ne Metodom Vyrishenya a Shlyachom Dosyahnenya', *Polityka I Chas*, May 1996, pp. 43–9.

Polityka Bezpieczenstwa I Strategia Obronna RP, 2 November 1992.

Przeglad Srodkowoeuropejski, Bezpieczenstwo Europy, Obronnosc, Integracja, No 14, Padziernik 1995.

Savchenko, N. *Anatomia Neobyalvlenoy Voyny* (Kyiv: Ukrainska Perspektiva 1997).

Shmanko, H. and E. Kish, 'Vishegradski Chotyrykutnyk', *Polityka I Chas*, January 1994, p. 50.

Tkachenko, V. *Spivdruznist Nezaleznych Derzav ta Natsionalni Interesy Ukrainy* (Kyiv: Institut Hromadskoho Suspilstva 1998).

Valevsky, O. L. and M. M. Honchar, *Struktura Heopolitichnych Interesiv Ukrainy*, Vypusk 45 (Kyiv: Natsionalny Institut Stratehichnych Doslidzen 1995).

Ukraina na Mizhnarodny Areni. Zbirnik Dokumentiv I Materialiv 1991–1995. Knyha 1, Ministerstvo Zakordonnych Sprav Ukrainy (Kyiv: Yurinkom Inter 1998).

Zolnayi, A. 'Uhorski Partnery Chekayut na Propozytsiyi', *Polityka I Chas*, May 1995, pp. 56–9.

Index